THE RISE AND FALL OF
THE GREAT
EMPIRES

THE RISE AND FALL OF
THE GREAT
EMPIRES

ANDREW TAYLOR

Quercus

CONTENTS

Genghis Khan

Bust of Alexander the Great

The Great Exhibition of 1851, a showcase of the British empire

Portrait of Napoleon on the imperial throne, by Jean-Auguste-Dominique Ingres, 1806

Empires seem to have gone out of fashion. *'The wind of change is blowing through this continent,'* declared Prime Minister Harold Macmillan on a visit to Africa in 1960, in belated acceptance of the fact that the African colonies of the British empire would soon be independent states in their own right. Britain had found itself effectively bankrupted by the Second World War, while the nations over which it had once held sway had been increasingly clamouring for their freedom.

INTRODUCTION

In the late 19th century, Canadian prime minister Alexander Mackenzie proclaimed: *'English supremacy should last until the end of time, because it means universal freedom, universal liberty, emancipation from everything degrading'*. Perhaps it did for an influential politician of western European parentage, although Native Americans, blacks in Africa, and millions of Indians in the Subcontinent might have disagreed – but in any case, the *'end of time'* proved just a few decades away. Britain was merely the latest in a long line of great powers that had seen their glory slip away. Many rulers dreamed that their empires would embrace the whole world and last for ever. Alexander the Great famously wept because he had no more worlds left to conquer; the Mongol Great Khans believed it was their destiny to rule the world. And the Nazis referred to their 'Thousand-Year Reich', whose realm extended beyond Germany's own borders for barely six years.

Various factors have motivated the creation of empire – some imperialists, like Alexander the Great, conquered apparently for the sake of conquest, and created military empires that died with them; others, like the Portuguese in the 16th and 17th centuries, were driven by trade. Some empires, like that of the Spanish in South America, involved the wholesale destruction and enslavement of civilizations that lacked the advanced weapons of their conquerors, while others, like the Third Reich, were created by the ruthless conquest of neighbouring states with similar cultures and backgrounds.

Early empires, such as that of the Romans, were necessarily limited by the sea. Though wielding some naval power in *Mare Nostrum* ('our sea', the Mediterranean), the Romans relied overwhelmingly on the movement of their troops across land to impose their will – all roads really did lead to Rome. It was only the development of sea transport and the new understanding of navigation and cartography in the 16th century that enabled powerful nations to extend their influence around the world and create empires on which, they boasted, the sun never set.

Many imperial powers – notably the Romans and the British – have relied on élite or leading groups among their subject peoples to rule on their behalf; such groups may reap even greater rewards than the imperial power itself. Even so, empires have often been hated and resented by the people who were ruled – and unpopular, too, sometimes, with the nations that ruled them. *'Guns will make us powerful – butter will only make us fat,'* declared the leading Nazi Hermann Goering in 1936. Political leaders and generals may prefer guns, but unsurprisingly, many people would opt for butter. The need to protect empires, the cost in both men and money of foreign wars, the dislocation of trade and the effects on domestic industry all exact a continuing price at home. And for Germany, of course, the eventual price of guns was far higher than the peaceful pursuit of commerce. It is worth reflecting that, whereas the Third Reich lasted for just 12 years, the German-led trading empire of the Hanseatic League endured for over three hundred.

For all their perceived disadvantages, however, empires can also be enormously lucrative. Historians may argue over whether the flood of gold and silver from Spain's American empire caused the rampant inflation that swept 16th-century Europe, but in the short term at least, it certainly brought Spain great riches. The British also gained raw materials, new lands for their growing population to settle in and vast wealth from their empire.

But in 1945, the days of empire seemed over for good. The two nations that emerged from the Second World War with their power enhanced – the USA and the USSR – both declared themselves implacably opposed, from their different political viewpoints, to the idea of empire. The creation of the UN on 24 October, 1945 raised hopes of a new world order. Yet the power and influence of the UN proved patchy at best. For all their anti-imperialist rhetoric, both the Americans and the Russians avidly carved out areas of influence that were empires in all but name. The collapse of the Soviet Union in 1991 ended Russia's imperial aspirations, at least for a time, and left the US as the world's sole military superpower. But will its dominance last? All it is possible to say at the start of the 21st century is that other nations have seemed to hold unchallengeable power before. Empires, even the greatest ones, do not last for ever.

The empires covered here do not appear in a totally chronological sequence; while the fall of some may clearly lead to the rise of others, the fact that most may be considered free-standing entities argued in favour of a less linear approach. Certain start or end dates may appear contentious, but the rationale for their placement is consistently explained. For example, the beginning of the Roman empire is set at 264 BC; though more than two centuries before the accession of the first emperor, this was the date when Rome truly began to cohere and face down the threat from Carthage, so laying the foundations for its later imperial greatness. Likewise, the choice of which empires to include is anything but arbitrary; irrespective of their duration or geographical extent, the 25 discussed here have all left an indelible imprint on world history.

Andrew Taylor,
2008

The earliest empire known to have existed grew up around the Tigris and Euphrates rivers in modern Iraq, some 4500 years ago. A few names, a few inscriptions and a number of stories and legends are all that remain, but it is possible to trace the rise and fall of an empire based in the city of Adab (modern Bismaya) in southern-central Iraq. Archaeologists have the records of a sequence of rulers, a number of revolts and defeats, and the eventual growth of a new empire under a ruler in the nearby city of Akkad on the Euphrates, probably somewhere close to modern Baghdad.

THE SUMERIAN EMPIRE
c.2490 – c.2200 BC

THE FIRST NAME THAT CAN BE ESTABLISHED IN THE LONG LIST OF RULERS who have pushed out their power to form an empire is that of the early Bronze Age king Lugal-anne-mundu of Adab in the third millennium BC. The fact that he is supposed to have ruled for 90 years may say more about the reliability of the records than his longevity – possibly implying that an entire dynasty has been represented by a single name. Later documents suggest, however, that around 2490 BC Lugal-anne-mundu controlled much of Mesopotamia, from the Arabian Gulf to the Mediterranean, and was known by his people as 'King of the Four Quarters of the Universe'.

Archaeological remains indicate that Mesopotamia, with its fertile soil and warm climate, had been inhabited by the same peoples from as early as 6000 BC, so Lugal-anne-mundu and his people were almost certainly natives of the region rather than invaders from outside. There may well have been earlier alliances between individual city-states, or even other powerful cities that exerted their influence over a wide area, but Adab was the first known to have unified the whole region.

SARGON OF AKKAD
Lugal-anne-mundu may be the first recognized emperor, but his empire crumbled with his death, and the next great name from Mesopotamia – Sargon of Akkad (r. 2333–2279 BC) – is generally believed to have wielded more power. Around 2300

LEFT *This bronze sculpture head from c.2250 BC represents an Akkadian king – possibly Sargon or his grandson, Naram-sin.*

TIMELINE

2700 BC First Akkadian
language records

2490 BC Lugal-anne-mundu
founds empire of Adab

2350 BC Sargon founds
Akkadian empire

2294 BC Death of Sargon

2150 BC Supposed end of
Akkadian empire

BC, Sargon established a standing army of some 5000 men and set out to defeat neighbouring cities and tear down their walls so they could no longer resist him. Having established his power base, he extended his rule throughout Mesopotamia and also east into present-day Iran, north towards Syria and possibly even into Asia Minor. Among the cities whose names are recorded in inscriptions as conquests are Mari in modern Syria, Yarmuti on the Mediterranean coast and Tuttul on the Euphrates in Syria.

There are no historical records of Sargon's reign, but the language of Akkad, which was preserved in stone carvings and memorials, spread throughout the region. The city remained dependent on the productive agricultural lands through the region, which were protected by a chain of stone-built fortresses, but it also developed into a trading centre, with ships from the Arabian Gulf and the Indian Ocean sailing up the Euphrates to unload in its port. Silver came from the mines of Anatolia to the north, and metal ores from Oman. Tin and copper had to be imported for the army's bronze weapons, as well as timber and stone for building, which could have provided the initial impetus for extending Sargon's domination across the region.

EROSION OF EMPIRE

Towards the end of Sargon's life there are records of opposition to his rule, which was renewed during the brief reigns of his two sons, Rimush (r. 2279–2270 BC) and Manishtushu (r. 2270–2255 BC). His grandson, Naram-sin (r. 2255–2219 BC), seems to have put down the revolts and to have extended the empire in northern Syria, and possibly also into the Arabian Peninsula; but, by the end of his reign, it was being pillaged by barbarian tribesmen from the Zagros Mountains. It is likely that drought and famine also played a part in the destruction, but the famous army and the network of trading links were destroyed; the forts and outposts that the people of Akkad had built were abandoned and fell into disuse.

Naram-sin's successor, Shar-kali-sharri (whose regnal dates are uncertain), held onto power for a little longer, despite a renewal of the internal struggles that had plagued the empire earlier. However, 100 years or so after Sargon had first

BELOW *The kings of Akkad ruled over an empire that reached from the shores of the Mediterranean to present-day Iran.*

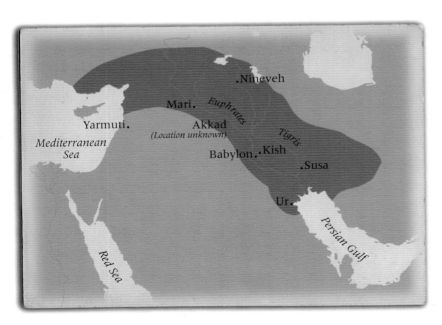

Nineveh

Mari.

Euphrates

Yarmuti.

Akkad
(Location unknown)

Mediterranean Sea

Tigris

Babylon. Kish

.Susa

Ur.

Persian Gulf

Red Sea

THE EARLIEST DAYS

Much of the history of Sargon (r. 2333–2279 BC) and his Sumerian empire is conjecture – but by building on information from inscriptions and ancient legends, it is possible to go back further, even before Lugal-anne-mundu. By around 3000 BC, as many as 12 separate city-states were struggling for power in Mesopotamia.

Some, such as Akshak and Bad-tibera, are known only from mentions in inscriptions, and descriptions of victories or defeats. Others, such as Erech and Ur in the southeast of modern Iraq, have been thoroughly excavated. It seems likely that each city would have had its walled defences, its own god and eventually its own king, with surrounding villages and settlements depending on him for protection. In the centuries before Sargon's rise to power, the cities of Lagash, Erech, Ur and Kish were trading with each other, occasionally fighting and struggling for ascendancy, but no one king was powerful enough to rule the whole area.

Seven centuries later, Sargon's city of Akkad was destroyed and lost, probably for ever, but his name remains as the first in a long line of rulers to achieve international domination – the first emperor about whom anything is known.

The ziggurat of Nanna at Ur. This large temple dedicated to the god Nanna was built c.2100 BC by King Ur-Nammu at the ancient city of Ur.

begun to bring other cities under his control, the Sumerian empire vanished as suddenly as it had grown up.

It lingered on in myth – for instance, the account of how Sargon himself was left as a baby in a basket of rushes reappears as the story of Moses in Old Testament tradition. The stories of the empire were written hundreds of years later, describing battles, victories and conquests that may or may not have happened. The point is that Sargon, like many emperors who followed him in later centuries all over the world, created not only an empire but also a legend.

The Assyrian Empire grew out of a period of confusion and unrest in the Mesopotamian region, where different cities, kings, and peoples were struggling for dominance. A succession of strong kings, and a highly trained army, enabled the Assyrians to establish an empire which, although under constant pressure from foreign invaders and local revolts, lasted for nearly half a millennium.

THE
ASSYRIAN EMPIRE
2000 – 612 BC

A COMMON THEME FROM ITS BEGINNING TO ITS END WAS THE POSITION OF BABYLON, considered a holy city in Mesopotamia, and almost always accorded special status by the ruling Assyrians. Occasionally, control of the city was seized by foreign nations, and occasionally it revolted against Assyrian rule; one king, infuriated by yet another revolt, actually ordered its destruction.

It was built again, but another revolt followed, led this time by its governor, the Assyrian king's own brother. Once more, the city was besieged and conquered – but a few years later, as the Assyrian leaders fought each other in a bloody internal struggle, the Babylonians took their revenge. Joining other nations in an alliance against their rulers, they marched up the Tigris Valley towards the Assyrian capital of Nineveh. The city and the empire were utterly destroyed.

FIRST STIRRINGS OF EMPIRE

The Assyrians took their name from the city of Ashur in northern Mesopotamia, which was their capital from around 2500 BC, when it was ruled by a governor from the Sumerian city of Akkad. Sometime around 2000 BC, with the rulers from Akkad driven out and the Sumerian empire in ruins, a new and cooler city was built further north at the ancient settlement of Nineveh, on the eastern bank of the River Tigris. It was the total destruction of this city, some 1400 years later, that would finally signal the end of the Assyrian empire.

LEFT *Ancient sculpture of Assyrian soldiers marching to battle.*

TIMELINE

c.2000 BC Assyrian capital moves to Nineveh

c.1800 BC Shamsi-adad establishes empire stretching to Mediterranean

c.1750 BC Collapse of Shamsi-adad's empire; start of period of foreign dominance

mid-14th century BC Ashur-uballit regains Assyrian independence

late 13th century BC Tikulti-ninurta captures Babylon

early 12th century BC Collapse of Tikulti-ninurti's empire

late tenth century BC Tiglath-pileser conquers lands towards Mediterranean, in Asia Minor and towards Babylon

late ninth century BC Ashur-nasir-pal reorganizes Assyrian army

879 BC Ashur-nasir-pal completes Kalakh palace

740 BC Tiglath-pileser takes Arpad

729 BC Tiglath-pileser takes crown of Babylon

689 BC Destruction of Babylon

681 BC Esarhaddon orders rebuilding of Babylon

671 BC Nile Valley added to empire under Esarhaddon

645 BC Capture of Babylon; death of Shamash-shum-ukin

614 BC Medes capture Ashur

612 BC Kalakh and Nineveh fall

609 BC Harran falls; Ashur-uballit II killed

From the first, the Assyrians were a warrior people, whose history was written primarily in the stories of their battles, victories, defeats and conquests. One early king, Shamsi-adad, at the start of the 18th century BC, conquered the lands to the west as far as the Mediterranean, to establish the first Assyrian empire. That collapsed within about 50 years, and the Assyrians were consumed in the tumult of the 16th century BC, when the whole of Mesopotamia was invaded by a succession of tribes from the north and east.

For two centuries, they lived again under foreign domination, until King Ashur-uballit led an uprising that drove the foreigners out, and established Assyria again as a nation in its own right. The Assyrians were still surrounded by powerful and aggressive tribes and kingdoms, but a succession of determined monarchs defended their independence until King Tikulti-ninurta, late in the 13th century, captured and plundered the holy city of Babylon, to establish another short-lived empire, this time stretching south through Mesopotamia. This empire, like that of Shamsi-adad, collapsed within a few years, following a rebellion by the king's two sons, in which he was killed.

There followed another 200 years of relative obscurity before King Tiglath-pileser began yet another series of conquests, taking his armies west towards the Mediterranean again, east into Asia Minor, and south towards Babylon. Little is known of the 100 years that followed his reign, but it seems likely that it was his conquests that led eventually to the great empire which would establish the Assyrians as the dominant power in Mesopotamia and the Middle East for nearly 500 years.

ASHUR-NASIR-PAL

Again, it was a succession of strong kings that built up Assyrian power to the point where their armies could begin to establish a long-term presence in the surrounding lands. Adad-nirari II, in the ninth century, fought a series of defensive campaigns against would-be invaders from Arabia, and also seized extensive territories from the Babylonians. It was his grandson, Ashur-nasir-pal II, however, who finally established the empire in all its power and savagery.

ABOVE *King Ashur-nasir-pal II was a bloodythirsty leader, legendary for the merciless treatment of his conquered enemies.*

Ashur-nasir-pal came to the throne in 884 BC, and was the inspiration behind the development of the Assyrian army, which rapidly became by far the most feared in the region. Few cities could withstand the heavy battering rams of his forces, and once the walls were breached, the inhabitants could expect little mercy. Inscriptions that he left behind describe how his defeated enemies were flayed, beheaded or impaled on stakes. Conquered peoples were moved *en masse* from one part of the empire to another – an early example of ethnic cleansing, designed to pre-empt any unrest or revolt.

The king campaigned northwards through Mesopotamia and towards the Caspian Sea, as well as north-west into Syria. This time, the Assyrians were building an empire to last: apart from generals and military forces, the king sent in administrators and tax collectors, and began a massive programme of new building, mostly of royal palaces and temples dedicated to the Assyrian deities, establishing the permanence and majesty of his rule. His palace in the town of Kalakh was reputed to cover some 25,000 square metres (270,000 sq. ft), and around 70,000 people were brought in to marvel at the king's wealth and power during its opening ceremonies.

BELOW The Palaces of Nimrud were built by Ashur-nasir-pal II in the ninth century BC. Many of the carvings found in excavations in the 1850s are now housed in the British Museum.

The conquests of Ashur-nasir-pal's reign continued under his son, Shalmaneser III, who added to the empire great swathes of territory across what is now northern Syria, and also campaigned in the eastern border regions.

ASSYRIAN KINGS

1115–1077 BC Tiglath-pileser I
1076–1074 BC
    Asharid-apal-ekur
1074–1056 BC Ashur-bel-kala
1056–1054 BC Eriba-adad II
1054–1050 BC Shamsi-adad IV
1050–1031 BC Ashur-nasir-pal I
1031–1019 BC Shalmaneser II
1019–1013 BC Ashur-nirari IV
1013–972 BC Ashur-rabi II
972–967 BC Ashur-resh-ishi II
967–935 BC Tiglath-pileser II
934–912 BC Ashur-dan II
911–891 BC Adad-nirari II
891–884 BC Tikulti-ninurta II
884–859 BC Ashur-nasir-pal II
859–824 BC Shalmaneser III
824–811 BC Shamsi-adad V
811–783 BC Adad-nirari III
783–773 BC Shalmaneser IV
773–755 BC Ashur-dan III
755–745 BC Ashur-nirari V
745–727 BC Tiglath-pileser III
727–722 BC Shalmaneser V
721–705 BC Sargon II
705–681 BC Sennacherib
681–669 BC Esarhaddon
669–631 BC Ashurbanipal
631–627 BC Ashur-etil-Ilani
626 BC Sin-shumu-lishir
626–612 BC Sin-sharish-kun
612–609 BC Ashur-uballit II

MILITARY LEADERSHIP

But from the start of the eighth century BC, the empire started to fall apart. Large stretches of territory in the north were lost, and throughout Babylonia, Aramaean nomads from what is now Syria were plundering and raiding almost at will. It needed a strong military leader to halt the decline, and in 754 BC, a revolt by the army brought a military leader to power. He took the name Tiglath-pileser III, and immediately set about reorganizing the administration of the empire, re-equipping the army, and forming alliances to strike back against the raiders. With Babylonian help, for instance, he inflicted a succession of defeats on the Aramaeans, and then, campaigning in the north and north-west, he reasserted control over many of the lands that had fallen away from the empire. The city of Arpad, in the north-west of modern Syria, was taken after a three-year siege, and its inhabitants massacred. Damascus was captured too, and its king executed. The power of the army was such that, while some nations were defeated in battle, many others decided that the protection of the Assyrians was worth the payment of annual tribute and the acceptance of Assyrian dominance.

In 729 BC, after the death of his former ally King Nabonassar of Babylon, Tiglath-pileser assumed the crown of that city, and the title of Ruler of Asia. Decades of Assyrian influence in Babylonia were now marked by the formal take-over of power, and the Assyrian empire was at its greatest extent.

DESTRUCTION OF BABYLON

Sargon II, who came to the throne in 721, was probably Tiglath-pileser's younger son. He almost immediately lost control of Babylon, but revolts in Gaza, Egypt and Syria were brutally put down, and a major expedition conquered much of the kingdom of Urartu, south-east of the Black Sea. Sargon forced out the Aramaean king who had seized the throne of Babylon, and – careful to avoid offending the priests in holy temples there – announced himself to be simply the governor of the city.

However, the fighting in the outlying areas of the empire, and particularly Babylonia, had been almost constant. A failed campaign against Jerusalem cost the Assyrians an estimated 185,000 dead, and a fresh invasion of Babylon, this time by the people of Elam, in the southwest of modern Iran, drove the Assyrians out of the city once again. In 689 BC, Sargon's son Sennacherib ordered its complete destruction, and the course of a canal was diverted to run over the ruins.

Since Babylon was considered a holy place, this was a direct challenge to the priesthood, and it seems likely that some sort of religious revolt was behind Sennacherib's murder some years later. His son, Esarhaddon, ordered the rebuilding of the city, and worked to establish peaceful relations not only with the priesthood, but also with the other cities of Babylonia. He also signed a peace treaty with the king of the Scythians, a nation of nomadic raiders from beyond the Caspian Sea, in order to protect the northern and eastern borders.

ABOVE *The defeat of Sennacherib at Jerusalem was said in the Bible to be due to divine intervention. Sennacherib himself claimed that Judas paid him tribute and he left.*

CONQUESTS IN THE SOUTH

But this non-confrontational approach did not mean there was any lessening of the desire to extend the empire. In 671 BC, Esarhaddon took Memphis, the capital of Egypt, and added much of the Nile Valley – previously ruled by the Ethiopians – to his lands. There were sporadic revolts in Egypt over the next few

years – Esarhaddon was killed while campaigning to put down one of them – and it was left to his son, Ashurbanipal, finally to drive the Ethiopians south out of the region.

Ashurbanipal's greater victories, however, came in southern Babylonia, where his brother Shamash-shum-ukin had been installed as crown prince of Babylon. Shamash-shum-ukin formed an alliance with several other kingdoms from the south, which aimed to remove his brother from the throne. They had an early victory against the king's soldiers, but by 645 BC, Babylon was under siege by the Assyrian army. It stood firm for three years, but eventually fell amid scenes of destruction and carnage. Shamash-shum-ukin, according to one account, gathered all his treasures, his wives and concubines into his palace and set fire to it, to die with them in a final and bloody act of defiance.

ABOVE *Ashurbanipal, king of Assyria, in a bas-relief carving held at the British Museum.*

Another attack at the same time was directed on Elam, where the capital of Susa was burned to the ground, its people exiled to other parts of the empire, and Elam itself reduced to the status of an Assyrian province. These were great victories, and they brought huge caravans of tribute and plunder back to Nineveh. Carvings in Ashurbanipal's palace, and the surviving great library which he had built in Nineveh, all suggest that the regime was confident and powerful; tens of thousands of administrators were running the empire, reporting ultimately to Ashurbanipal himself. Talented artists and craftsmen and constant flows of tribute, including offerings from the Persians, ensured that Assyria was culturally as well as militarily without rival.

CIVIL WAR, INVASION AND DECLINE

But despite the victories, the need for such military action in Elam and Babylonia, and the constant revolts in other regions, suggest that Assyrian rule was less sure than it appeared.

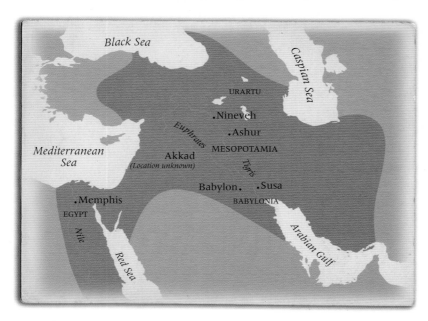

LEFT *At its peak, the Assyrian empire extended from west of the river Nile in Egypu to east of the Caspian Sea in Persia.*

ASTRONOMICAL OBSERVATORIES

The Assyrians were closely involved with the development of astronomy in ancient Babylon, which led to detailed predictions of the movements of planets and even of eclipses.

One of the temples at Kalakh, destroyed in the sack of the city in 612, is believed to have included an observatory at the top of one of its towers, or ziggurats, which dated back for hundreds of years. From there, priests would have made regular and detailed observations and measurements of the stars and planets, which were associated with the Mesopotamian gods. In this way, it was believed, it was possible to foretell the future.

By the time the empire collapsed, Assyrian astronomers had already established the regular occurrence of eclipses, and were familiar with the paths of the planets through the night sky. Astronomical diaries have been preserved which include detailed observations going back as far as 650 BC, but it is certain that the study of the skies had been going on centuries before that.

There are few inscriptions to tell the story of the decline of the empire, but it seems to have been precipitated by a civil war between Ashurbanipal's sons. For at least ten years, starting around 635 BC, there was chaos in government, with new kings announcing their accession and generals forcing them from power. Some time around 625 BC, Scythian raiders swept through Syria and Palestine, while in Persia, the Medes from the north-east were gradually seizing control of Assyrian provinces. Then they took most of Babylonia, and in 614 BC captured the former capital of Ashur. Two years later, in 612 BC, the palace of Kalakh and the city of Nineveh both fell, and shortly after that, the western city of Harran, where the last Assyrian king, Ashur-uballit II had tried to make a last stand.

The Assyrians had been known for the cruelty of their rule – one of their judicial punishments was to force a convicted man to eat a pound of wool, and then drink water until the wool swelled and split his stomach apart. The butchery which followed the capture of a city by the Assyrian army was notorious. It seems that they were treated in much the same way by their conquerors: many would have been exiled to distant lands, just as their enemies had been before, and many more would have been slaughtered. When the Greek historian, Xenophon, passed by the site of the city 200 years later, it was still an uninhabited ruin.

The Achaemenid empire of the Persians is a largely off-stage presence in the history of Europe. Because of Greek opposition, their power never extended westward – but the empire, though it lasted for only two centuries, had a marked effect on European civilization. It brought together the cultures of Greece, Babylon, Egypt and Persia – and even when the empire itself was destroyed by Alexander the Great, that mixture of influences survived into the age of Rome. The Achaemenids also have an important place in the history and culture of Iran, where they are often seen as the founders of the Iranian nation.

THE ACHAEMENID EMPIRE
559 – 331 BC

WHEN CYRUS II (r. 558–529 BC), KNOWN AS CYRUS THE GREAT, succeeded his father Cambyses I to the throne of Anshan, in the southwest of modern-day Iran, in 559 BC it was as a subject-monarch, owing allegiance to King Astyages (r. 584–*c*.550 BC) of the Medes. Yet within five years he was at war with Astyages, and within 20 he was ruler of an empire of his own that was greater and more powerful than the Medes had ever dreamed of. His Achaemenid dynasty claimed to trace its roots back to Achaemenes, a Persian king of the seventh century BC, of whom nothing is now known, but its rise to dominance throughout the region can be dated to Cyrus' defeat of the Medes. Exactly how this amazing explosion of power was achieved is uncertain, although the Greek historian Herodotus (*c*.484–*c*.425 BC) suggests that treachery among Astyages' own aristocracy helped Cyrus to his first victory, and other sources refer to an alliance with the king of Babylon, Nabonidus (r. 556–539 BC).

In 550 BC, after three years of fighting, Cyrus seized the Median capital of Ecbatana, taking Astyages alive and, according to ancient accounts, treating him with respect and honour. Whether or not Cyrus was planning to create an empire, he was taking

LEFT *A sculpture of King Darius I in the ruins of his palace, the Apadana, at his new capital of Persepolis.*

all the steps that would increase his standing at home and his power abroad, starting with the creation of a magnificent new city at Pasargadae, and mounting expeditions in the north to consolidate his frontiers.

First, he attacked King Croesus (r. c.560–546 BC), the famously rich king of Lydia, and rapidly took control of practically the whole of Asia Minor, with only a few scattered Greek colonies on the coast able to resist him. Then, in a six-year series of campaigns in the east, he marched through a string of provinces that would form a barrier between his homeland and the fierce nomadic tribesmen of Central Asia. In the east, he turned on his earlier ally Nabonidus, effectively bringing the whole of the Babylonian empire under his control (also, incidentally, allowing the Jews to go back to Palestine after nearly 50 years of Babylonian captivity). When Cyrus died in 529 BC, he was on his way east again to reinforce his control of the distant provinces there, and he was already planning his next campaign, in which his son Cambyses II (r. 529–522 BC) would lead an army to conquer Egypt. His empire included the whole of Mesopotamia, Syria, Phoenicia and Palestine, and stretched out to the east as far as the Hindu Kush in modern Afghanistan.

FOUNDATIONS OF EMPIRE

Conquering such a wide range of territories was an astonishing feat of arms – but Cyrus' achievements were more than just military. He laid the foundations of empire by setting up irrigation systems in the parched grazing lands to the east, and by a policy of religious tolerance. In Babylon, for instance, he had himself anointed as ruler by the priests of the local god Marduk, and promised the people that he would outlaw slavery, protect the rights of property and guarantee freedom of religion. Such promises – recorded in cuneiform writing on a baked-clay cylinder found in the ruins of Babylon in the 19th century – may have been cheap, and there is little evidence of the extent to which his practice matched his prescription, but it is perhaps significant that it is for those pledges that Cyrus wished to be remembered.

Cyrus also paid close attention to the administration of the empire he had acquired so quickly, building a series of fortified towns such as Marakanda (known today as Samarkand) to keep control of the far eastern borders, and linking his capital Susa to Sardis in Asia Minor and the Aegean by building a 1500 mile (2400 km) road. He also established a system of regional administration in which regional governors, or satraps, were allowed a considerable degree of independence.

CAMBYSES' EGYPTIAN CONQUEST

With Cyrus' death came an early sign of the dynastic infighting that would fatally weaken the empire within 200 years. His son, Cambyses (r. 529–522 BC), had been involved in government for at least eight years and had been governor of Babylon in his own right. Records suggest that he was worried about a possible challenge from his brother Bardiya, who was ruling in the eastern provinces. Bardiya was put to death, and in 525 BC Cambyses launched the attack that his father had planned against the Egyptian pharaoh Psammetichus III (r. 526–525 BC). The first phase of the campaign was successful: Cambyses led his forces across the Sinai Desert to win the Battle of Pelusium, and the Egyptian city of Memphis was taken within a few months. (About 100 years later, Herodotus claimed to have found the battlefield at Pelusium still scattered with the bones of the soldiers who fell there. The skulls of the Egyptians, he says, were much thicker and stronger than those of the Persians, and he suggests unconvincingly that this may be because the Persians weakened the bones by covering their heads with felt caps rather than leaving them exposed to the hot sun.)

ABOVE *A silver plaque, with the same text written in Old Persian, Elamite and Babylonian, defining the limits of the empire of King Darius I.*

After the defeat, Psammetichus was carried off as a captive to the city of Susa, and the whole of Egypt as far south as the island of Elephantine, which guarded the upper reaches of the Nile, was brought into the Persian empire. The Persian name of the new satrapy, Mudraya, survives in the Arabic name for Egypt, Misr.

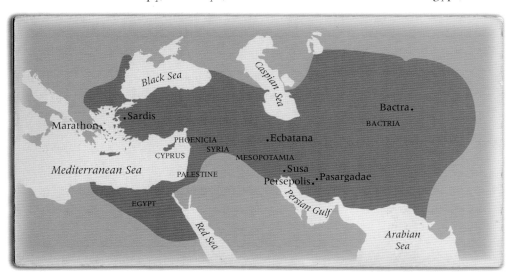

LEFT *Map showing the extent of the Achaemenid empire. Ancient Persepolis is located near the city of Shiraz in the south of modern-day Iran.*

ΔAPEIΟΣ

ΠΕΡΣΑΙ

Cambyses was declared the Egyptians' new pharaoh – although Herodotus says that unlike his father, who won much support in Babylon with his respect for the local deities, he outraged the Egyptian priesthood by killing their sacred bull and burning the body of the pharaoh Amasis (r. c.570–526 BC), Psammetichus' predecessor. Egypt would prove to be a constant source of trouble to Cambyses' successors. But as he travelled back to Persia, word came of an uprising in the east, where a mystic named Gaumata was reported to be claiming to be the reincarnation of Bardiya, and had won the support of several satrapies by promising to cancel their taxes. On his way to deal with this new rebellion, Cambyses died mysteriously, either by suicide or in a bizarre accident, according to the sources. One of his generals, Smerdis, a member of a different branch of the royal family, took over command.

DARIUS THE GREAT

One possibility is that Gaumata was one of the Mede aristocrats, who had been accepted at court ever since Cyrus' defeat of Asyages, which would mean that the seizure of power could have had wider implications for the future of the empire. In any case, Darius (c.549–485 BC r. 522–485 BC), with the battle-hardened troops from the Egyptian campaigns, quickly defeated and killed the usurper. It seems likely that Gaumata's attempt to take power had wider support, because the new 'Great King' was immediately faced with a series of revolts in different regions: in Elam in the heartland of Persia, in Babylon, in Egypt among the Medes, and in the eastern satrapies of Parthia and Margiana. For at least three years Darius was fighting a succession of battles to make his position secure, the final ones coming during an expedition to Egypt in 519 BC, where he re-asserted Persian power and reorganized the taxation and agricultural systems.

Although his own dynastic claims were tenuous, the new emperor was establishing a long-term empire on a firm base, in much the same way as Cyrus had tried to do before him. Like Cyrus, he began the construction of a city of his own, Persepolis, about 50 miles (80 km) southwest of Cyrus' city of Pasargadae – a magnificent construction designed to demonstrate his power and wealth, the ruins of which still stand about 40 miles (60 km) from the modern city of Shiraz. Darius was asserting his right to be considered an equal of his great predecessor, and in his inscriptions he stressed the dynastic connection that he claimed to trace right back to Achaemenes. He also built on Cyrus' administrative innovations. The system of regional government was developed with the satraps continuing to wield power but under the watchful eyes of separately appointed military governors, who reported directly to Darius' central government. Financial controllers were also appointed, with a brief to oversee the collection of taxes in gold or silver from each region – the use of coins made of gold, silver and copper revolutionized trade throughout the empire.

UNIFICATION AND EXPANSION OF THE EMPIRE

Darius also expanded the network of roads that Cyrus had started, and organized the digging of a canal from the Nile to Suez, linking the Mediterranean with the Persian Gulf and the Indian Ocean, and improving the links between the various parts of his vast empire. Royal inspectors toured the different satrapies constantly to report on local conditions, and military patrols were maintained along the roads, keeping them safe for travellers and for the king's own messenger service.

At the same time, Darius was ambitious to push the boundaries of the empire further afield. Persian nobles – as distinct from the inhabitants of subject cities and regions – enjoyed considerable political privileges, but were expected always to be available for military service. They commanded an army largely made

TIMELINE

359 BC Artaxerxes II dies; succession of Artaxerxes III

351 BC Rebellion in Phoenicia

343 BC Reconquest of Egypt

338 BC Death of Artaxerxes III; succession of Artaxerxes IV Arses

336 BC Death of Artaxerxes IV Arses; succession of Darius II

334 BC Alexander crosses the Hellespont

330 BC Alexander sacks Persepolis; Darius II killed

RULING OVER A DIVERSE EMPIRE

The great triumph of the Achaemenid emperors was that they maintained such a tolerant and inclusive rule over an empire that was so diverse that its official inscriptions were written in three languages – Old Persian, Babylonian and Elamite – while the most common language of the imperial administration was Aramaic.

This mix of languages reflects the fact that the empire was a generally tolerant amalgamation of different peoples under the rule of the Great King, whose court would travel from Susa north to Ecbatana, south to Persepolis and west to Babylon. The governors, or satraps, who ruled the provinces had considerable independence, and the conquered peoples retained their own religions, customs and much of their traditional legal frameworks – although the army remained centrally controlled. Cyrus the Great (r. 559–529 BC), who adopted a conciliatory attitude towards the conquered Babylonians, and thus eased the way to his acceptance as the legitimate heir to the deposed Nabonidus, was setting a precedent that would define the character of the empire.

Even though the central power of the empire had continually to be reasserted against rebellious provinces, the rule of Cyrus and his successors was based on a firm body of law. Darius I (r. 521–486 BC) in particular was known as a great law-giver – but despite using a consistent legal framework in the daily life of the empire, the succession was often bloodily contested between claimants; the tolerance and respect for law which marked the empire as a whole did not extend to the rulers themselves.

up of mercenaries and soldiers supplied by the various satraps and which included, according to Herodotus, a personal bodyguard for the Great King of 10,000 'Immortals'.

With this army, Darius campaigned first in the east, extending Cyrus' earlier conquests, and then in the west, where his forces moved along the western and northern shores of the Black Sea and established a bridgehead on the European shores of the Hellespont. In a revolt by several of the Greek cities in Asia Minor, Athenian forces supporting the rebels had sacked and burned the city of Sardis, leading Darius to swear vengeance. In the Aegean, several of the islands which had traditionally been ruled by the Greek city-states came under Persian rule: it was clear that Greece was the next objective of the expanding empire.

INVASION OF GREECE

The first push into mainland Greece was repulsed by the Athenian victory at the Battle of Marathon in 490 BC, in which the Athenians, although heavily outnumbered, lost 192 men compared with Persian losses of 6500. For the

Greeks, the victory was a defining moment, but for the Persians it seemed at the time to be little more than a temporary setback in a distant frontier skirmish. Their forces retreated towards Asia Minor, where Darius ruthlessly put down rebellions among the Greek settlements and began the planning of a second, more intensive invasion.

Before Darius could mount this new campaign, he fell ill and died. From among his 12 sons and six daughters, his eldest son Xerxes (r. 485–465 BC) had already been groomed to take over the crown. There were rebellions in both Babylon and Egypt, to which Xerxes had to travel in order to put down the resistance, but he inherited a kingdom which, despite the defeat at Marathon, remained inherently strong and stable.

Xerxes crushed the Babylonian and Egyptian uprisings brutally and then concentrated on building a huge army for the new attack on Greece. One estimate is that only about a tenth of it was made up of Persians, the rest coming from Scythia, Bactria and the other provinces of the empire. In 480 BC, he crossed the Hellespont with these forces, supported by a fleet of warships. The army forced their way through northern Greece, defeating the heroic Spartan resistance at Thermopylae, and marched on Athens. They sacked the city and burned the Acropolis, but their fleet was defeated by the smaller but more manoeuvrable Greek vessels at the Battle of Salamis.

HUMILIATION AT THE HANDS OF THE GREEKS

Unable to find supplies for his army without naval support, Xerxes was forced to pull back to the Hellespont. He returned to Persia, leaving his commander Mardonius (d.479 BC) with orders to hold the parts of Greece that had already been conquered. But although he managed to recapture Athens, the Greek city-states united against the Persian threat and defeated the Persian army and navy on the same day in 479 BC, in the Battles of Plataea and Mycale.

Greek historians, who are responsible for most of today's knowledge about the Persians, suggest that Xerxes then settled for a comfortable royal life in the cities of Ecbatana, Susa and Persepolis. The degeneracy and self-indulgence of their enemies was a common theme of the Greeks – Herodotus' claim that Persian skulls were weaker than those of the Egyptians because of

BELOW *In a show of strength, as represented by this sculpture of a Greek soldier from the temple of Aphaea, the Greeks defeated both the Persian army and navy on the same day, in the Battles of Plataea and Mycale.*

their habit of wearing hats in the sun is one example – but it does seem that Xerxes made no more efforts to extend his empire. He was assassinated in 465 BC, possibly on the orders of his son Artaxerxes (r. 465–424 BC), who inherited the crown.

Persian rule in Egypt and elsewhere was now under increasing pressure, with constant attempts to seize power in palace coups and revolts in different parts of the empire. Soon after his accession, Artaxerxes was fighting his own brother Hystaspes in the satrapy of Bactria. There are few details about the reigns of the succeeding kings – Darius II (r. 424–405 BC), Artaxerxes II (405–359 BC), Artaxerxes III (r. 358–338 BC), Artaxerxes IV Arses (r. 338–336 BC) and Darius III (r. 336–330 BC) – and the Greek authors whose accounts survive are often confused and contradictory, but it is clear that the internal unrest continued.

BELOW *Cyrus II, the first king of the Achaemenid empire, liberated the exiled Jews after defeating the Babylonians, allowing them to return to their homes.*

BLOOD-LETTING IN THE PALACE

Darius II only won the throne after a brief but savage period of blood-letting among the illegitimate sons of Artaxerxes. The one legitimate son, Xerxes II, was allegedly murdered within days of his succession in 424 BC as he lay drunk in the palace, and Darius seized power in the ensuing struggle. Immediately, he had to put down more revolts, first in Lydia, Asia Minor and then in Egypt; and the 20 years of his reign seem to have been filled with different uprisings all over his empire. He was on his way to deal with more trouble in the mountainous northern region when he fell ill and died. His successor, Artaxerxes II, then faced an insurrection by his younger brother Cyrus, who raised an army with a large contingent of Greek mercenaries in an attempt to take Babylon as a stepping stone to the throne. Cyrus was defeated and killed at the Battle of Cunaxa (401 BC), about 50 miles (80 km) north of Babylon, but the unrest continued. During a rare spell of relative peace and stability, Artaxerxes reasserted his control over the Greek cities of Asia Minor, but control over Egypt had slipped away. In Athens, meanwhile, there were repeated calls for a war of revenge on an empire that was seen as weak and decadent.

The empire struggled on. Artaxerxes III, according to one source, came to power only after burying alive his sister, who was also his step-mother, and having his uncle and more than 100 sons and grandsons massacred by archers after they had been locked in a palace courtyard – an extreme way of securing his position, even by the standards of the time. Subsequently, he commanded an army which finally defeated the rebellious Egyptians and their Greek mercenary allies at the Battle of Pelusium in 343 BC, and put down rebellions in Phoenicia and Cyprus. For a short time the Achaemenid empire seemed to have regained its earlier power and glory – but the power was a mirage.

ABOVE *Artaxerxes I, son of Xerxes, on the Tripylon (Council Hall) in Persepolis. It has been suggested that he ordered the assassination of his father, Xerxes, in order to take the throne.*

DARIUS III AND THE FALL OF THE EMPIRE

Each succession seemed to have its own horrific story of murder and betrayal. Darius III, according to the Greek historian Diodorus Siculus (c.90–c.27 BC), writing about 300 years later, came to power after the eunuch Bagoas, a mysterious but senior military commander at the Great King's court, had poisoned first Artaxerxes III and then his successor Artaxerxes IV Arses and his children. Darius III only escaped a similar fate by tricking Bagoas into drinking his own poison.

Once again, though, he was plagued by insurrections and revolts, and he was in Egypt when news first arrived of the invasion of Asia Minor by the Macedonian forces of Alexander the Great (r. 336–323 BC). (See Alexander the Great, pages 38–47.) His defeat of troops from the northern satraps at the Battle of the Granicus (334 BC) gave Alexander unchallenged control of Asia Minor, and he had reached the town of Issus before Darius III himself at the head of his army managed to bring him to battle again. Once more the Macedonians were victorious, and after rampaging down the Mediterranean coast and through Egypt, Alexander finally destroyed Darius III's power in 331 BC at Gaugamela, near the modern city of Mosul. From there he marched eastwards down the Royal Road that Cyrus the Great had built 200 years before, towards Darius I's city of Persepolis. The city, said to be the richest in the world, was sacked and looted, with the Palace of Xerxes (the king who had plundered Athens and burned the Parthenon) singled out for complete destruction.

Darius III himself had escaped from the disaster of Gaugamela and was planning a desperate last stand against the invaders when he was murdered by one of his satraps. Alexander, with the respect for a defeated opponent that Cyrus had shown, had his body buried with dignity in the ruins of Persepolis, and travelled north to Pasargadae to pay homage at the tomb of Cyrus. After his own death, one of his commanders-in-chief would establish the Seleucid dynasty, ruling not only Persia but the whole eastern half of Alexander's empire from Babylon. The Achaemenid empire, along with the glories of Cyrus and Darius, had perished in the flames of Persepolis.

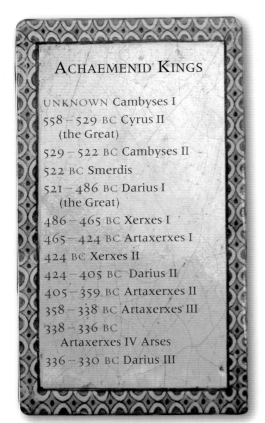

ACHAEMENID KINGS

UNKNOWN Cambyses I
558 – 529 BC Cyrus II
    (the Great)
529 – 522 BC Cambyses II
522 BC Smerdis
521 – 486 BC Darius I
    (the Great)
486 – 465 BC Xerxes I
465 – 424 BC Artaxerxes I
424 BC Xerxes II
424 – 405 BC Darius II
405 – 359 BC Artaxerxes II
358 – 338 BC Artaxerxes III
338 – 336 BC
    Artaxerxes IV Arses
336 – 330 BC Darius III

WHY DID THE EMPIRE FALL?

There were clear military reasons for the defeat by the Macedonians – Alexander's troops were better armed and more manoeuvrable than the Persians, and he was a brilliant and daring military commander. And while the Persians were used to putting down internal dissension, they had never before faced an invasion by an outside army that was determined to destroy their power. The Greeks, on the other hand, were in no doubt as to the reason for the fall of the Persian empire: its leaders had lost the martial spirit of their predecessors and become soft and self-indulgent. Xenophon (c.431–355 BC), writing during the reign of Artaxerxes II, told of 'those carpets on which the Persians love to loll lazily', and the orator Isocrates (436–338 BC) declared scornfully, 'It is impossible for people raised and governed as they [the Persians] are to have any virtue ... They indulge their bodies in the luxury of their riches'.

It is certainly true that the years following the defeat at Salamis in 480 BC saw fewer efforts at military expansion, although there were still occasional military victories abroad, such as the defeat by the Persian naval commander Conon of the Spartans at Cnidus (394 BC) during the

campaigning of Artaxerxes II in Asia Minor, which led to their expulsion from
the coastal settlements and the islands of the Aegean. It is also true that the
relative calm of Artaxexes II's reign saw the construction of many magnificent
monuments, such as the golden columns and silver roof tiles of Ecbatana and the
lavish expansion of the fabulously wealthy city of Persepolis. Less biased
observers than the Greeks, particularly today, might describe such achievements
as civilized rather than decadent.

In fact, it was the endemic revolts, insurrections and palace infighting that
weakened the empire rather than any supposed moral decline. Every Great King
had to reassert his authority over the various satraps by force of arms –
significantly, there was never any attempt to weld them into a single culture.
The Achaemenid empire, which at its height extended across three continents
and covered an area of around 3 million square miles (8 million sq km), was
multi-ethnic, multi-cultural and multi-lingual: when Alexander appeared, the
satraps were simply exchanging one overlord for another. Once Darius III had
been put to flight in battle, the only unifying force holding the empire together
had been shattered. It would be more than 900 years before the game of chess
first appeared in Persia, but the loss of the king ended the Achaemenid empire
just as surely as a checkmate.

ABOVE *This detail from the*
Alexander Mosaic *shows*
Persians fleeing from the Battle
of Issus. Although heavily
outnumbered, the Macedonians
succeeded in breaking Darius'
defences, forcing his army to
break ranks and retreat in
disarray.

The Delian League, formed originally to defend the Greeks against Persian attack, gradually took on the characteristics of an Athenian empire around the Aegean Sea. Cities that had once supplied ships and men for the joint defence of the league began to pay money to Athens instead. But in mainland Greece, without the support of their navy, the Athenians were vulnerable to attack. Despite attempts to construct fortifications, their city was eventually conquered by their militaristic and highly disciplined rival, Sparta, supported by the Persians.

THE ATHENIAN EMPIRE
c.500–400 BC

For the Athenians, victory over the invading Persian army at the Battle of Marathon in 490 BC was the defining moment in their history. But the Persians took their revenge, returning under King Xerxes (r. 485–465 BC) less than ten years later to sack Athens and tear down its walls. Even though that disgrace was followed by their eventual defeat and expulsion from Greece, it left the Greek city-states terrified of repeated attacks. To the victorious Greeks, the defeats of the rampaging Persian army and navy in 479 BC at the Battles of Plataea and Mycale respectively seemed at best like a brief respite. There was always a sense that the city-states would have to band together again in the future to beat off more attacks. The Spartans, who had taken the leading military role in the Persian wars, wanted to pull Greek settlers back from Asia Minor – but one of the first acts of the Athenians was to besiege and capture the Persian settlement of Sestos on the Hellespont.

DEFENSIVE ALLIANCE

Fear of the Persians, mixed with hatred and contempt for what the Greeks believed was an effete and degenerate nation, led them to band together for their defence in what became known as the Delian League, after the holy island of Delos, where its meetings were held. While the Spartans had a powerful army, it was the Athenian navy that was likely to form the strongest defence against any return of the Persians.

LEFT *Athenian merchants grew rich on the proceeds of trade, and architectural triumphs, such as the Parthenon, were financed with the tribute sent to Athens by members of the league.*

According to the Greek historian Thucydides (c.460–395 BC), the other city-states and the settlers in Asia Minor asked Athens to take the leadership of the league. From the outset, although each member had in theory one vote in deciding league policy, the Athenians enjoyed a clear dominance. There was an early campaign against a Persian settlement at Eion in northern Greece, but there was also an attack on the city of Carystus on the island of Euboea, a traditional enemy of the Athenians, and another on the island of Naxos. The pretext for both raids was to encourage membership of the league – Carystus did not want to join, and Naxos had announced its intention to secede – but the savage punishment brought to bear on Naxos, which was forced to tear down its city walls and which saw its citizens enslaved, does not sound like an attempt to establish an effective defensive barrier against Persian attack.

It was not only by the threat of force that the Athenians won more support. Successful expeditions against the Persians demonstrated how effective the league could be. A naval expedition to southern Anatolia, under the Athenian general Cimon, forced a number of coastal cities to swear loyalty, and then clashed with a Persian fleet near the River Eurymedon. The Greeks sank many of the Persian vessels and captured others, effectively ending the naval threat of the Persians in the Aegean for ten years or more. More importantly, news of the victories encouraged several more cities, such as the trading centre of Phaselis in Asia Minor, to join the league.

PEACE WITH PERSIA

The Athenians were deliberately concentrating all the resources of the league within their own treasury. They were responsible for producing the overwhelming majority of the ships and soldiers needed by the league; and in return they demanded tribute from the other members. Thucydides suggests that this tactic of encouraging members to commute their contributions of ships and men into money was a deliberate policy to prevent the members of the league from drifting away. *'While Athens was strengthening her navy with the money they sent, a revolt never had enough resources or experienced generals for war'*, he said.

About 460 BC the Greek general Pericles ordered a disastrous attack on the Persian province of Egypt, in which a Greek force that had been sent to support an uprising against Persian rule was defeated with the loss of thousands of men. Around the same time, the Athenians were entering into an alliance with the city of Segesta on the island of Sicily. The two moves typified their activities around this time: attempting to push the frontiers of their sphere of influence outward, by means of either war or diplomacy.

In 454 BC, the league's treasury was moved from Delos to Athens. The reason given was that renewed Persian activity in the Mediterranean following the defeat in Egypt meant that the undefended island of Delos was no longer a safe place to store the booty and tribute that had been gathered. But from this time onwards, the league appears even more like an empire, with the other city-states paying tribute directly to Athens.

Defeat in Egypt was followed by an uneasy peace with the Persians. Each side seems to have recognized that it could not achieve a conclusive victory over the other. Although the details of their agreement are unclear – some historians even doubt whether a formal peace was ever agreed – it seems that the Persians agreed to end their activities around the Aegean, while the Greeks renounced any interest in Persian possessions in Asia Minor, Cyprus or North Africa.

BATTLES IN GREECE

With the end of hostilities against the Persians, the original reason for the existence of the Delian League had gone, but tensions had been growing on the Greek mainland. Sparta, the southern Greek city which had long been a

ABOVE *The Greeks and Persians fought for nearly 50 years, before eventually reaching an uneasy stalemate. This illustration shows the Battle of Thermopylae in 480 BC, when an outnumbered Greek army held off the Persian forces in one of history's most famous last stands.*

ATHENIAN DEMOCRACY

The city-state of Athens had one of the first known functioning democratic systems in the world. The aristocrat Cleisthenes (fl.510 BC) is usually credited with instituting the constitutional reforms of the late sixth century BC which required new laws to be approved by the citizens at a mass assembly. He also established a council, or boule, of 50 members, chosen by lot from among the ten tribes of Athens.

It was far from any modern idea of a democracy. Of an estimated population of around 250,000 during the fourth century BC, only about 30,000 adult male citizens had the vote. Only about 6000 of them could fit at any one time onto the Pnyx, a rocky hill near the Acropolis, which was used as a meeting place.

Pericles had such a profound influence on Athenian society that Thucydides deemed him to be 'the first citizen of Athens'.

The rest of the population – mainly women and slaves – was excluded. A voter had to have completed military training and to have Athenian ancestry on both sides of his family, although citizens from elsewhere in Greece could be granted voting rights *en masse*.

The assembly made political decisions such as those about war and peace. It also voted to accept or reject new laws proposed by the boule, and it tried political crimes. Most public officials were chosen by lot rather than by election, but the assembly also elected juries of citizens aged over 30 to try civil and criminal cases. If individuals seemed to be acquiring too much power or influence, it could vote to ostracize or expel them for ten years.

traditional rival, had remained in an uneasy alliance with Athens in the aftermath of the Persian invasion, but the growth in Athenian power and influence had caused concern among the Spartans. There had been sporadic skirmishing, and only revolts by the helots, the state-owned Spartan serfs, had prevented several outbreaks of war between the two cities.

To increased Spartan antagonism, the Athenians had starting reinforcing the defences of their own city by building long walls from the city itself to its port of Piraeus. In 458 BC, before the project was completed, Spartans and Athenians clashed at the Battle of Tanagra, to the north of Athens. The Athenians were defeated, but the Spartans lacked the strength to follow up their advantage and had to retreat to their home city. Despite their defeat at Tanagra, the Athenian army continued to push west into Boeotia, where they won the Battle of Oenophyta, giving them control of much of the northern shore of the Gulf of Corinth.

But the clashes continued, with alliances among the different states forming, breaking and re-forming over the next few years. While Athenian sea power meant that the more distant Aegean islands could still be kept within the league, the mainland city-states were starting to break away. A revolt by the Boeotians, some ten years after the Battle of Oenophyta, forced Athens to send a new army of several thousand men to recapture the cities that had broken away. Initial successes were followed by a catastrophic defeat at the Battle of Coronea in 447 BC.

ABOVE *The Athenian empire at its peak, c.450 BC.*

Other revolts on the large island of Euboea, close to the mainland, and in the city of Megara on the isthmus of Corinth, encouraged fresh intervention from the Spartans. By 431 BC, years of skirmishing and minor confrontations culminated in the outbreak of full-scale war between Sparta and her allies in the Peloponnesian League on one side, and Athens and the loyal members of the Delian League on the other.

DEFEAT AND SURRENDER

In the early phases of the Peloponnesian War, continued Athenian naval superiority meant that raids could be carried out on the shores of the Peloponnese almost at will, while the Spartans in return launched repeated land assaults. But a massive naval attack by the Athenians on Sparta's ally, Syracuse, in Sicily resulted in a catastrophic defeat in 413 BC, after the Greek ships were trapped in the harbour of Syracuse and destroyed.

BELOW *An Athenian trireme: a battleship with three rows of oars on each side. This was the predominant type of vessel used in the Peloponnesian War.*

The Spartans, meanwhile, were growing in strength, largely thanks to a new alliance with the Persians, and in 404 BC a Spartan naval force met the Athenian ships at the Battle of Aegospotami, close to the Hellespont. The Athenian fleet was destroyed and thousands of prisoners executed.

With no fleet, the Athenians were defenceless, and they were forced to surrender their city to the Spartans after a siege. The city walls were destroyed, and democratic government was replaced by a brutal Spartan-backed oligarchy. Although Athens recovered within 30 years to found another confederation of Aegean cities, the era of her greatest power was past.

At its height the empire of Alexander the Great extended from Punjab and the foothills of the Himalayas in the east through the former Persian empire and the Greek city-states to the fringes of the Balkans and North Africa in the west. But more than any other empire in history, Alexander's was the product of the energy, determination and sheer brute force of a single man; within a few months of his death it had been split among his warring generals, and by the first century BC most of the Hellenistic territories in the west had been assimilated into the growing power of Rome. The Greek city-states to the south saw the Macedonians as barbarians, and Alexander's military conquests during his 13-year reign showed why.

ALEXANDER
THE GREAT
336 – 323 BC

ALEXANDER (r. 336–323 BC) CAME TO THE THRONE AFTER HIS FATHER, Philip II of Macedonia (r. 359–336 BC), had unified the city-states of Greece to form the League of Corinth, hoping to lead them against the Persian empire. There had been bitter rivalry between the king and his young, ambitious son ever since Alexander's success in the Battle of Chaeronea (338 BC) when, at the age of 18, he had led the Macedonian cavalry which wiped out the finest soldiers in the army of Thebes. Later reports describe him cutting his way through the Theban lines at the front of a tight wedge of horsemen: true or false, this was the start of a lifetime of legend-building and astonishing military success. Philip, jealous of his own reputation and concerned at the emergence of a possible rival, sought to contain the young upstart, and even sent him briefly into exile with his mother, Olympias.

Just two years later, Philip was dead – assassinated during a ceremony at the ancient Macedonian capital of Aegae as he sought the gods' approval for a new war on Persia. Alexander was at his father's side, and rumours persisted that he or his mother might have been responsible. The assassin was conveniently butchered on the spot.

LEFT *Detail of a floor mosaic found at the House of the Faun, Pompeii, depicting Alexander the Great at the Battle of Issus in 333 BC.*

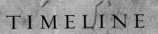
356 BC Born in Pella, Macedonia

340 BC Regent of Macedonia while Philip II campaigns in Byzantium

338 BC Commands cavalry at defeat of Athens and Thebes at Battle of Chaeronea

336 BC Philip assassinated; Alexander succeeds

335 BC Defeats Thrace and Illyria

334 BC Battle of the River Granicus starts Persian campaigns

333 BC Defeats Darius III at Battle of Issus; besieges Tyre and Gaza

332 BC Welcomed in Egypt as liberator

331 BC Founds Alexandria; marches into Assyria; forces Darius to flee at the Battle of Gaugamela

330 BC Sack of Persepolis; founds new cities across Afghanistan and Central Asia

326 BC Tribes of northern Pakistan submit; Ora, Massaga and Aornos destroyed; conquers Punjab at Battle of Hydaspes; army rebels at River Hyphasis

323 BC Dies at Babylon; conflict among generals

301 BC Empire divided into four after Battle of Ipsus

In the months that followed, the 20-year-old king asserted his authority with exemplary violence when the citizens of Thebes rose in revolt, razing the city to the ground and selling its inhabitants into slavery. Bribery, intrigue and summary execution dealt with old allies of his father who might prove a threat; Thrace and Illyria on the northern boundaries of his kingdom were defeated, and Athens, which had also been threatening rebellion, accepted his rule.

AN INSPIRED GENERAL

Those initial campaigns also established another aspect of the new king's character. He might have had the savagery of a psychopathic gangster but he also had the military brilliance of an inspired general. When he took his armies south into Greece, he was confronted by an army from Thessalia which had seized control of the Vale of Tempe, a narrow pass through the mountains. Rather than fight them on unfavourable terms, he held his army back until his engineers had cut steps in the mountain side to their flank, and then led his troops around behind the Thessalian forces.

With his position secure and the Greek city-states intimidated into submission, Alexander was ready to revive the campaign that his father had planned against the Persians. In the spring of 334 BC, at the head of an army of 50,000 foot soldiers, cavalry, sling-shot men and archers drawn from across Greece, he marched out of Macedonia towards the Hellespont, 300 miles (480 km) away, which was the crossing into Asia Minor. Significantly, he also took with him his own historian, Callisthenes (360–328 BC), who was to write the account of Alexander's great triumphs (and who, incidentally, died in prison six years later after making the mistake of criticizing his master).

ABOVE *A gold coin from Tarsus (a city in modern Turkey) featuring a sculpted relief of Philip II of Macedonia, dating from c.359–336 BC.*

For Alexander, it was the start of an unbroken 11 years of military campaigning across most of the known world. He would destroy the Persian empire, take Greek power and Greek culture to countries that the Greeks had never even heard of and establish cities that would last for 2000 years and more. As was his wish, his name would never be forgotten: to the defeated Persians he would become known as Alexander the Accursed; in

Arabic he would be remembered as Al-Iskander al Makadoni, in Hebrew as Alexander Mokdon, in Aramaic as Tre-Qarnayia, in Urdu as Sikander and in Pushtu as Skandar – but he would never return to Greece.

THE GATEWAY TO ASIA

Philip's forces had already established a bridgehead on the Asian side of the Hellespont, but they had been forced to pull back. Alexander himself had executed one of the joint leaders of the expedition in his initial purge of his father's supporters. Now, in 334 BC, at the Battle of the Granicus River, near the modern-day Turkish town of Ergili, he faced the troops of his Persian enemies for the first time.

He drew up his élite cavalry, known as the Companions, in the same wedge-shaped formation they had adopted at Chaeronea, and led them in a charge at the Persian army, which was reinforced by experienced Greek mercenaries. In the fighting, he was stunned by a blow on the head from an axe and only saved from death by the intervention of a Greek officer named Clitus. Like Callisthenes, Clitus would die a few years later, killed by Alexander in a quarrel after the officer suggested that he was a lesser man than his father. Around 4000 Persians were killed as their lines broke and soldiers fled, and at least 2000 were taken prisoner. The Macedonians suffered casualties of around 400.

The battle had opened the gateway to Asia, and Alexander marched southwards unopposed to take the Persian provincial capital of Sardis, where the gates and the treasury were thrown open to him without a fight. His forces rampaged along the southwestern coast of Asia Minor, blockading the ancient town of Halicarnassus (modern Bodrum) on his way, so that it could not be used by the

BELOW *The ruins of Sardis; once a Persian provincial capital, Sardis was captured by Alexander in 334 BC. It continued to thrive and remained a major city for another 1000 years thereafter.*

THE LEGEND OF ALEXANDER

Many ancient sources tell the story of Alexander's meeting with the Cynic philosopher Diogenes of Sinope (*c.*412 – 323 BC), who lived for a period in a barrel to demonstrate his contempt for luxury and comfort. Alexander went to see him in Corinth and asked if there was anything that he, as prince of Macedonia, could do for him, a penniless vagabond.

Diogenes – who believed passionately in the virtue of honesty – squinted up at the future ruler of one of the greatest empires in history. '*Yes*', he replied. '*You could stand aside out of the sunlight*'. Alexander's response, according to the sources, was to tell his attendants that if he had not been born Alexander of Macedon, he would like to have been Diogenes.

This is only one of scores of legends and stories which surrounded Alexander during his life and in the centuries after his death. One early source was a verse epic – now lost – written in Alexandria in the second century AD, but other versions appeared in Old English, German, Irish and Middle English. Arab and Persian poets also wove the stories into romances.

The philosopher Diogenes demonstrates to Alexander, conqueror of the world, that frugality leads to happiness..

Persian navy. Then he turned into the mountains of Lycia, moving from town to town with impunity. With the Persian army destroyed at the Granicus, there was no one to stop him.

LEGENDARY EXPLOITS

Apart from the military effect of his campaigns, Alexander's reputation was spreading as more stories about his remorseless power were created. At the town of Gordium, where his army paused for the winter, there was an intricate knot tied with rope made from either tree bark or vines, which legend said would only ever be untied by the future king of Asia – a challenge that was irresistible to the young general. Some accounts say he managed to untie it, others that he simply sliced through it with his sword, but the end result was the same, identifying the young general as a mighty conqueror. With one great victory and a series of defeated towns behind him, Alexander was master of these provinces of the Persian empire and well on his way to fulfilling the prophecy.

The decisive battle came a few months later, when the Persian king Darius III (c.380–330 BC) led his armies in person to meet this new young challenger. The estimate by the first-century Greek historian Plutarch (AD 46–120) that Darius' forces were 600,000 strong are clearly exaggerated, but it seems likely that the Macedonians may have been outnumbered by as many as two to one. Even so, when the two sides met near the town of Issus in 333 BC, the Persians, hemmed in by unfavourable terrain, were again put to flight by Alexander's battle-hardened soldiers. Plutarch quotes reports that Alexander was wounded in the battle by Darius himself, but the Persian king was forced to flee for his life, leaving behind his mother, his wife and his daughters as well as large quantities of gold, silver and other treasures.

ABOVE *Alexander reportedly treated Darius' family well after they were captured in 333 BC. This romanticized version of events was painted by the Italian Baroque artist Sebastiano Ricci in about 1710.*

According to Plutarch, Alexander treated the emperor's family well – but there was no mercy for his soldiers. Thousands of them – as many as 16,000 according to some estimates – were killed either in the battle or the massacre that followed. Although Darius himself escaped to lead a third Persian army against Alexander, his power had been effectively broken. According to the second-century Greek author Arrian (d. AD 180), he offered to make peace with Alexander, only to receive the following contemptuous reply:

> *'In future when you write to me, call me King of Asia. Do not address me as an equal.'*

There was to be no peace. The invaders moved on down the Mediterranean coast, laying siege to the prosperous port cities of Tyre and Gaza on their way towards Egypt – Tyre was razed to the ground, and the governor of Gaza dragged by a chariot around the walls of his city until he died.

ALEXANDRIA, EGYPT'S NEW CITY

In Egypt, not surprisingly, Alexander's reputation had gone before him, and the Egyptians welcomed him as a liberator into what had been the richest province in the Persian empire. Their priests declared him to be the son of Ammon (an oracle god). He had already founded cities in his own name after the Battle of Chaeronea and at Issus, but now he gave his name to the most famous Alexandria, which was to become the Ptolemaic capital of Egypt. Yet before work had even begun on the new city, Alexander was on the move again. Despite word of an uprising in Greece led by the citizens of Sparta against the general he had left in control there, he set off to the east again, crossing the Tigris and the Euphrates without opposition as he marched to face Darius again at the battle which would finally destroy the Persian empire.

Again, Alexander was heavily outnumbered, and this time Darius had taken care to choose a wide-open battleground which, unlike that at Issus, would give his forces room to manoeuvre. Here at Gaugamela in 331 BC he had war elephants from India and scythed chariots in his lines, and his generals had tried to deny Alexander's forces food and supplies by laying waste to the countryside through which they had to march. But what Darius could not control was the moon, and a lunar eclipse spread panic among his forces. Once again, he offered Alexander peace terms, this time including half his empire and his daughter's hand in marriage.

'That part of the world which has not looked upon Alexander has remained without sunlight.'

PLUTARCH, *in his biography of Alexander the Great*

For the third time, the Persian forces were broken and, although Darius escaped, he was never again any threat. Alexander chased and harried him until a few months later he was betrayed and murdered by a Persian nobleman. But now the Macedonian forces were heading south towards the fabled riches of the Persian capital of Persepolis, passing through Babylon, where Alexander ordered his troops to respect the houses of the ancient city, and also Susa, where he added the contents of the Royal Treasury to his plunder. Persepolis, though, was the greatest prize, and after making sure that the main mountain passes were under his control, he stormed into the city.

Persepolis was not only reputed to be the richest city in the world, it was also the ancient capital of the race that had invaded Greece and laid Athens to waste 150 years before, and Alexander took a terrible revenge. His soldiers plundered the city itself, killing the men and selling the women as slaves, and then burning the royal palaces to the ground. Gold, silver and other treasures were carried away by trains of camels and mules. *'As Persepolis had surpassed all other cities in prosperity, so she now exceeded them in misfortune'*, wrote the Greek historian Diodorus of Sicily (*c*.90–*c*.27 BC) some 300 years later. At 26 years of age, Alexander was ruler of the Persian empire and the avenger of what he claimed had been the violent rape of Greece by the Persian armies.

ON INTO INDIA

Now the Persian resistance was reduced to a guerrilla campaign, largely led by Bessus (d.329 BC), the nobleman who had murdered Darius and declared himself to be the new emperor under the name of Artaxerxes V. Alexander moved eastwards through modern Afghanistan to the foothills of the Himalayas, founding city after city and naming them in his own honour. Between Alexandria in northern Egypt and Alexandria Eschate ('Alexandria the Furthest') 3000 miles (4800 km) to the east, in what is now Tajikistan, at least 14 more towns named in his honour were scattered across Asia Minor.

He used diplomacy as well as force to coerce the tribes into submission. In the province of Balkh in what is now northern Afghanistan, he married a local princess, Roshanak, in an attempt to cement his control. When he decided to head further east and south into the Indian subcontinent, he urged the chieftains of what had been the Persian province of Gandhara to accept his rule without resistance. Those who refused, mostly hillsmen living in what is now Pakistan, were battered into submission not just for the sake of more conquests, but also to protect the lengthening Macedonian supply lines. Mountain strongholds like Ora, Massaga and Bazira (modern Barikot) were all taken after determined resistance. As each settlement fell, so the defenders were butchered until, having fought his way across the Indus, Alexander found himself at the Hydaspes river (now the River Jhelum), facing the soldiers of Raja Puru (r. 340–317 BC), ruler of a Punjab kingdom called Pauravaa.

BELOW *Amid the ruins of the ancient city of Persepolis stand the remains of Xerxes' winter palace. Known as the Tachara, the building was begun by his father, Darius I.*

Raja Puru's forces were split by Alexander's tactic of leading part of his army upriver to find a crossing point and were forced to surrender after a bitter fight. But the Macedonians lost at least 4000 men, with another 12,000 wounded, according to modern estimates. Many of them died in bitter fighting with Raja Puru's war elephants, which terrified the horses and slaughtered the men. The soldiers had been campaigning for seven years; they were far from home and increasingly unlikely ever to return; they had fought at least a dozen major battles and innumerable skirmishes. Further to the east, beyond the Hyphasis river (now known as the River Beas), was the powerful

northern Indian Nanda empire, which had a vast army with hundreds, perhaps thousands, of the feared war elephants. Alexander's men refused to go any further: the Hydaspes River had been the site of their last major battle, and the Hyphasis marked the eastern limit of Alexander's power.

RETREAT AND DEATH

His army would still have to fight its way out, but now at least it was heading back towards Persia, along the coast of the Indian Ocean. Alexander wanted to leave an empire behind him, not just a trail of military victories, and he appointed officers to act as satraps, or governors – when he discovered that many of those he had appointed earlier in his campaigning had abused their authority, he had them executed. In the Persian city of Susa he took two more wives for himself, and organized marriages for nearly 100 of his officers.

From Susa Alexander marched on to Babylon, perhaps with a view to extending his rule over Arabia – he had already sent a fleet to explore the coastline of the Persian Gulf. But whatever plans he might have had came to nothing: in Babylon, while staying in the ancient palace of the seventh-century-BC king Nebuchadnezzar (r. 604–561 BC), he retired to his bed after a party. Twelve days later, a month before his 33rd birthday, he was dead. Inevitably, there were rumours that Alexander was poisoned, but he had contracted malaria a few years before, he had been wounded several times during his years of campaigning and there had been many opportunities to pick up infections that could have caused his death.

ABOVE *Folio from a 14th-century manuscript of the* Shahnama (Book of Kings) *by the poet Firdawsi (d.1020). Commissioned by the Mongol Il-Khanid dynasty, this version contains illustrations of the exploits of Alexander the Great. This page shows Alexander (also known as Iskander) supervising the building of an iron rampart.*

But whether he was assassinated or died of natural causes, there were plenty of generals to take advantage of his death. First Perdiccas (c.360–320 BC) and Craterus (c.362–321 BC) took joint power as regents on behalf of Alexander's mentally ill half-brother Philip Arrhidaeus (r. 323–317 BC) before Perdiccas eliminated Craterus, along with some 30 other potential rivals. He was assassinated by his own troops and the various contenders for the imperial crown fought each other in the so-called Wars of the Diadochi, or Successors. One of the casualties was Alexander's son, known as Alexander IV (323–309 BC), who was born two months after his father's death and was shuffled around from one would-be regent to another until he was poisoned at the age of 13 to remove him from the

> *'They were told that the kings of the Ganderites and Praesii were waiting for them with eighty thousand cavalry, two hundred thousand foot soldiers, eight thousand chariots and six thousand war elephants.'*

PLUTARCH, *describing reports of the northern Indian Nanda forces*

reckoning. The wars culminated in the Battle of Ipsus in central Turkey in 301 BC, which finally settled the break-up of Alexander's legacy into three unstable blocks: the Antigonid and Selencid empires and the Ptolemaic kingdom. Just 33 years after the victory at the River Granicus which had opened the way for his amazing campaign of conquests, Alexander's empire had ceased to exist.

AFTERMATH AND LEGACY

By the first century BC, most of the western territories which Alexander had conquered were under Roman domination, and in the east the Parthians, a nomadic people of the Central Asian steppes, had taken control of much of what remained. But the cultural legacy of Alexander's short-lived empire was even more widespread and more long-lasting than his military domination. Greek influence remained strong for centuries in many of the cities he established, and Greek culture and thought were spread through Persia into Central Europe and as far as northern India. There are clear Greek influences on early Buddhist art, which spread out of Central Asia in the centuries after Alexander; and the survival of Greek culture and the Greek language helped the spread of trade and ideas – including, four centuries after Alexander's death, that of Christianity.

Alexander's reputation far outlived his empire. His savagery towards political rivals and defeated foes, his obsession with his own greatness and supposed descent from the gods, and his unpredictable mood changes may all be part of a legend created to subdue and terrify surrounding nations, but they sound today like the qualities of a man who was barely sane. To the Romans, who effectively inherited and recreated his empire, he was a hero and the model of a military leader, and his name has remained synonymous with power and conquest into modern times.

BELOW *Alexander's campaigns of conquest expanded the Macedonian empire from its heartland in Greece, south to Egypt and east as far as India.*

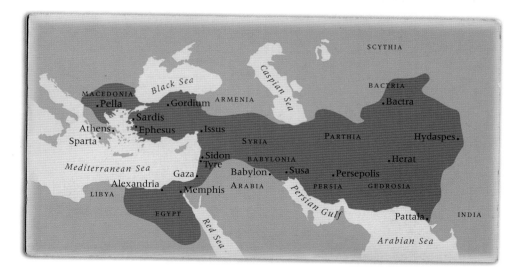

The Roman empire grew from an alliance of city states in the fourth
century BC to dominate the whole of western Europe, the Middle
East and North Africa. Its rise was punctuated by many setbacks,
including devastating military defeats and even the sack of Rome
itself, but the Romans regrouped after each disaster. Their strategy
was to keep their disciplined, well-equipped legions in the frontier
regions of their empire, where they could repel attacks from the
barbarian tribes outside. Within those frontiers, order was generally
kept by alliances with trusted local rulers coupled with the threat
of terrible military retribution for any revolts.

THE ROMAN EMPIRE
264 BC—AD 476

ROMAN MILITARY GENIUS CONQUERED EUROPE but it was Roman roads, Roman
architecture and Roman laws that transformed it. It is almost impossible to
exaggerate the influence that the Romans had on the lands they ruled. But for
much of the empire's seven centuries there was no agreed line of succession. Power
was held by the man who could command the strongest loyalty among the army,
particularly within the élite Praetorian Guard. This led to prolonged periods of conflict,
as rival generals fought for dominance, and also undermined the military discipline
that had first secured Rome her empire. When German tribes serving in the legions
revolted in the fifth century, there was no unified command to resist them. The empire
survived in the east to become the Byzantine empire, but in the west it collapsed as the
tribal leaders seized power.

DOMINANCE IN ITALY

The Romans had an empire long before they had an emperor. A series of victories in
wars against neighbouring tribes led first to the establishment of the Latin League of
allied city-states, with Rome as the most powerful partner, and then to Roman rule.
By the mid-third century BC, the Romans had achieved dominance over rival Italic
peoples such as the Latins and Samnites and conquered the Greek cities of southern
Italy, giving them control of the whole Italian peninsula.

LEFT *Detail from the sarcophagus of Roman emperor Marcus Aurelius
(second century AD), showing Roman legionaries crushing a barbarian force.*

By this stage, the Romans had already come into conflict with the Carthaginians, a people of Phoenician origin who dominated trade throughout the Mediterranean from the city-state they had established on the coast of modern Tunisia. The first of a series of three wars between the two would-be imperial powers – the Punic Wars (from the Latin *Poeni*, 'Phoenicians') – began in 264 BC, with a local conflict in Sicily. The conflict rapidly escalated into a war on land and sea that lasted sporadically for 23 years. The Roman legions, recruited largely from Rome's Italian possessions, were virtually invincible on land in Sicily and North Africa, but the Carthaginians' strong navy assured them control of the seas for much of the war. Rome's eventual victory marked the start of a period of dominance in the Mediterranean, which became known as *Mare Nostrum*, or 'Our Sea'. Perhaps this, the start of expansion outside Italy, marks the real start of the Roman empire.

MEDITERRANEAN POWER

The Second Punic War, which started in 218 BC, was fought mainly in Italy, where the Carthaginian general Hannibal (247–c.183 BC) – with his war elephants – inflicted a series of defeats on the Roman legions. Despite his victories, most of the Italian towns remained loyal to Rome, and Hannibal was unable to take the city. The war continued for 17 years, as Rome first attacked Carthaginian colonies in Spain and then, under the general Scipio (236–183 BC) moved against Carthage itself. Forced to return to defend the city, Hannibal was defeated at the Battle of Zama in 202 BC. Once again, the Carthaginians sued for peace.

In their war against Hannibal, the Romans had been fighting on two fronts, since Philip V of Macedonia (r. 221–179 BC) had allied himself with Carthage, but their overwhelming victory effectively ended Carthage's imperial ambitions. Humiliating peace terms left the city forbidden to maintain military forces, and committed to paying a huge indemnity to Rome. Eventually, worried by resurgent Carthaginian militarism, the Romans instigated the Third Punic War. After a long siege, Carthage was taken in 146 BC and burned to the ground.

In the east, meanwhile, the distrust between Rome and Philip of Macedonia following Philip's alliance with Carthage had burst out into open warfare again in 200 BC. In a series of conflicts over the next 50 years, the Romans first defeated Philip and forced him to withdraw from his Greek territories outside Macedonia, and then established their own Greek colonies of Achaea, Epirus and Macedonia. In 146 BC, the same year that Carthage was destroyed, the city of Corinth – one of the most beautiful and luxurious of the ancient Greek city-states – was razed to the ground and its inhabitants either killed or sold into slavery.

The Greeks had been shown in a most brutal way how they would be treated if they resisted Roman power. More lands were seized from the Seleucids – a dynasty founded by a former general of Alexander the Great (r. 336–323 BC), who had set up an empire from Asia Minor to Persia on territory originally conquered by the great Macedonian commander. In 133 BC, Attalus III of Pergamon (r. 138–133 BC) in modern Turkey bequeathed his entire kingdom to the Romans in the hope of avoiding civil war among his would-be heirs. The new province of Asia created there became one of the greatest sources of wealth for the growing Roman empire and, together with the colonies in Greece and the former Seleucid empire, established a permanent Roman presence in the eastern Mediterranean.

LEFT *Bust of the Carthaginian general Hannibal, from the first century BC. Despite his military prowess, the Roman republic proved strong enough to withstand his brilliant campaign of conquest during the Second Punic War.*

ROMAN GOVERNMENT

The government of the Roman republic evolved over time, but generally it was composed of the senate, an assembly of the wealthy and influential upper class (patricians); the assembly of the common people (plebeians), which could propose and pass legislation; and two consuls, who were elected each year to serve as joint heads of government. Together these groups made up the *Senatus Populusque Romanus*, or 'the Senate and Roman People', whose initials SPQR were mounted on the eagle-topped standard that Roman legions carried before them into battle.

BELOW *A 19th-century mural depicting an impassioned speech to the Roman senate by the renowned orator Cicero (106–43 BC). The supreme seat of power in the republic, the senate found its power steadily curtailed under imperial rule.*

ABOVE *Bas-relief carving of a Gaulish warrior. Rome struggled long and hard to subjugate Gaul. The decisive Roman victory came at the Battle of Alesia in 52 BC.*

For many centuries, this apparently complex and sophisticated form of government ensured relative peace and stability, but the rapid acquisition of new lands around the Mediterranean threatened to cause conflict. Much of the wealth flooding back to Rome was channelled into the hands of a few powerful families. At the same time, soldiers in the legions – most of whom were farmers and small landowners from Rome or its Italian vassal cities – could be away from home for years on campaign, during which time their families often fell into debt and lost their lands. Roman society was being dangerously polarized. Attempts at land reform, resisted by the members of the senate, caused bitter rioting in the late second century BC.

The new colonies, however, offered the prospect of huge wealth and power to the governors appointed to run them. Military commanders who won the blind loyalty of their soldiers would be able to exert irresistible influence over the government at home. These changes in society would put the republic under increasing strain over the next 100 years, and lead to its eventual destruction.

ROME UNDER THREAT

Early in Rome's history, in 390 BC, Gauls from the north had sacked the city itself, a humiliation that imprinted itself deep on the Roman psyche. Since then, the Romans had established a buffer zone south of the Alps, in Cisalpine Gaul ('Gaul this side of the Alps'; also called *Gallia Togata*, 'toga-wearing Gaul') and extended their rule north into Provincia (modern Provence in the south of France).

But the Gauls were not prepared to accept Roman rule, and in 105 BC, after a rebellion in the town of Tolosa (Toulouse), some 200,000 Gaulish tribesmen confronted two Roman armies at Arausio, close to the River Rhône. For the Romans, it was the worst military disaster in the history of the republic. Their armies, around 120,000 strong, including some 40,000 auxiliaries and non-combatants, were annihilated. The historian Livy (59 BC–AD 17) put the number of Roman dead at 80,000; hardly any of the legionaries escaped the slaughter.

Once again, Rome appeared to be at the mercy of a terrifying barbarian invasion; 285 years after the first Gaulish sack of the city, another such calamity seemed to be a real possibility. But the victorious armies turned instead towards the Pyrenees, giving the Romans time to raise fresh legions and defeat them first at the Battle of Aquae Sextae (modern Aix-en-Provence) in 101 BC, where 90,000 Gauls were reported to have been killed, and then a few months later at Vercellae (modern Vercelli), where up to 130,000 were said to have died. The two victories ended the immediate threat, but it would be another 50 years before Julius Caesar (r. 49–44 BC) finally conquered the Gauls.

REVOLT AND CIVIL WAR

That intervening period was marked by a succession of rebellions, insurrections and civil wars. First, in 91 BC the other Italian cities, which had been allied with Rome since the early days of the Latin League, rose up in protest at Rome's refusal to grant them full citizenship, equal rights and a share in the plunder brought back from military victories. Their armies were made up of tough veterans of the Romans' own legions, and they won a series of victories. It was more than a year before the rebellion (known as the 'Social War', from the Latin term *Socii* to denote their erstwhile allies) was put down, and even then the Romans were forced to accede to many of the cities' demands.

When Roman interests in the east were threatened the next year by Mithridates VI of Pontus (r. 120–63 BC) – a kingdom on the northern coast of Asia Minor – the consul Sulla (*c.*138–78 BC) was given command of the army sent to quell it. However, while he was recruiting

---

TIMELINE

AD 9 Battle of Teutoburg Forest

43 Claudius orders the invasion of Britain

60–61 Boudicca's revolt of Iceni in Britain crushed

64 Much of Rome destroyed by fire

66 Start of the Great Jewish Revolt against Roman rule

68 Revolt against Nero starts 12 months' civil war and anarchy

69 Vespasian starts rebuilding of Rome after civil war

***c.*105** Trajan adds new eastern provinces to the empire

122 Hadrian's Wall built in northern Britain

192 Murder of Commodus starts five years of fighting for succession

193 Septimius Severus takes power; campaigns in Britain and the east

235 Death of Alexander Severus sparks 50 years of fighting; 25 emperors rule in rapid succession

284 Diocletian establishes firm government; decides to divide empire

394 Invasion of western empire by eastern emperor Theodosius

395 Theodosius dies; generals take power

476 German tribes revolt; Romulus Augustulus deposed by the Germanic leader Odoacer

his legions among the Italian cities, Gaius Marius (157–86 BC), the general who had led the campaign against the Gauls, attempted to stage a coup in Rome. Sulla brought his troops back to Rome and forced his rival to flee after capturing the city in a brief but bloody assault.

When Sulla eventually left for Pontus, Marius came back, provoking a fresh round of slaughter. It was another two years before Sulla returned to mount a full-scale military campaign to regain power. By this time, Marius was dead, but his supporters persuaded several of the Italian cities to resist Sulla. Rome had sunk into civil war, with its allies taking sides against each other.

In November 82 BC, after many months of skirmishing in the Italian countryside, Sulla finally defeated his opponents at the Battle of the Colline Gate in Rome, and took power again. The senate, worried about a potential popular uprising, named him as dictator, which gave him effectively unlimited power to deal with the crisis. Over the next two years, he reorganized the constitution to give more power to the senate, at the expense of the plebeians, and also inflicted a bloody revenge on his opponents, thousands of whom were executed. This period witnessed the institution of the dreaded 'proscriptions,' public lists of men whom Sulla summarily condemned to death.

BELOW *A stone relief of gladiators fighting. These fighters, whose name derives from the short sword* (gladius) *many of them used in combat, put on hugely popular displays of martial skill in public arenas throughout the empire.*

After Sulla's death in 78 BC, there were two more insurrections. The first was instigated by another consul who tried to seize power at the end of his term of office; the second took the form of a massive slave revolt, led by a former Roman auxiliary soldier, Spartacus (*c.*120–*c.*70 BC), who had deserted the legions, been recaptured and sent as a slave to fight as a gladiator. In 73 BC he led an army of more than 70,000 slaves that terrorized the Roman countryside for several months. It was two years before this uprising was defeated; some 6000 of the rebels were crucified as a savage warning to other slaves not to rebel.

The real danger to the republic, however, came not from its slaves but from its politicians and generals. In 70 BC two generals led armies to the walls of Rome, demanding that they be elected as consuls. Both were former close allies of Sulla: Gnaeus Pompeius Magnus (106–48 BC) – known to history as Pompey the Great – a young commander who had won his spurs doing Sulla's butchery, and another former confederate of Sulla, Marcus Licinius Crassus (*c.*115–53 BC), who marched his troops back from the defeat of Spartacus' rebellion to press his own claim.

The senate, faced by military might to which it had no answer, was forced to acquiesce, and the two men were appointed to serve together. The republic's constitution had been stretched almost to breaking point.

THE FIRST TRIUMVIRATE

Sulla's loyalty had been to the patricians in the senate, but Pompey and Crassus allied themselves firmly with the plebeians. Their consulship was marked by lavish expenditure on entertainments and hand-outs for the Roman people – the historian Plutarch says that, out of his own pocket, Crassus gave every Roman enough grain to live on for three months. In addition, they abandoned Sulla's changes to the constitution and restored the powers of the plebeian assembly. To the patricians, it seemed that two powerful generals, with the support of battle-hardened and loyal troops, were deliberately cultivating a mass popular following.

Pompey added to his popularity two years after his consulship, first by conducting a successful operation against pirates who were plaguing Italy's coast, and then by commanding a victorious military campaign against Mithridates VI of Pontus, which saw the Roman empire extend its territory to the shores of the Black Sea.

His victories caused the final downfall of the rump Seleucid kingdom in what is now Syria, brought huge new wealth to the empire and left Pompey himself not only the richest man in Rome, but also the most popular – at least among the common people. He was awarded the honour of a triumphal procession through the city; street festivities at his expense, which went on for two days, further boosted his popularity.

Despite the fears of the senate that Pompey would use his celebrity to install himself as dictator, he disbanded his army when he returned to Italy. Now, in a masterstroke of political management, a young politician named Julius Caesar brought together Pompey and his old rival Crassus, and established a political alliance of the three men known as the triumvirate.

One of Caesar's first priorities was to be elected as consul, which he achieved in 59 BC. Next, he forced through a law distributing large tracts of public land to the common people. At the end of his consulship, he left Rome to take up his appointment as governor of the provinces of Cisalpine Gaul, Transalpine Gaul and Illyricum (present-day Croatia).

Caesar embarked at once on a series of campaigns against the barbarians who had once threatened Rome. Over the next seven years, he systematically conquered the Gaulish tribes through a series of alliances and piecemeal military operations, recruiting new legions to his ranks from among the Gauls themselves. By the time his Gallic wars were finished in 52 BC, tens of thousands of his enemies had been either killed or sold into slavery, and Caesar had made his first incursion across the Rhine. He had also crossed the Channel to land in Britain.

RETURN TO CIVIL WAR

But Caesar's political relationship with Pompey was under strain. Crassus' death while campaigning against the Parthians in the east now made Pompey and Caesar direct rivals. Caesar's governorship of Gaul, which carried with it immunity from prosecution, was coming to an end, and he was concerned that he might be charged with violating the constitution both in his consulship and in recruiting extra legions from among the Gauls. In 49 BC, news reached him that the senate – supported by his ally, Pompey – had declared him to be an enemy of Rome, and demanded that he return to stand trial.

With his battle-hardened troops, Caesar now seized the initiative. As a provincial governor, he was forbidden from entering Italy at the head of an army, but he defied this convention and crossed the River Rubicon, which marked the frontier, and headed for Rome. The empire that controlled most of the known world once again faced looming civil war.

At first, there was no significant opposition, and Pompey and his army were forced to flee to Greece, where they planned to continue the fight in the eastern colonies. But Caesar followed him, having destroyed all the forces that were loyal to Pompey in the western Mediterranean, and crushed him at the Battle of Pharsalus (48 BC). From there, he travelled to Egypt, where his support helped Cleopatra VII (r. 51–30 BC) gain the throne. He also won military victories in Asia Minor, North Africa and Spain, returning to Rome to be formally named dictator for ten years.

The appointment simply acknowledged the reality that Caesar was unchallenged as the most powerful figure in Rome. But a group of senators, worried about the possible collapse of the republic if all power rested with a single man, conspired to assassinate him. On the Ides of March (March 15) in 44 BC, he was stabbed to death on his way to address the senate.

THE REPUBLIC IN RUINS

The Roman constitution had been in turmoil for nearly 50 years, ever since Sulla's troops marched on Rome. The senate had accepted the demands of one military strong man after another, while still maintaining the fiction that power was divided among consuls, senate and plebeian assembly. Now, as Julius Caesar's friend Mark Antony (83–30 BC) whipped up the common people against the conspirators, the republic was effectively dead. As his heir, Caesar had named his great-nephew and adopted son Octavian (r. 27 BC–AD 14), who now joined with Mark Antony and a senator named Marcus Aemilius Lepidus (d.13 BC), another old supporter of Caesar's, to form the Second Triumvirate. Lepidus remained in Rome, but Mark Antony and Octavian – the latter still aged only 18 – followed the conspirators to Greece and defeated them at the Battle of Philippi (42 BC).

ABOVE *Mark Antony (depicted here in an undated sketch) lost crucial support in Rome and the army as a result of his debauched lifestyle at the court of Cleopatra VII of Egypt. He committed suicide after defeat at the Battle of Actium.*

The three victorious generals agreed to rule the empire together, Antony taking the eastern provinces, Octavian the north and west and Lepidus North Africa. But the civil wars were not over yet: first, Octavian bribed Lepidus' legions to desert him and effectively seized control of his fiefdom of North Africa; then, in 31 BC, war broke out between Octavian and Mark Antony.

Octavian's forces defeated Mark Antony and his lover Cleopatra at the naval Battle of Actium (31 BC), off the Greek coast. Octavian, sole survivor of the three men who had shared out the empire, was left as the unchallenged ruler of Rome. To protect himself against any fresh attempt to seize power, he placed his chosen men as governors in control of the legions in the key provinces, and packed the senate with his own supporters. From now on, every important decision about the government of Rome or the empire was taken by Octavian himself.

In 27 BC, in a finely judged piece of political theatre, he offered to relinquish the powers he had seized. The senate unanimously – and wisely – declined and acknowledged his power for life, with the honorific title of 'Augustus', meaning 'noble' or 'revered'. His play-acting – such as his refusal to adopt Julius Caesar's title of dictator – was designed to suggest that he was simply restoring the traditional republic. But Rome and its empire had its emperor at last.

'FIRST CITIZEN' AUGUSTUS

Augustus accepted the title of *imperator*, which meant 'leader', or 'commander-in-chief', but did not at that time have the connotation of emperor. Rather, it was a title bestowed on a successful general by the troops under his command – Pompey and Julius Caesar were among other leaders who had been so honoured. It was only after Augustus that successive emperors started to use the title as a prefix to their names and it thus began to take on its modern meaning. The formal title he was given was *princeps*, which meant 'first citizen'. Ever since the expulsion of the Etruscan tyrant Tarquinius Superbus from Rome in 509 BC, the term *rex* ('king'), was one of the most hated words among Romans – one reason the conspirators gave for assassinating Julius Caesar was that he was preparing to assume kingship.

With that precedent in mind, Augustus was at pains to maintain the fiction of continued republican rule. In fact, he not only assumed supreme power but also introduced a hereditary element into the Roman leadership. In all but name – a crucial distinction for the Romans – he was both king and emperor of Rome.

Part of Augustus' strategy to pretend that the republic was still alive and well was to share the administration of the provinces of the empire between governors chosen by himself and those chosen by the senate. Significantly, though, the imperial provinces were those along the borders of the empire, where the legions were stationed, while those controlled by the senate had very few soldiers. Augustus was careful to keep close personal control of the army.

After the decades of civil war, Augustus' assumption of power marked the start of over 150 years of relative peace, without significant military expansion of the empire. The British historian Edward Gibbon (1737–94) described the period that started in 27 BC, when Augustus declared the civil wars to be at an end, as the *pax Romana*, or 'Roman peace'. There were occasional outbreaks of political unrest and sporadic wars against Persian and German tribes; rebellions, such as that of the British Iceni tribe under Queen Boudicca (d. AD 60), were put down by force. But, apart from a brief spasm of civil warfare when military commanders competed for power after the fall of Nero, the vast majority of the conflicts for nearly 200 years took place far from Rome: for the inhabitants of the city and Italy in general, it did indeed seem like a welcome period of tranquillity.

The policy of maintaining the existing frontiers of the empire, rather than trying to extend them by conquest, was foisted on Augustus by a bloody defeat in his one major attempt at expansion. An expedition to cross the Rhine and establish a Roman province of Germania on the east bank collapsed when three full legions – between 15,000 and 20,000 men – were ambushed and slaughtered by an alliance of Germanic tribes at the Battle of Teutoburg Forest in AD 9. Later attempts to avenge the defeat also resulted in heavy losses, and so the Rhine was accepted as a natural boundary to the empire.

THE RELUCTANT TIBERIUS

Augustus died in AD 14, and was succeeded by his stepson Tiberius (r. 14–37; the son of Augustus' scheming wife Livia from her first marriage). The new *princeps* adopted the same tactic as his stepfather before the senate, and affected reluctance to take up his new role. Tiberius was an accomplished general: he had been dispatched to strengthen the Rhine frontier after the disaster of Teutoburg. He had, however, been repeatedly warned by Augustus not to try to extend the frontiers of the empire, and military action during his reign was confined to limited manoeuvres on the Rhine and Danube, the suppression of a revolt in Gaul and campaigns against troublesome tribes in North Africa.

Tiberius seemed to be indifferent to the duties of his imperial role – for much of his reign, he retired to the island of Capri (possibly to escape his domineering mother), leaving Rome to be governed by his officials – but when a plot against him was unmasked in 31, his rage and paranoia knew no bounds. The purges, arrests and executions that followed were a foretaste of what was to come for the Romans under certain of the later emperors. When the dour Tiberius died in 37 at the age of 77, the crowds in the street were reported to have celebrated wildly. They did not know then what sort of man was to follow him.

PURGES AND PROSECUTIONS UNDER CALIGULA

Gaius Julius Caesar Germanicus (r. 37–41) – better known by his childhood nickname of Caligula, or 'Little Boot', since he was shown to the troops wearing military uniform as a child – was the son of Tiberius' adopted son Germanicus (15 BC–AD 19). The Roman historian Suetonius (c.69–130) quotes unconfirmed reports that he was personally responsible for the death of Tiberius by ordering

ABOVE *This 18th-century engraving of the Battle of Actium shows the squadron of the Egyptian queen Cleopatra fleeing the fight, abandoning the stricken ships of her ally Mark Antony to their fate.*

LEFT *A cameo portrait of Octavian (Augustus). His ascendancy brought the long period of civil war in Rome to a close and laid the foundations of the empire.*

ABOVE *Caligula was a highly unstable personality, whose rule became infamous for its capricious cruelty. The Praetorian Guard, which he had alienated by surrounding himself with German troops, engineered his violent downfall.*

him to be smothered. Caligula was originally named as joint heir with Tiberius' own grandson, the 18-year-old Gemellus (19–37), but he had him executed within a few months of Tiberius' death.

For those outside the inner ruling circle, Caligula's reign started well. There were lavish entertainments for the people, the promise of an end to the treason trials and an invitation to return for those exiled by Tiberius. He also, shrewdly, ensured the loyalty of the élite Praetorian Guard with generous bonuses. But he was determined to reassert the authority of the *princeps* over a senate that had become used to governing without Tiberius in Rome. So, despite his promises, he began a new round of purges, prosecutions and executions. Several conspiracies against him were broken up and the conspirators executed.

Many Roman authors claim that Caligula was mad – Suetonius, for instance, claims that he planned to make his favourite horse Incitatus a consul – and also tell stories of sexual depravity and cruelty. Many modern scholars doubt these accounts, which are similar to many told of autocratic rulers. What is certain is that several major public works projects were started in Rome, including improvements to the harbours to speed up the import of grain and large aqueducts to bring fresh water to the city. Throughout the empire, Caligula also started a programme of rebuilding and maintaining the roads that the army had built to help their military operations.

Caligula also seems to have planned to abandon Augustus' policy of holding to the existing frontier of the empire, gathering troops along the Rhine apparently for a renewed invasion of Germany. However, only four years after his accession, he was stabbed to death by officers of his own guard. His rule demonstrated the reality behind the mock false modesty displayed in the senate by both Augustus and Tiberius: there was, in truth, no political check on the power of the *princeps*. Only the force of arms could prevent him from doing whatever he chose.

CLAUDIUS — A COSMOPOLITAN EMPEROR

Claudius (r. 41–54), Caligula's uncle, succeeded by default. Frail, and possibly afflicted by cerebral palsy, he was the last surviving male member of his family after Caligula's purges. Born in Gaul, he was also the first of the Roman emperors to be born outside Italy – a sign of the increasingly cosmopolitan nature of the empire – and the first for whom the title Caesar was a mark of rank rather than a family name. From now on, all Roman emperors would refer to themselves as Caesar, although they had no direct connection with the ancient family of Julius Caesar.

There is no direct evidence that Claudius was involved in the plot to assassinate Caligula – although, perhaps suspiciously, one of his first acts was to order the immediate execution of all the assassins – but his succession reinforced the lesson of Caligula's reign. Claudius was imposed upon the senate at sword point by the Praetorian Guard. Real power now rested in the hands of the military élite.

His reign also demonstrated how the empire had developed. In the face of opposition from the patricians in the senate, he extended Roman citizenship to inhabitants of the wider empire and even brought Gauls into the senate. He also took a direct role in the administration of the provinces.

But without a doubt Claudius' greatest achievement was the first major expansion of the empire since Augustus. In the east, he

ABOVE *First-century AD fresco of guests at a Roman banquet. Increasing wealth in the growing empire ensured a lavish lifestyle for Rome's patrician élite.*

annexed territories in the Balkans, Asia Minor and modern Palestine to the empire, and in the west, he began the occupation of Britain. Julius Caesar had visited the island of Britannia and Caligula had made a half-hearted attempt to send the legions in Gaul there, but under Claudius, Roman Britain became a fact. Preparations for a concerted operation started early in his reign, with four legions arriving in the southeast of the country, probably in Kent, in 43. Claudius himself travelled to Britain a few months later.

Even though the Romans never managed to take control of the whole island, the occupation was to last for more than 350 years. For Claudius it was important because it established his credentials as a military leader; for the empire it marked its furthest northern outpost, and a valuable source of raw materials.

REVOLTS UNDER NERO

Claudius died in 54 – probably poisoned at the instigation of his wife Agrippina, according to the Roman historian Tacitus (c.56–117), to prevent him revoking his choice of her 16-year-old son, Nero (r. 54–68), as his successor. One of Nero's first acts was to announce the formal deification of his stepfather, in what had become a traditional act of homage to a dead emperor.

BELOW *Under Claudius, shown on this coin from his reign, stability returned to Rome after years of upheaval. He instigated important public works and organized an extremely efficient invasion of Britain.*

Initially, Nero promised to restore to the senate all the powers it had enjoyed under the republic, but before his reign was over he had seized still more power for himself. Potential rivals and critics were exiled or executed without mercy. There was also a great fire in Rome in 64, almost certainly caused accidentally, but blamed by Nero on members of the newly formed Christian sect. Some were dressed in animal skins and torn apart by dogs, while others were crucified.

Abroad, Nero faced a wave of unrest across the empire. In 60–61, Queen Boudicca led her British Iceni and Trinovantes tribesmen in an uprising that nearly caused the loss of the new province; he had to send three legions to suppress a major revolt that erupted in Judaea in 66; and in Gaul and Spain, too, there were brief but bloody insurrections. All these revolts were successfully put down, but their significance was that they required individual governors to have much larger bodies of troops under their command than usual. This made them potentially dangerous and in 68 the senate, alienated by its loss of influence, joined with the governors of one of the Spanish provinces, Servius Sulpicius Galba (r. 68–9), to remove Nero from office.

CHAOS AT THE HEART OF ROME

Nero's suicide, when faced with execution by members of his own Praetorian Guard, marked the start of 12 months of near anarchy in Roman public life. Nero had made no provision for the succession – but in any case, the emperors who followed him made no serious claim to any legitimacy other than brute force. The army, in effect, was choosing who should rule and overthrowing them if they failed to prove generous enough with their bribes.

Galba, who had been behind the plot against Nero, took his place, but was killed within six months, having alienated even the soldiers who had supported his coup by failing to pay them money they believed they were owed. Then came Otho (r. 69), governor of Lusitania in the Iberian Peninsula, who had marched with Galba to Rome. He lasted for just three months before he was overthrown by Vitellius (r. 69), whose province was on the Rhine. By now, different factions of the army were openly fighting each other, simply to force their own nominee onto the throne.

After only a few more months, there was another insurrection, this time by troops based in Egypt and Syria, in support of their own governor, Titus Flavius Sabinus Vespasianus (r. 69–79). As the emperor Vespasian, he ruled for ten years, ending the anarchy in Rome and establishing a new dynasty.

ORDER RESTORED BY VESPASIAN

The first challenge of the new Flavian dynasty was to restore order. The new emperor, who had seen fighting in Britain and in the dangerous Jewish Revolt, had an impressive military pedigree. Rome was once again headed by a strong emperor with the military power to put his plans into effect.

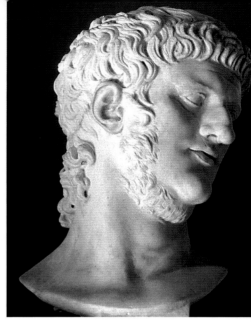

ABOVE *The last of the Julio-Claudian line, Nero, became a byword for vain excess and megalomania. His massive new imperial palace (the 'Golden House') dominated the heart of Rome.*

Inside the city, Vespasian began to repair the ravages of the fighting. Rebuilding was started at the Temple of Jupiter and the Capitol – both burned during the civil wars – and other temples and public buildings were constructed, including the magnificent Colosseum (or Flavian Amphitheatre) for games, gladiatorial contests and public spectacles.

At the same time, Vespasian introduced new Roman and provincial candidates into the senate, reaffirming its role in government, although always stressing his own supremacy, and purged the army of units which had shown support for Vitellius. His contribution to the empire was also considerable: more legions were sent to the east to ensure that the recent Jewish uprising caused no wider unrest while, in Britain, Roman power was extended into northern England, Wales and Scotland. Provinces that had demonstrated their loyalty, such as Spain, were rewarded with more civic rights.

Both in Rome and abroad Vespasian followed a dual policy of firm military control, coupled with impressive building and a restrained but relatively liberal attitude towards the political rights of both Romans and conquered peoples. He had also carefully groomed his son, Titus (r. 79–81), for the succession. As a result, he was the first Roman emperor to die peacefully, in his bed, and without rumours of foul play.

But though Titus had acquired a reputation as a military leader alongside his father, he ruled for barely two years. Suetonius claims that he contracted a fever, and that his brother Domitian (r. 81–96) forbade doctors to tend him.

BELOW *View of the central arena of the Roman Colosseum. Construction of this magnificent amphitheatre, which could seat some 50,000 spectators, was begun by Vespasian in* AD 70.

DOMITIAN — LAST OF THE FLAVIANS

Whether or not he was partly responsible for his brother's death, Domitian lost no time in deifying him and building up the standing of the whole Flavian dynasty. But Domitian, unlike his father and his brother, was no general – even though he usually insisted on appearing in full military regalia.

He continued the policy of pacifying the people with games and spectacles in the Colosseum, with big building projects and even with personal donations to every citizen. However, following a rebellion in Germany in 89, his rule became more bloodthirsty and unpredictable, with sudden arrests, executions and the seizure of private property. He had open contempt for the senate and the patricians, and relied increasingly on a coterie of friends and courtiers. It was one of these, Marcus Cocceius Nerva (r. 96–8), who led a plot to assassinate him in 96.

THE ANTONINE DYNASTY

Nerva's rule was brief, but marked another important change in the nature of the empire. Coming to power in the wake of Domitian's terror, he was the first in a succession of stable rulers known as the 'Five Good Emperors', who ruled Rome from 96 to 180. Nerva made few changes to the frontiers, but in bringing the senate back into day-to-day government and abandoning the policy of dynastic succession, he set the precedent for the next 100 years.

His successor Trajan (r. 98–117), a commander on the Rhine frontier, extended the boundaries of the Roman empire to their farthest extent, concentrating his forces against the Parthians, who had been mounting constant raids on the eastern colonies. Armenia was captured and annexed to the empire, and thereafter the ancient cities of Babylon, Seleucia and the western Parthian capital of Ctesiphon. His forces continued through Mesopotamia, declaring it to be a new province of the empire, and sacked the city of Susa.

It was a conquest – or several conquests – too far. Trajan's successor, Hadrian (r. 117–38), abandoned the new province in favour of consolidating the empire behind secure, defensible borders. As part of the same policy, he ordered the construction of the great wall that bears his name across the north of England, establishing a firm northern border for Roman Britain. This state of relative peace and stability endured in the empire for a further 50 years. There were occasional revolts and some readjustment of the boundaries – Hadrian's successor Antoninus Pius (r. 138–61) built a new wall across Scotland, 100 miles (160 km) north of Hadrian's Wall, as a new frontier; once again, however, it proved too difficult and costly to defend.

During the reigns of the next two Caesars, Marcus Aurelius (r. 161–80, the last of the Five Good Emperors) and Commodus (r. 180–92), tribal raids in Gaul and along the eastern frontier became more common and more serious. Even behind the less ambitious borders that Hadrian had drawn, the empire was too big to be maintained solely by military occupation. Throughout its history, the legions were based mostly at the frontiers, preventing incursions by barbarian tribes, rather than garrisoned throughout the conquered lands. A network of alliances and client kingdoms took some of the pressure off these frontier troops, but there was little spare capacity. Crises at one point on the border had to be met by moving troops from elsewhere, or raising fresh legions.

The maintenance of Roman power in the countryside and cities of the interior was achieved largely by co-operation with local rulers, and by civil authorities backed by little more than the threat of possible retaliation. Once that system broke down, as it began to do under Commodus, the survival of the empire was under increasing pressure. The *pax Romana*, which had started with Augustus two centuries before, began to disintegrate.

THE LONG DECLINE

In 192, the murder of the cruel and capricious Commodus, who had instigated a reign of terror similar to that of Domitian, sparked another round of political violence in Rome. Over the next five years various military commanders fought

ROMAN EMPERORS

27 BC Augustus
AD 14 Tiberius
37 Gaius (Caligula)
41 Claudius
54 Nero
68 Galba
69 Otho and Vitellius
69 Vespasian
79 Titus
81 Domitian
96 Nerva
98 Trajan
117 Hadrian
138 Antoninus Pius
161 Marcus Aurelius
180 Commodus
192 Pertinax
193 Septimius Severus
211 Caracalla
217 Macrinus
218 Elagabalus
222 Alexander Severus

After the death of Alexander Severus, 25 emperors followed over the next 50 years. Emperor Diocletian divided the empire in 285. The last emperor of the western Roman empire, Romulus Augustulus, was deposed in 476.

LINGUISTIC LEGACY

The Romans left their mark on the language and culture of the whole of western Europe. Both the Byzantine and the Holy Roman empires claimed to be their heirs. The so-called Romance languages, ranging from Spanish, Portuguese and French in the west to Romanian in the east, are all direct descendants of Latin; English, although a Germanic language descended from Anglo-Saxon, still derives at least a third of its words from the Romans. Until well into the 16th century, more than 1100 years after the fall of the empire, theirs was the language of scholarly debate throughout Europe.

A lictor, *one of the men who guarded Roman magistrates, carrying his badge of office – a bundle of rods and an axe known as the* fasces.

Lawyers still quibble in it, and for millions of members of the Roman Catholic Church around the world it remains the language of worship: in less peaceable times, the argument over whether it should be used in church and in printing the Bible was played out in blood and fire.

The titles of Europe's rulers bore witness to their desire to cloak themselves in the borrowed glory of the ancient emperors. The Russian *Tsar* and the German *Kaiser* are both variants of the Roman 'Caesar'; The English word 'king' may be Germanic in origin, but their princes clearly derive from the Latin *princeps*; today, the United States has both a capitol and a senate. Less reputably, the fascist parties of Europe can trace the term for their ideology back to the *fasces*, a bundle of birch rods tied together as a symbol of the strength through unity of the state, and carried through Rome by the *lictors* in formal processions. The symbol even appears today on the official seal of the US Senate, as well as on various European coats of arms.

to succeed him as emperor, openly bribing the Praetorian Guard for its support. It was Septimius Severus (r. 193–211), governor of the province of Pannonia on the Danube, who emerged victorious and established the new Severan dynasty, which would rule Rome for the next 42 years.

The empire was by now little more than a military dictatorship. Severus replaced the Praetorian Guard with his own loyal troops from the Danube, and the power of the senate dwindled. He tried to maintain the borders, with a major expedition to defeat the Parthians and reclaim Mesopotamia as a colony, and travelled to Britain in 209 to subdue tribes there who had broken through the Antonine Wall. After falling ill and dying in Eboracum (York), he was succeeded by his son Caracalla (r. 211–17), but the five following members of his dynasty faced increasing unrest both in the empire and at home.

The last Severan, Alexander Severus (r. 222–35), died in 235. His reign was followed by 50 years of turmoil, as rival claimants vied for power. Over that time, there were no fewer than 25 emperors, none of whom ruled for long, and all but two of whom were either murdered or killed in battle. The empire was clearly falling apart, plagued by rampant inflation, repeated raids and full-scale invasions by various barbarian tribes, as well as constant civil war.

ABOVE *Map of the Roman empire at the death of Diocletian in 305, showing the 12 'dioceses' into which he divided his realm.*

Diocletian (r. 285–305) became emperor in 285, and decided that it was impossible to defend the empire in the east and the west at the same time. He remained as emperor of the eastern half, handing rule in the west to his fellow general Maximian (r. 286–305). This arrangement proved to be permanent, resulting in the creation of the Byzantine empire, which lasted in the east for almost 1200 years (see The Byzantine Empire, pages 84–95). In the west, there were further divisions, revolts, military coups and invasions – including one by the eastern emperor Theodosius I (r. 379–95) in 394, after he refused to recognize his western counterpart, Eugenius (r. 392–4). Theodosius defeated his rival at the Battle of the Frigidus in the Balkans and became the last emperor to rule, albeit briefly, over the whole Roman empire.

After his death a year later, a succession of generals took power, while emperors served as figureheads, with no real power. In 476 a revolt of German tribes who had been serving as mercenaries captured and killed their Roman commander, and then stormed Ravenna to depose the reigning emperor, Romulus Augustulus (r. 475–6).

Since the sack of Rome by the Gauls, the Romans had built an empire that extended throughout Europe, North Africa and the Middle East. They had conquered the Gauls and brought them into their own armed forces. Now, finally, descendants of those Gauls had returned to deliver the final blow.

China is probably the world's oldest continuous civilization, with records of some of the kings of a great dynasty, the Xia, dating back to *c*.2070 BC. Royal tombs have been found from a succeeding dynasty, the Shang, whose ancient capital has been excavated at the modern town of Anyang, about 300 miles (500 km) southwest of Beijing. According to Chinese legend, they were toppled by a semi-nomadic tribe from the west, who formed the Zhou dynasty sometime in the mid-tenth century BC. The great Chinese thinker Kong Fuzi (Confucius), the originator of a philosophy that dominated much of Chinese thought throughout the history of the empire, is thought to have lived during the Zhou period.

THE
CHINESE EMPIRE
c.221 BC – AD 1644

ACCOUNTS OF ALL THESE EARLY DYNASTIES MINGLE HISTORICAL RECORDS with the interpretation of artefacts that have been unearthed, along with ancient tales from Chinese myth and legend. The traditional date given for the unification of China as a single country or empire is 221 BC; before then, there had been at least 300 years of political chaos, with a constant state of war between rival kingdoms.

This date is usually taken as the beginning of early imperial China, which was dominated by two dynasties: the Qin, from whose name (once transliterated as Ch'in in English) the name of the country is thought to derive, and the Han. Although Chinese scholars have in the past presented the history of their country as an unbroken succession of dynasties, in reality there have been lengthy periods of near-anarchy, with local warlords, rival kingdoms and rebel generals all vying for power. Allowing for such gaps, it is possible to trace nearly 1900 years of imperial Chinese history, from the unification under the Qin to the suicide of the last Ming emperor in 1644.

The defeat of the Ming dynasty, after a series of wars that cost an estimated 25 million lives, brought the Manchu (Qing) from the north. Once again, China was under foreign rule, and many historians consider the fall of the Ming to mark the end of the

LEFT *The first Chinese emperor Shi Huangdi, shown here in a 19th-century painting, initiated a pattern of centralized totalitarian government that still, in a different ideological guise, pertains in modern China.*

TIMELINE

551–479 BC Traditional dates of life of Confucius

221 BC Traditional date for unification of China under Qin Shi Huangdi

c.220 BC Start of construction of Great Wall of China

210 BC Death of Qin Shi Huangdi; terracotta army

210–206 BC Period of conflict

206 BC Liu Bang seizes power as Emperor Gaozu; start of Han dynasty

141 BC onwards Emperor Wudi extends empire north, south and west

AD 2–11 Disastrous flooding of Yellow River

23 Red Eyebrows topple Wang Mang

36 Guangwu moves capital from Xi'an to Luoyang

c.150 First known translation of Buddhist scriptures into Chinese

184 Yellow Turbans revolt

220–589 Overthrow of Emperor Xian; period of Three Kingdoms and conflict

589 Yang Jian invades from north, rules as first Sui emperor, Wendi

early seventh century Failed attempts to invade Korea

617 Liyuan rebels; later (619) seizes power as Emperor Gaozu

mid-seventh century First Chinese mosque and church established

continued

Chinese empire. The Qing dynasty ruled China until 1911, when it was toppled in the nationalist revolution that established the Republic of China, the first of a series of political upheavals culminating in the victory of Mao Zedong (Mao Tse-tung 1893–1976) in 1949, and the establishment of communist rule in the People's Republic of China.

Today, the Chinese state extends over the whole area once ruled by the Qing. It has 22 provinces, five autonomous regions (Guangxi, Inner Mongolia, Ningxia, Xinjiang and Tibet), four municipalities (Beijing, Tianjin, Shanghai and Chongqing) and two special administrative regions (Hong Kong and Macau) with a degree of political and economic autonomy. The island of Taiwan (formerly Formosa), which is still ruled by the successors of the nationalist government defeated in 1949, is claimed by the People's Republic as the 23rd province.

BIRTH OF AN EMPIRE

The third century BC was a time of constant warfare across much of China, but the Qin, who had developed a strong central government and a powerful army, emerged supreme among the rival peoples. Their leader, born as Zhao Zheng, took the name Qin Shi Huangdi (r. 221–210 BC), which means 'First Emperor of the Qin', so announcing his intention that he and his successors should rule over the whole area. He sent his armies to conquer lands as far south as the Red River in Vietnam, and also committed forces to the north and west to subdue the nomadic tribes which threatened him.

Qin's rule at home was merciless. Laws were applied strictly, with death the most common penalty for transgressions. In a purge on dissenters, Qin ordered the burning of all books that advocated any form of government other than his own autocracy, and had hundreds of scholars – accounts of the numbers vary from 400 to 1100 – buried alive.

RIGHT *Territories under Qin rule in 206 BC. In just 150 years, the Qin had expanded from a small area around Chang'an to control large areas of central and southern China.*

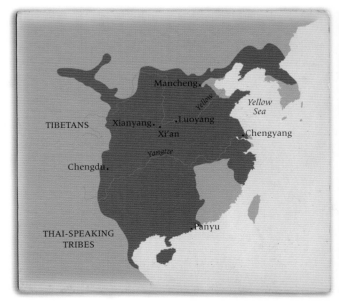

THE TERRACOTTA ARMY

In March 1974, a group of seven Chinese peasant farmers in the village of Yang, near the city of Xi'an, were digging a well to water their fields when they broke into a pit containing life-sized terracotta figures standing in rows. Further excavations over the next two years revealed two more pits with similar figures, and additional discoveries have been made since, taking the number of ancient carvings so far unearthed to over 1000. As many as 7000 more are believed to lie buried under the ground.

This was the terracotta army of Emperor Qin Shi Huangdi, buried with him late in the third century BC so that he would be able to rule another empire in the afterlife. According to ancient sources, the emperor's mausoleum nearby took hundreds of thousands of labourers nearly 40 years to build. When he was finally interred there in 210 BC, the model army of soldiers, archers, horsemen and even secretaries and scribes was ranged on guard several hundred yards from the entrance.

Qin Shi Huangdi, the first emperor to rule over a united China, was a feared autocrat in life; but within five years of his death, Chinese historians say the mausoleum was raided and burned, and many of the terracotta soldiers damaged. Almost all of the bright paint that once covered them is gone, but the fine details of the carving – the individual faces and the texture of the shoe soles, for instance – remain.

Two of the finely crafted warriors from the terracotta army of the first Qin emperor, one of the most spectacular archaeological finds of all time.

Qin was the emperor responsible for the famous terracotta army of 7,000 life-size sculpted soldiers, lined up to guard his body in its magnificent mausoleum. Other sculptures included horses, chariots and figures believed to represent officials and administrators – everything that might be necessary to recreate Qin's empire in the afterlife. The mausoleum and the other grandiose building projects he undertook, including a wall to keep the northern nomads out of the kingdom (a precursor to the famous Great Wall of China) required heavy taxation and forced labour. In addition, Qin's personal rule alienated the traditional aristocracy and, although he retained power as long as he lived, the Qin dynasty was overthrown within a few years of his death.

EXPANSION UNDER THE HAN

Qin's great achievement was to unify the Chinese, but with his death the different factions collapsed again into internal conflict. The general Liu Bang, who led one of the factions rising up against Qin in 206 BC, took the name of Han Gaozu (r. 202–195 BC), or 'Noble Emperor of the Han'. The Han dynasty lasted for more than two centuries, and recreated a centralized state in which access to power and influence was widened to a much greater proportion of the population.

Under the Han the laws were less strict, while the administration of the state, under the central rule of the emperor himself, was divided into small provinces run by individual lords. The ancient Chinese philosophy of Confucianism, a secular system of thought encouraging love, piety, duty and virtue, which had been so brutally repressed under Qin, became central to Han government and remained a key element of Chinese thought throughout the imperial era.

The Han emperors were also militarily strong and outward-looking. Emperor Han Wudi (r. 141–87 BC), for instance, who came to power at the age of 16, sent armies south into Vietnam and north to Korea, pushing back the boundaries of the empire. He also colonized vast tracts of land to the west to discourage attacks from the nomads living there. The westward spread of Chinese culture was influential in establishing the trade routes towards Central Asia and eventually Europe that became known as the Silk Road. Han Wudi ruled for 54 years and was responsible for a succession of ambitious public projects, including a canal to link the Yellow River to his capital at Xi'an in central China, about 400 miles (640 km) southwest of Beijing.

Programmes of land reform, aimed at distributing land to the peasants, were bitterly unpopular with traditional landowners, while heavy taxes began to cause unrest among the peasants as well. Floods and famine

brought more misery, and nomadic tribes seized large areas of the empire in the north. Revolts spread around the country in the last years of the first century BC, and a secret society known as the Red Eyebrows launched a successful attack on the capital. Wang Mang (r. AD 9–23), a court official who had ruled on behalf of the infant emperor and who had recently declared himself emperor instead, was killed by the rebels.

Another period of chaos and anarchy ensued, until a wealthy landowner related to the Han family seized power as Emperor Guangwu (r. AD 25–57), with the aim of restoring order and rebuilding imperial authority. One by one, he defeated his regional rivals for power, and by AD 36 he seemed to have succeeded, marking the break from the earlier Han emperors by settling his capital at Luoyang, some 200 miles (320 km) east of Xi'an.

ABOVE First Emperor of the Han Dynasty Entering Kuan Tang, *by the painter Chao Po-chu (fl. 1119–63).*

The development of the army, and shrewd alliances with neighbouring tribes, enabled Guangwu to drive back many of the northern nomads who had been threatening the empire from the west, pushing Chinese power almost to the Caspian Sea, and gaining control of large areas of central Asia. At home, however, the contentious issue of land reform and Guangwu's inability to levy sufficient taxes remained a constant problem. In 184 another peasant rebellion, this time led by a secret society named the Yellow Turbans, overthrew the Han dynasty for a second time. For the next three decades, the Han remained only as figurehead emperors, unable to assert any significant control, until Emperor Xian (r. 189–220) was finally overthrown in 220.

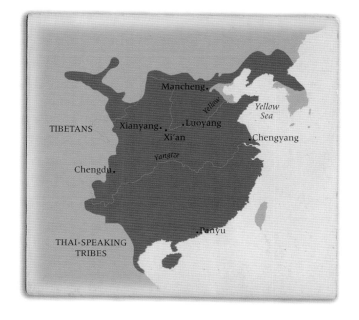

RIGHT *Map showing the extent of the Han dynasty, which ruled China from 202 BC to AD 220.*

THE SUI DYNASTY

Again, the fall of the dynasty sparked lengthy internal conflict, with warlords competing for control of their own individual areas. During what became known as the Period of Three Kingdoms, the Han civilization survived, but the northern and southern regions of the empire were effectively split for nearly four centuries. During this period, the new religion of Buddhism gradually spread through China, after being introduced from India, and when the era of political disunity came to an end, it was through the actions of a Buddhist palace official and administrator from northern China, Yang Jian. Having seized power there in 581, he invaded the south in 589, declaring himself to be the leader anointed by heaven.

Ruling as Emperor Wendi (r. 581–604) of the Sui dynasty, the first of a series of Buddhist emperors, he immediately took pains to lessen the rivalries between north and south, widening access to government posts and reorganizing the administration of the empire. Wendi tackled the problem of land reform by distributing land to farmers according to the size of their families. They were allowed to farm these lands, but not to sell them, and agricultural production increased rapidly. New granaries were built, and the country's existing canal network expanded.

Wendi strengthened the empire's borders with a strong and well-paid army, but avoided ambitious schemes to conquer neighbouring lands. However, his son, Yangdi (r. 605–17), not only extended the building programmes his father had initiated but also launched a series of costly foreign campaigns. In the south, these military expeditions were largely successful, but four attempts to conquer the northern region of what is now Korea (Koguryo) failed, leading to intense unrest throughout the country. A series of natural disasters brought dissatisfaction to a head, and Yangdi was assassinated after a military coup in which one of his generals, Li Yuan, seized power.

TANG MILITARY STRENGTH

Li Yuan's Tang dynasty held power in China for nearly 300 years, but the first emperor, who reigned as Gaozu (r. 618–26) was ousted after only a few months by his son, who took the reign name Taizong (r. 627–49). The infrastructure of canals and granaries left behind by the Sui were crucial in enabling the Tang emperors to transport rice and other crops around the empire in times of famine.

Greater efficiency, better equipment and high-yield varieties of rice brought rapid growth in production; the consequent increase in taxes paid to the central treasury meant that the Tang could maintain a large and well-equipped army of aristocrats and peasants. While armies in the north deterred the attacks of the nomadic tribes who had plagued the settlements for centuries and also extended the empire through almost the whole of the Korean Peninsula, campaigns to the west were pushing Chinese influence through Central Asia to the borders of Persia.

ABOVE *Emperor Wendi, the first of China's Sui rulers, won the support of the country's Confucian scholarly élite and embarked on a series of social, military, religious and bureaucratic reforms to consolidate his control. Wendi's reign was a time of great prosperity; some accounts record that enough food was stored in the state granaries to last 50 years.*

RIGHT *A painted stucco model of a Tang dynasty warrior from the reign of Taizong, found at a military outpost guarding the northern Silk Road. Some modern estimates put the number of soldiers under arms during the Tang dynasty at around 500,000.*

CHINA'S FEMALE EMPEROR

In 690, China's only woman emperor came to the throne when the Buddhist Wu Zhou, a former concubine of the two previous emperors, deposed her own son and took power as Empress Zetian (r. 690–705). Over the next few decades, China enjoyed a golden age of art and poetry, and the imperial court became known throughout Asia for its splendour and richness. In central Europe, there were clashes with the powerful Turkic tribes, which saw vast areas of Mongolia added to the empire. By the middle of the eighth century the kingdoms paying tribute to the emperor included Nepal, Kashmir, Vietnam, Korea and Japan.

Military reforms included the abandonment of forced service in the army and the development of a professional force of long-serving soldiers, who were posted to military provinces along the empire's growing borders.

At the same time, the development of trading links along the Silk Road and through port cities such as Guangzhou (Canton) in southern China brought new ceramics, silverware and other goods from Persia and India. Despite the strict border controls, writings, ideas and travellers thronged to the Tang capital of Xi'an, making it one of the most cosmopolitan cities in the world. In the mid-seventh century, China's first mosque and its first Christian church were established at Guangzhou and Xi'an respectively.

But even the powerful Tang army was stretched by its western conquests and by the length of the borders it had to defend. Individual generals, commanding troops far from home, began to take power for themselves, and in the middle of the eighth century one of them, An Lushan (c.703–57), started a revolt in which he captured Xi'an itself. This breakdown in discipline saw much of the territory that had been gained lost once more. Mongols in Manchuria, Turks to the west and Tibetans to the south gradually forced their way back into the territory they had surrendered.

After the defeat of An Lushan's revolt – only achieved by forming an alliance with the Turks, who drove him out of Xi'an and then plundered the city themselves – the Tang managed several decades of relative peace within their greatly contracted borders. But then, during the ninth century, provincial governors began to assume greater powers, and central

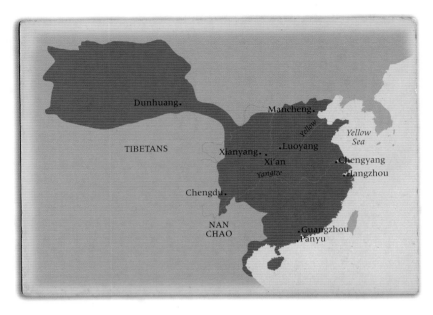

authority was compromised. A series of peasant uprisings further increased pressure on the Tang government: in one of these, in 874, a peasant leader named Huang Chao (d.884) sacked first Guangzhou, where tens of thousands of people were butchered, and then Luoyang and Xi'an. The emperor, Xizong (r. 862–88), was forced to flee, and although the fighting went on for another 30 years, the Tang dynasty was effectively over.

For 50 years after the fall of the Tang, China was divided. In the north, five dynasties quickly rose and fell as rival claimants vied for power, all the while fending off continued attacks by central Asian tribes. In the south, though, five separate kingdoms grew up under military governors from the Tang army.

TRADE AND TECHNOLOGY UNDER THE SONG

Around 960, Zhao Kuangyin, one of the generals who ruled in the south, gained supremacy and established a capital at Kaifeng on the Yellow River, from which he would rule over most of China as Emperor Taizu (r. 960–76). Though he took control of the south by military force, Taizu accepted the necessity of paying tribute to the northern tribes, a policy upheld by his successors. The rulers of the Song dynasty, as they were called, were among the least militaristic in Chinese history.

After about 170 years of ruling from Kaifeng, the Song were forced out by an attack from the north, and had to re-establish themselves further south, at Hangzhou. The vast expanse of territory that the Tang had ruled seemed to have been lost forever; but behind their reduced frontiers, the Song exploited technological advances made in the previous decades to preside over an age of invention and scientific discovery. Gunpowder began to be used in siege weapons, while there was a great leap forward in shipbuilding skills, as six-masted ships with crews of up to 500 sailors were built to carry the rapidly increasing cargoes of goods traded around Asia and as far afield as Africa and the Middle East.

FOREIGN MASTERS — THE YUAN

But to the north, there was a new threat. For the Song rulers, the growth in power of the nomadic armies of Mongolia, which had spread through Central Asia to the frontiers of Europe, seemed to offer a diplomatic opportunity of the kind they had exploited many times before in dealing with their enemies, and they reached an alliance aimed at defeating their northern enemies, the Jin of Manchuria.

The strategy was successful at first, and the Jin were comprehensively defeated. But then, instead of staying in the north, Kublai Khan and his Mongol armies swept south to destroy the Song dynasty and overrun the whole of China. In 1279, Kublai Khan, Great Khan of the Mongol empire (r. 1260–71), announced that he was the first emperor of the Chinese Yuan dynasty (r. 1271–94).

The Yuan was the first dynasty to rule the whole of China from the former Jin capital, Beijing – later renamed Cambuluc, or 'the great residence of the khan'. By the Chinese, they were never considered anything other than an army of occupation, and seem to have made little effort to integrate with the indigenous population. Although Kublai Khan was the last Great Khan, and his Yuan successors saw themselves as emperors of China rather than khans of the Mongols, they spoke a different language from the Chinese and appointed their countrymen to positions of authority in the government, while treating the Chinese as an inferior race. There was little investment – the grandeur of Kublai Khan's private palace and the magnificence of his court, which so impressed the Venetian explorer Marco Polo (1254–1324), was built on wealth seized from the people rather than earned through trade or agriculture. Unsuccessful attempts to seize territory in Japan and Vietnam were expensive in terms of money, lives and prestige. On the other hand, there was considerable cultural diversity. Buddhism, Islam and Christianity were tolerated, and traditional Chinese Confucianism gradually re-emerged as a widespread philosophy.

ABOVE Section of a panoramic painting entitled Going Upriver at the Qingming Festival *by the Song dynasty artist Zhang Zeduan (1085–1145).*

BELOW Map showing the Song empire of the tenth and eleventh centuries, prior to the loss of Kaifeng and northern territories to the Jin in 1127.

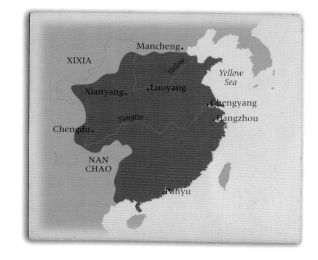

But having lost the support of many Mongolians, and with the hostility of many Chinese, the short rule of the Yuan was punctuated by sporadic rebellions by Mongols and by Chinese peasants. A succession of palace coups in the early 14th century cut short the reigns of the last Yuan emperors, and in 1368 Zhu Yuanzhang led a peasant revolution that forced them back north to Mongolia.

THE MOST POWERFUL NATION ON EARTH — THE MING DYNASTY

Zhu Yuanzhang ruled under the name of Hongwu (r. 1368–98), or 'Great Military Leader', and started a new dynasty, the Ming. Large and frequently neglected estates which had grown up under the Yuan were broken up and distributed to the peasants, and the third Ming emperor, Yongle (r. 1402–24), resumed attempts to expand the empire, building a huge navy and recruiting a standing army of a million men. The Song and Yuan had built ships both for war and for trade, but nothing on this scale. Ancient records suggest that over 1600 new ships were built, creating a navy of some 3750 vessels.

Other Asian nations sent tribute to the Ming emperor – in 1421, a fleet of ships brought rulers and envoys of 28 nations from as far away as Arabia, Africa and India to pay homage – and the army pushed west and south, recovering some of the lands once ruled by the Tang and Han dynasties. In the north, an invasion of the Mongol heartlands in 1380 led to the capture of tens of thousands of prisoners, and the sacking and destruction of the capital city, Karakorum.

But the Ming's priority was to extend their influence and increase their wealth by trade and diplomacy rather than by conquest. Chinese merchants travelled along the Silk Road once more, rebuilding the profitable trading empire of the Tang from 500 years before. Meanwhile, the Chinese merchant fleet traded widely.

This combination of an efficient agricultural base, a strong military and an interest in exploration and discovery helped the Ming to create one of the richest nations in the world. In the north, where the greatest threat to the empire was believed to lie, they restored and rebuilt the ancient Great Wall, so that the watchtowers and battlements which survive today are almost all of Ming construction.

DECLINE OF THE MING

But internal struggles for power weakened the authority of the emperor, and the empire began to be inward-looking and distrustful of scientific discovery. Sometime towards the end of the 15th century all contact with foreigners was discouraged, and laws were announced forbidding the construction of ocean-going ships. Around the same time, Mongol raiders began making incursions into the empire in the north, while some years later in the east an invading Japanese army was repelled with huge loss of life. When the Ming were threatened by a new enemy, the Manchu, who had unified many of the tribes in Manchuria and the surrounding area, they dispatched a huge army north, only to see it defeated by the smaller but highly mobile Manchu forces. The 16th century saw continual raids from the north. Some accounts claim that up to 25 million people died fighting the Manchu.

ABOVE *Map showing Ming China in around 1600, following years of expansion under later emperors of this dynasty.*

The Ming dynasty was falling apart. Once again, it was the Chinese peasantry who dealt the final blow, after another of China's perennial famines: in the early years of the 17th century, popular unrest sparked repeated revolts and outbreaks of violence, and the last Ming emperor committed suicide in 1644 as a peasant army stormed his palace. Sensing their opportunity, the Manchu swept through the kingdom within weeks, to establish the Qing dynasty. It was the second time that the empire had been ruled by foreigners.

At least in the early years of their rule, the Qing – like the Mongols of the Yuan dynasty – retained their own culture and treated the Chinese as a subject people. The wearing of Manchu clothing and hairstyles – the hair worn in a long pigtail, for example – were enforced on pain of death. But this time, unlike the Mongols of the Yuan dynasty, the Qing stayed in control for centuries. The Chinese empire, which had endured for nearly 2000 years, had finally been superseded.

BELOW *The Forbidden City in Beijing, built from 1406 to 1420, was home to China's emperors until the end of imperial rule in 1911.*

During the early Christian era, the northern Ethiopian kingdom of Aksum stood on one of the world's great sea trading routes between Europe, India, Arabia and the Far East, and it also controlled the overland route to the prosperous ancient cities of Nubia and the hinterland of Africa. At its height, it stretched along the southern Red Sea coast as far as Egypt in the north and to modern Djibouti in the south. Today, all that remains of the empire is the town of Aksum itself, close to the Ethiopian border with Eritrea, while the only monuments to Aksum's legendary greatness are 119 massive granite obelisks (stelae) in the central square – some still standing, others lying broken on the ground.

THE EMPIRE OF AKSUM
C.500 BC – AD 600

BY THE TIME THE GREEKS AND ROMANS WERE WRITING ABOUT THE IMPORTANT TRADING city of Aksum in the first century AD, people of the kingdom had been settled in the Ethiopian highlands for some six centuries. As well as dealing in merchandise from India, China and the Far East, the cities of Aksum – its port Adulis and the southern settlement of Matara, apart from the capital itself – were a melting pot of Egyptian, Middle Eastern, Indian, African and Arabic cultures.

A PROSPEROUS TRADE CENTRE

Adulis, which housed communities of Greek and Roman traders, was five days' march from the city of Aksum across the Tigray Plateau. From there, precious stones, copper, glassware and textiles from merchant vessels were brought inland by caravan, along with the iron needed to equip the army of a ruler who claimed the title 'King of Kings'. In return for imported goods, the traders of Aksum would export such treasures as incense, emeralds and rhinoceros horn from the Red Sea hills and the lands to the west, around modern Sudan. Obsidian and tortoiseshell came from islands in the Red Sea, and ivory from the lands to the west of the Nile. Gold, paid for with salt from the salt flats of the Danakil Desert, and another commodity – slaves – were also transported to the coast, making the city a prosperous centre for the East African slave trade.

LEFT *Ruins of the palace of King Kaleb at Aksum in highland Ethiopia. This sixth-century ruler presided over the zenith of Aksumite power.*

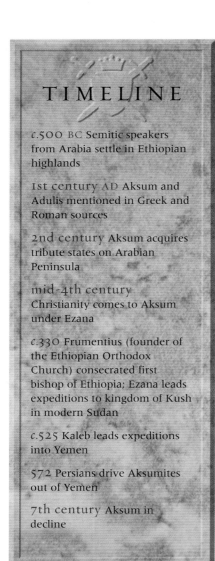

Archaeologists estimate that the city of Aksum at its height may have had a population as large as 20,000, many of them officials and servants of the king's court, supported by tributes from vassal states and taxes levied on the merchant traffic of the Red Sea. In the sixth century one of the ambassadors of the Byzantine emperor reported back in amazement that the Aksumite King Kaleb (d.*c.*540) rode in a great carriage drawn by elephants. The rulers of Aksum were the first in Africa to issue their own coinage, an achievement that points to a progressive and ambitious economic and political outlook. Inscriptions on the coins which have been found are in both the local language of Ge'ez and Greek, demonstrating the cosmopolitan nature of the trade that passed through Adulis.

A MYSTERIOUS EMPIRE

Yet our knowledge of the empire's growth, the battles it must have fought as it extended its influence over northern Ethiopia and across the Red Sea, its power and its decline is scanty, gleaned from coins, inscriptions, archaeological investigations and passing mentions in various ancient texts. One early king, mentioned by the Greeks, was named Zoskales (*c.*100), who was said to be 'miserly by nature'; another, Endybis (*c.*270–300), is known because coins with his image still survive. A later ruler, Ezana (*c.*330–56), brought Christianity to Aksum in the mid-fourth century.

Inscriptions bearing Ezana's name have been found at the ancient city of Meroe on the east bank of the Nile, which might suggest that the Aksumites were responsible for the destruction of the kingdom of Kush, a prosperous Nile Valley civilization which had begun its decline during the second and third centuries.

However, by the seventh century, the power of what had once been the richest and most powerful state in the region was in decline. Early in the sixth century, King Kaleb had mounted a successful invasion of Yemen, on the other side of the Red Sea, but those lands were lost in a counter-invasion by the Persians in 572. They were followed about 50 years later by the Arabs, as they spread the word of Muhammad.

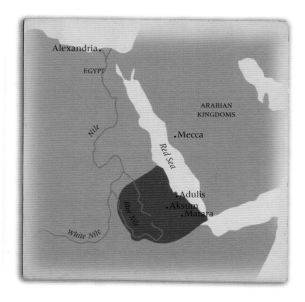

RIGHT Map showing the extent of the Aksumite empire during its decline in the sixth century AD.

THE STELAE OF AKSUM

In 2005, in an important act of cultural repatriation, an Aksumite stele was finally returned to the town from which dictator Benito Mussolini's fascist troops seized it when Italian forces invaded Ethiopia in the 1930s. The 1700-year-old, 24-metre- (78-ft-) tall carved stone pillar, which weighs some 160 tonnes, was one of more than 100 such structures dating from the early days of the Aksumite empire.

The stelae of Aksum, which are intricately decorated to resemble actual buildings, with false windows and doors carved into them, were positioned to mark the underground burial chambers of royal and aristocratic figures from the king's court.

The biggest stele still standing is around 23 metres (75 ft) tall, but one of the broken specimens that now lie in pieces on the ground would once have stood well over 30 metres (100 ft) high. Many have what appear to be stone altars carved out of their bases, carefully aligned to face the rising sun.

Were they associated with pre-Christian sun worship? Their purpose is now as mysterious as the whole history of the Aksumite empire.

The tallest standing obelisk in the Stelae Park at Aksum is the stele of King Ezana, named in honour of the first monarch of Aksum to embrace Christianity.

Gradually, the Aksumites lost control of the trade routes that had been their lifeblood, as the whole economic system on which they had relied began to crumble. The steady stream of merchant vessels sailing into the open harbour of Adulis became a trickle; and then, suddenly and inexplicably, the port was abandoned, probably sometime late in the sixth century. The centre of power in Ethiopia shifted south to the region around Lalibela and the great city of Aksum began its long descent into obscurity.

None of the emperors who ruled in Constantinople for nearly 1,400 years would have recognized the word 'Byzantine', a term first used more than 100 years after the last emperor died fighting in the ruins of his doomed capital. The emperors thought of themselves as Romaoi, a Greek word for a Roman idea and a useful starting point for understanding the character of the empire – a Roman tradition, carried on by Greeks from a heartland in Asia Minor. Modern research suggests that the empire displayed considerable military strength, impressive political flexibility, and provided a crucial cultural link between the ancient world and modern civilization.

THE BYZANTINE EMPIRE
c.330 – 1453

THE BYZANTINE EMPIRE GREW SLOWLY OUT OF THE ROMAN EMPIRE, its emperors considering themselves not just to be heirs to the emperors of Rome, but Roman emperors in their own right. The emperor Constantine (r. 306–37) transferred his capital to Byzantium in 330, renaming the city Constantinople. The fortifications that he began turned his new capital on the Bosphorus into a virtually impregnable fortress, and established its military character for the next nine centuries.

DIVISION OF THE ROMAN EMPIRE

Theodosius I (r. 379–95) was the last emperor to rule over both halves of the Roman empire. On his death in 395, it was formally divided between his two sons. The western capital was then Milan, and the rampant Visigoths, led by Alaric I (r. 395–410), sacked and pillaged Rome in 410. Meanwhile, the richer and more settled eastern half of the empire, based in Constantinople, maintained an uneasy peace by making huge payments of tribute to the Gothic tribes and by recruiting large numbers of foreign mercenaries to protect its borders.

In the sixth century the emperor Justinian I (r. 527–65) sought to exert his authority over the whole of the old empire, even though much of the western half was occupied by Vandals, Ostrogoths and other Gothic tribes. He extended his rule north to the

LEFT *A sixth-century mosaic from San Vitale cathedral in Ravenna, Italy, shows the Byzantine emperor Justinian the Great and his retinue.*

Danube, around the Mediterranean to the southern coast of Spain and the Pillars of Hercules (or modern Gibraltar), and also to all the main Mediterranean islands – the farthest-flung boundaries in the history of the empire. Justinian conquered the Vandals in North Africa and drove the Ostrogoths from Italy – at the price of the complete devastation of the Italian countryside. Only three years after his death in 565, another German tribe, the Langobardi or 'Longbeards', later to become the Lombards, seized the Italian territories again. There were no more serious attempts to extend the power of Constantinople back over the lands of the western empire. The division of the old Roman empire was final and complete.

JUSTINIAN'S LEGACY

Justinian's military adventures may have carried a high price, but he also left a lasting legacy, both in the magnificent basilica of Hagia Sophia, and in his codification of Roman law in the *Corpus iuris civilis*, which brought the Roman legal system together with Christianity. To this day, European law across most of the continent – although not in Britain – is based on the Roman principles and practices first set out by Justinian.

But his invasion of Italy had drained the imperial coffers. By the time Heraclius (r. 610–41) seized power to found a new dynasty in 610, barbarian tribes were forcing their way further and further into the Balkans to the west and, in the east, Persian troops were seeking to impose their own candidate as emperor. The situation was so serious that Heraclius considered moving the capital again, this time to Carthage in North Africa.

Instead, he reached a settlement with the barbarians in the west, under which he hoped they would remain in the empire's Balkan lands and effectively protect them from further invasion, while he turned his attention to the Persian threat. Over several years' campaigning, he gradually drove the Persians back out of Asia Minor, and in 627 he led his forces against those of the Persian emperor Khosrau II (r. 590–628) at the Battle of Nineveh, on the eastern bank of the River Tigris. An overwhelming victory destroyed the Persian army, and for a brief spell the Byzantine empire was restored to its position of power and strength in the Middle East.

ISLAM'S QUEST FOR CONSTANTINOPLE

While Heraclius had been campaigning across Asia Minor, another threat to his empire had been gathering strength 1000 miles (1600 km) further south. The birth of Islam was sending Arab armies north with

HAGIA SOPHIA

The emperor Justinian (r. 527–65) had more than 10,000 people working for five years to create the Megala Ecclesia, or Great Church, which would later be named the Church of Hagia Sophia, or Holy Wisdom. It was completed in 537 with materials brought from all over the empire, including columns from the Roman temples of Baalbeck in Lebanon, and its massive dome was seen as a monument to Justinian's imperial power.

An earthquake in 558 caused the collapse of the magnificent dome – the first of several occasions during succeeding centuries in which it had to be rebuilt – but the church remained as the official seat of the patriarch of Constantinople and the setting for all the great ceremonies of state of the Byzantine empire. It was decorated by mosaics, to which later emperors added, making the interior of the church a showcase for Byzantine art.

In 1453, the Turks converted the building into a mosque, covering many of the Christian mosaics with white plaster and beginning the process of adding more decorations and artefacts brought from different provinces of the Ottoman empire. When Mustafa Kemal Atatürk (1881–1938), the founder of the modern Turkish Republic, ordered its transformation into a museum in 1935, the plaster was removed, and the ancient decorations were revealed.

Hagia Sophia, with its towering dome and ornate, arched interior, is widely accepted as one of the greatest surviving examples of Byzantine architecture and engineering, and its mosaics, figurative paintings and icons include some of the ancient empire's greatest treasures.

Hagia Sophia was the largest cathedral in the world for almost a millennium, and is considered by many to be the epitome of Byzantine architecture.

news of the new religion. First the Persian empire and then the Byzantines felt the edge of their swords in a series of battles that would roll sporadically across the continent with varying intensity for nearly 900 years, and eventually breach the supposedly impregnable walls of Constantinople.

For the Arabs, it was the start of an obsession with capturing the Byzantine capital that would last for centuries. After a naval battle in 655 at Finike in the Mediterranean in which hundreds of Byzantine ships were destroyed, only the outbreak of civil war between rival claimants to the title of caliph in the Islamic empire prevented the Muslims from launching an all-out attack. In the following decades, there were repeated naval attacks by Arab fleets which sought to blockade the city, but these were beaten off by the use of so-called Greek fire, a primitive form of flame-thrower mounted on the Byzantine ships. One such attempt came in 674, when the Arabs were forced to withdraw by the onset of winter; in 717, an army of 80,000 men mounted a 12-month siege of the town by land, while around 1800 warships attacked from the sea. This time the Byzantines were aided by attacks on the Arabs from Bulgar tribesmen behind their lines, which some reports suggest cost as many as 30,000 Arab lives. Still Constantine's walls held firm and, for a while at least, the Islamic attacks on the Byzantines became less intense.

RELIGIOUS HEARTLAND

Alongside their political and military strength, the emperors also retained ecclesiastical and religious authority – unlike in the west, where this passed to the pope in Rome. In the eighth century, for instance, Emperor Leo III (r. 717–41) instituted a ban on the use of statues, paintings and icons in religious worship. This policy was in line with Islamic practices, and may have been adopted partly to make it easier to regain authority in the areas where the Muslims had exerted influence. It angered the pope, however, who saw it as a direct attack on the Latin faith and his own authority. The conflict lasted for more than 120 years, causing sporadic revolts across the empire and bedevilling relations with Rome, until Empress Theodora (r. 842–55) finally accepted in 843 that the icons could be brought back into church.

THE MACEDONIAN DYNASTY

The Byzantine empire reached its height over the next 300 years – although not as extensive as it had been under Justinian, it was much stronger and more stable. Under the successors of Basil I (r. 867–86), who initiated the Macedonian dynasty when he murdered his predecessor Michael III (r. 842–67) to seize power in 867, the population of the empire increased and trade developed, bringing with it wealth. At home, there was a new religious unity following the settlement of the dispute over icons, while abroad, in the Muslim lands, there was continuing struggle and internal warfare as different regional dynasties struggled for control. It was time to start taking back the lands that had been lost to the Arabs.

But it was not that easy. During the first decade of his reign, Basil launched a series of raids towards the Euphrates, where a renegade Christian sect had formed an alliance with the Muslims. They were defeated, and in another campaign, the island of Cyprus was briefly recaptured. Then, in 904, an Arab fleet plundered the Greek city of Thessalonica. The sea fighting and raids continued, bursting out at different points in the Mediterranean and the Aegean, with neither side able to strike a decisive blow.

BASIL THE BULGAR-SLAYER

Other enemies were appearing on the borders as well: first the Rus, a tall, fair race from the eastern Slav lands to the north, and then the Bulgars, who defeated a Byzantine army at the Battle of Bulgarophygon in northern Turkey in 896 and forced them to pay an annual tribute. It was more than another 100 years before the Bulgars were finally defeated by the soldier-emperor Basil II (r. 976–1025) at the Battle of Kleidion in 1014, on the northern fringes of the empire. The savagery of the battle – after which, according to one legend, nine out of every ten Bulgar prisoners were blinded, with the tenth left with just one eye to show his comrades the way home – gave Basil the name of the 'Bulgar Slayer'. A few years later, the Bulgars surrendered and accepted the authority of the emperor – for the first time in 300 years, the northern border of the empire ran once more along the River Danube.

With secure borders around lands that now covered the whole of Asia Minor, the Balkans and part of southern Italy – also re-taken by Basil's armies – the Byzantines should have been about to embark on a period of strength and prosperity when Basil died in 1025.

ABOVE *The 11th century frontispiece of a psalter, showing Basil II standing triumphantly over the conquered Bulgarian chiefs. His conquest was so violent and bloodthirsty that it bestowed upon him the title of 'Bulgar-Slayer'.*

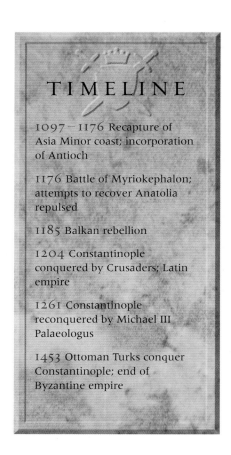
EMPIRE IN CRISIS

Basil's younger brother, who succeeded him as Emperor Constantine VIII (r. 1025–8), was the first of a series of weak and incompetent rulers who saw the armies disbanded and the wealth that Basil had built up squandered. Instead of military power, the empire began to rely on paying foreign mercenaries to defend its borders, and civilians rather than generals controlled the state.

It was a bad time to lose the protection of military efficiency and determination, because two new powerful enemies were starting to raid the fringes of the empire. First, in around 1040, the settlements of southern Italy were attacked and plundered by Norman raiders from northern France – the same Normans who, 26 years later, would conquer England at the Battle of Hastings. Over a period of about 30 years, the raiders gradually established themselves, until by 1072 the Byzantines had once more been forced out of the Italian Peninsula.

In Asia Minor, meanwhile, the Seljuk Turks, originally from Central Asia, had been conducting forays into Armenia and Anatolia. A crushing defeat at the Battle of Manzikert in 1071 was followed by the effective annexation of the entire region, as the Turks moved thousands of settlers in without opposition. By 1080, some 300,000 square miles (777,000 sq km) of Byzantine territory, in the east and the west, had been seized by foreign enemies.

The empire was in crisis. Trade had largely ground to a halt, inflation was rampant and the emperors were effectively bankrupt. Invaders were swarming through the Balkans: it was clear that the empire did not have the strength to face the Turkish threat in the east.

When Emperor Alexios I Komnenos (r. 1081-1118) sent ambassadors to Pope Urban II (1035–99) in Rome to appeal for help from western Christendom, the news that the western church was calling for an armed pilgrimage to drive the Turks out of Jerusalem must have seemed like a cure for all his ills. It was the start of the Crusades – a cure that would eventually spell death to the Byzantine empire.

ABOVE *Seljuk relief sculpture of a warrior. The Byzantine empire was shrinking: the Turks invaded Asia Minor in the east and the Normans took the Italian peninsula in the west.*

UNRULY CRUSADERS

For Pope Urban, the conquest of Jerusalem offered the prospect of Christendom reunited under papal authority, and at the Council of Clermont in 1095 he

set the First Crusade in motion. But the first group to reach Constantinople consisted not of disciplined troops, but a ragtag army of peasants gathered in France by the inspirational preacher Peter the Hermit (c.1050–1115), who led them on a three-month trek across Europe, murdering and looting on the way. Alexios, horrified by the appearance of this dangerous and unruly rabble, sent them into Asia Minor with instructions to wait for more forces. Set upon by the Turks, the largely unarmed horde of would-be Crusaders was butchered. It was an inauspicious start to the campaign to drive the Muslims away.

Two months later, though, the main body of soldiers, led by knights from France, Italy and England, gathered at the walls of Constantinople. Well armed and disciplined, but entirely dependent on Alexios for food and supplies, they set off south for Jerusalem. Over the next two years, despite constant arguments and

ABOVE *The 19th century artist Eugenio Lucas Velasquez depicted* The Crusaders Before Jerusalem, *where they hoped to reunite Christianity under papal authority.*

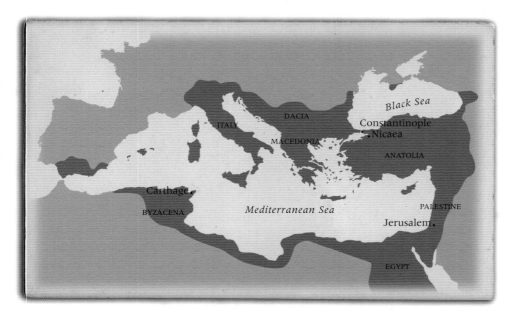

mistrust among the Crusaders themselves and between the Crusaders and the emperor, they recovered much of western Asia Minor for the empire. In 1099 they reached Jerusalem and, after a lengthy siege, they sacked the city, murdering Muslims, Jews and Eastern Christians indiscriminately.

The Byzantine empire had regained much of its former territory in Asia Minor, and instead of the threatening presence of Muslim armies further south, there was now a network of independent Crusader statelets. There was a rare spell of peace. The 12th century was one of growth and stability as the emperors built a network of fortifications across Asia Minor to cement their control, and the cities of the Byzantine empire continued to grow rich with trade from the western European maritime powers.

ABOVE Map showing the Byzantine empire at its greatest extent, in the early seventh century following its war against Persia.

There were two more Crusades, both of them less successful than the first, and Jerusalem fell to the Kurdish Muslim leader Salah-ed-Din Yusuf ibn Ayyub, known as Saladin (r. 1174–93), in 1187. The immediate significance of that was not so much that it signalled a resurgence of Muslim power as that it inspired the Fourth Crusade of 1203: the Crusade that gave the first unmistakable sign that, for all the apparent strength and confidence of the 12th century, the end of the Byzantine empire was imminent.

THE LAST YEARS

The disaster came at a time when the empire was least able to cope with it. The strong, capable Komnenos dynasty, which had overseen the flowering of the past 100 years, collapsed in a welter of infighting and palace intrigue. The first three emperors of the dynasty reigned for a total of 99 years; the fourth, Alexios II Komnenos (r. 1180–3), was murdered after three years and the fifth, Andronikos I Komnenos (r. 1183–5), was deposed and murdered after two more.

When a new emperor, Isaac II Angelos (r. 1185–95; 1203–4), seized power in 1185, it was the start of a fresh dynasty that would be marked by weak government, rebellion and intrigue. Isaac was deposed and blinded by his own brother, the first of a series of violent changes of power in the next few years. In the west, meanwhile, the Serbs and Hungarians were breaking away from the empire, and a revolt in Bulgaria further weakened Byzantine power. By the time the soldiers of the Fourth Crusade arrived at the walls of Constantinople in 1204, the empire was weaker and more divided than it had ever been.

This time, rather than attacking the Muslims or seeking to free Jerusalem, the Crusaders' swords were turned against the Eastern Christians of Byzantium. They accepted a bribe from the deposed and blinded Isaac and his son in return for putting them back on the throne, and then stormed and sacked the city. The Crusaders rampaged through the streets for three days, murdering, raping and plundering. Priceless ancient bronzes were melted down and precious stones ripped from their settings as Christian soldiers grabbed what they could from Christian churches. The famous bronze horses that now stand in Venice's Basilica di San Marco were among the precious artefacts ripped out of the shattered city and shipped off to the west.

A SLOW DEATH

The empire was formally dissolved and its territories split into three. Emperors, at least in name, continued to reign from the city of Nicaea on the northern coast of Asia Minor – the modern Turkish city of Iznik – but even when Michael VIII Palaeologus (1261–82) managed to recapture Constantinople itself 57 years after the sacking, there was no wealth and no political strength to back up his

BELOW *16th-century fresco painting of the siege of Constantinople. The city was torn apart by the Fourth Crusade in 1204, signalling the beginning of the end of the ancient Byzantine empire.*

authority. Through the 14th and early 15th centuries, Michael's descendants managed to maintain their grip on the imperial crown, but little else.

It was a slow-motion death, spread out over two centuries, but when the end came it was dramatic and spectacular. It may be hard to find a precise date for the start of the Byzantine empire, but it is easy to put a date on the ending of it: Tuesday 29 May, 1453. The famous city walls were still standing, but inside them was a defending army of less than 8000 men, many of them foreign mercenaries. The Turkish armies who had finally come to storm the city were between 150,000 and 200,000 strong, with a fleet to blockade the city from the sea, and gunpowder and cannon to batter the walls from the landward side.

Even so, the defenders had repulsed repeated frontal attacks for more than eight weeks. Some reports suggest that the end came when a door in the walls was left unlocked, so the ancient walls were never actually breached – but all that is certain is that the Turkish forces finally burst through into the city. The last Byzantine emperor, Constantine XI Palaeologus (r. 1449–53), was seen to throw aside his purple regalia and hurl himself into the melée, determined to die as his city fell. The empire of Byzantium, whose history had seen so much dissembling, deception and intrigue, had finally died with a last, desperate act of hopeless bravery.

AFTERMATH OF EMPIRE

The seizure of Constantinople was a defining moment in the growth of the Ottoman empire, which effectively took over the role of the Byzantines as the dominant power in the Middle East. Their empire, with Constantinople as its capital, lasted into the 20th century.

The split in the Christian church survives to this day, with Eastern Orthodox churches, rather than Roman Catholic ones, predominant in Russia, the Balkans and eastern Europe. These churches trace their ancestry back to the Eastern Church of the Byzantine empire.

CULTURAL LEGACY

But the lasting significance in the west of the Turkish victory was cultural rather than military or political. It is hard to exaggerate the empire's importance in preserving and passing on classical culture, much of which would have been lost without it. Greek

ANCIENT BYZANTIUM, MODERN ISTANBUL

According to legend, the ancient city of Byzantium was named after a Greek king Byzas of the sixth century BC, who captured the strategic peninsula jutting out into the Black Sea from its Thracian inhabitants. In about 200 BC, the city was razed to the ground and then rebuilt by the Roman emperor Septimus Severus (r. AD 193–211), who renamed it Augusta Antonina in honour of his son.

Its name was changed again in 330, when Emperor Constantine I (r. 306-37), moving the capital of his empire to the city, ordered that it should be called New Rome, but it became Constantinopolis in his memory shortly after his death in 337. That remained its official name for 1600 years, as capital first of the Byzantine and then the Ottoman empire.

However, legend has it that Arabs in the 13th century – believing that the Greek phrase *eis ten polin*, which actually means 'in the city' was its name – began to call it Istinpolin. This name gradually changed into Istanbul and was the official name given to the city in 1930 when it became the capital of the Turkish Republic.

Like Rome, the city has seven hills. It commands the Bosphorus, which is the channel connecting the Black Sea to the Mediterranean.

and Latin literature, science, philosophy and theology were virtually forgotten in western Europe after the collapse of Rome, but the writings of Homer, Plato, Aristotle and almost all the ancient Greek literature we still have today were preserved in the libraries of Constantinople. So were the mathematical works of Euclid, the histories of Herodotus and the textbooks that formed the basis of much ancient Arab medicine.

Greek scholars had been travelling westwards with ancient manuscripts from the city's libraries for more than two centuries – for at least 50 years before the fall of the city, it was obvious that Constantinople was doomed. But in 1453 an exodus into Italy started which helped to define the character of the Renaissance over the succeeding decades. Constantinople itself may have been lost to Christianity, but the classical spirit of the ancient Byzantine empire, transformed by western learning and western translators, was spreading across Europe.

BELOW *The Ortaköy mosque, Istanbul and the bridge across the Bosphorus that links Europe with Asia.*

Charles the Great – Charlemagne – the king of the Germanic Frankish people, built an empire in eighth-century Europe which reached from the Danube in the east to Spain, Germany and Italy and included scores of different tribes, nationalities and languages. In theory, the empire survived for almost 1000 years after Charlemagne's death, but its real imperial power ended with the death of Frederick II in 1250; after that, it was little more than a confederation of German states under the hereditary leadership of the Austrian Habsburg family. By the time Napoleon oversaw its dissolution in 1805, the Holy Roman Empire had become an anachronism – a survival of the Middle Ages, just as the shape of modern Europe was beginning to emerge.

THE HOLY ROMAN EMPIRE
496–1805

AMONG THE VARIOUS TRIBES AND NATIONS WHO FOUGHT FOR POWER AFTER THE FALL OF THE Roman empire in AD 476 the Franks, under their leader Clovis I (r. 481–511), gradually emerged as the most powerful. Clovis' conversion to Christianity was a link with his Roman predecessors, and he accepted Roman titles from the Byzantine emperor in Constantinople (see The Byzantine Empire, pages 84–95), who claimed to be the inheritor of the authority and privileges of the Roman empire. There was no thought at that time, however, that the empire might find a true heir in western Europe.

THE MEROVINGIAN DYNASTY EMERGES

Clovis' successors – known as the Merovingian dynasty, after Clovis' grandfather, Merovich – extended their power eastwards into central Europe. But the Frankish tradition was for lands and powers to be shared among the king's children when he died, which resulted in almost constant internal fighting and the loss of royal authority as they struggled for pre-eminence. In the eighth century (by which time

LEFT *A heavily jewelled reliquary bust, c.1350, of Emperor Charlemagne, the architect of the Holy Roman Empire.*

TIMELINE

476 Fall of Roman empire

496 Clovis converts the Franks to Christianity

732 Charles Martel stops Muslim invasion of Europe at Battle of Tours

755 Donation of Pippin

774 Charlemagne seizes Lombard territory

778 Charlemagne attacks Muslims in Spain

781 Charlemagne's sons appointed kings of Italy and Aquitaine

784 Saxons defeated in Germany

800 Pope crowns Charlemagne emperor of the Holy Roman Empire

840 Death of Louis the Pious leads to civil war

843 Treaty of Verdun splits the empire into three

887 Frankish aristocrats overthrow Carolingian dynasty

936 Otto I accedes to throne of eastern empire

954 Otto I defeats Hungarians at the Battle of Lechfeld

961 Pope asks Otto I for protection

962 Otto I invades Italy and is crowned emperor by the pope

962 onwards Ottonian Renaissance

963 Otto deposes the pope; installs his own candidate

continued

the Franks ruled most of western Europe) power was slipping away from the central authority of the king towards the princes and the aristocracy. A palace official named Pippin – known subsequently, slightly disrespectfully, as Pippin the Short – seized power to make himself Pippin III, king of the Franks (751–68), and establish a new dynasty, the Carolingian.

When Pope Stephen II (r. 752-7) needed protection from the Langobardi tribes (later to become the Lombards) who had invaded northern Italy, he turned to Pippin, who defeated the Langobardi and handed over to the pope lands they had seized from the Byzantines. This transaction, known as the Donation of Pippin, was the origin of the Papal States, the territory in central Italy that still remains under direct papal authority. Pippin had effectively formed a powerful alliance with the papacy, the start of a volatile relationship between temporal power and religious authority that would last for centuries.

When Pippin died in 768, his aim was to divide his kingdom, as the Franks had traditionally done, between his sons Charles and Carloman. It seemed briefly as if rivalry between the two would destroy this new dynasty as it had the last, but the death of Carloman (r. 754–71) in 771 left Charles as the sole ruler of Pippin's legacy. It was Charles – Charlemagne, or Charles the Great (r. 771–814) – who laid the foundations for the Holy Roman Empire.

CHARLEMAGNE'S CAMPAIGNS OF EXPANSION

Brushing aside the claims of Carloman's heirs, the 24-year-old Charlemagne embarked on a 30-year series of military operations designed to bolster his authority among the various tribes and nations of his new realm. His first campaign, which lasted well into his 50s, was against the Saxons east of the Rhine. Charlemagne's forces rampaged repeatedly across their lands, burning villages, slaughtering their inhabitants and forcing both the Saxons and their Frisian allies along the North Sea coast to embrace Christianity.

While the fighting continued beyond the Rhine, Charlemagne also sent forces into northern Italy, incorporating the lands of the Langobardi into his possessions. In 781 he declared a new kingdom of Italy, subject to his own overlordship, with his son Pippin as king.

From Italy, he moved on to Spain, where Umayyad refugees from the 'Abbasid revolution in Arabia had established Muslim rule and were making inroads into the Frankish lands of southern Gaul. (See The

'Abbasid Empire, pages 122–129.)
After three years of fighting,
Charlemagne had extended his
power as far as the Ebro river,
creating an effective buffer against
attacks on Gaul in what became
known as the 'Spanish March',
and allowing him to create a
neighbouring kingdom of
Aquitaine for his son Louis in 781.
For the first time in decades, the
lands ruled by the Franks were
relatively peaceful.

In 788, it was the turn of the
Bavarians, who had traditionally
been fiercely independent.
Annexation of their lands brought
Charlemagne into contact with the
Avars, Central Asian nomadic
tribesmen who had conquered
much of the territory along the
Danube. Over the next eight years
they too were conquered and
forced to accept Christianity.
Charlemagne took more treasure
for himself and added another
stretch of land south of the
Danube to his rapidly growing
empire. Where his father had been

ABOVE *14th-century painting of
Charlemagne's Spanish march,
when he retook southern Gaul
from Umayyad refugees, creating
the kingdom of Aquitaine.*

a successful regional king, Charlemagne had established himself, in fact if not
yet in name, as an emperor.

The title seems to have been bestowed on him almost against his will. In 799
an uprising in Rome forced Pope Leo III (r. 795–816) to seek Charlemagne's
protection. In return, it was agreed that Leo would consecrate Charlemagne's
son Pippin as king of Italy under his father. But, apparently without any
consultation, the pope suddenly placed a crown on Charlemagne's own head,
and announced him in the traditional Roman terms as *Augustus et imperator*.
According to contemporary reports, Charlemagne was angered rather than
flattered: Leo had publicly enrolled the Franks, their king, and – most
importantly – their armies as his defenders, but Charlemagne himself had been
placed in an invidious position with the Byzantine emperors, who would not
accept any rivals as inheritors of the authority of the Caesars.

LOUIS THE PIOUS AND THE EMPIRE IN ECLIPSE

The newly crowned emperor was in his 60s; his armies, virtually invincible on land, were facing new threats from the sea, with raiding parties of Vikings harassing the Franks' possessions while, from Spain, Muslim Saracen warriors continued to attack his borders. Although he began to call himself 'emperor governing the Roman empire', and launched a determined military and diplomatic campaign to persuade the Byzantine emperor Michael I (r. 811–13) in Constantinople to recognize his Roman titles, there is little evidence that Charlemagne expected his empire to survive him. In 806 he followed the old Frankish tradition of declaring that his lands would be divided among his three sons on his death.

However, his sons Charles and Pippin died before him, and in 813 he arranged the imperial coronation of Louis (r. 814–40), whom he had earlier installed as king of Aquitaine. A few months later, Charlemagne died. He had left his son, who became known as Louis the Pious, ruler of an empire that stretched from modern Barcelona in Spain to the Danube, and from Italy to the North Sea. It included not only Franks, but also Saxons, Jews, Spaniards, Lombards, Romans, Bavarians, Avars, Slavs and other conquered tribes and nations. Keeping that mixture of races, languages and cultures together was enough of a challenge; but, despite Constantinople's grudging acknowledgement of the imperial titles, Louis had also inherited a festering rivalry with the Byzantines that would last for hundreds of years.

ABOVE *14th-century painting of the coronation of Louis I. He was crowned king of Aquitaine as a child, later becoming Holy Roman Emperor after his father, Charlemagne, died.*

RIGHT *Detail of Charles II (the Bald) receiving the monk and scholar Alcuin of York.*

There was also a damaging ambiguity at the heart of the empire itself. Charlemagne's empire was an aggressively Christian bulwark against the Muslims in Spain – but was it simply built on Charlemagne's Frankish ancestry and the Franks' rule over the other nations of Europe, or was it an expression of the earthly power of Christianity, with the pope and the Catholic Church embodying the final moral authority? Charlemagne had tried to establish his independence from Rome by organizing his son's coronation in Germany, not Rome, and by crowning him himself, rather than involving the papacy. Yet both Louis and his son Lothair (r. 840–55), whom he raised to the rank of emperor alongside him, later sought papal approval of their titles.

Louis' plan was that his son should inherit all the lands as Lothair I, with his other two sons reigning as inferior kings in Aquitaine and Bavaria. He tried to settle the uncertainties and the disunity of the empire by presenting himself as a Christian emperor ruling over a single Christian people, united by their religion with the help of the pope, whom he named as his assistant, or *adiutor*.

Louis crushed opposition to his rule ruthlessly – some of those who conspired against him were killed, some were exiled, some had their eyes put out and others were sent to monasteries. Even so, he faced constant opposition, both from his own family and from the subject peoples of the empire, and when he died in 840 the quarrelling between the sons of his two marriages led to the break-up of the empire into three separate parts at the Treaty of Verdun in 843. The imperial title survived, passed from Louis to Lothair, then to his son Louis II (r. 855–75), and on to the engagingly named Charles II the Bald (875–7), followed by Charles III the Fat (r. 881–7). Over time, however, respect for the family of Charlemagne diminished and the weakened Carolingian dynasty was overthrown by Frankish aristocrats in 887.

HOLY, ROMAN AND EMPIRE

'Neither holy, nor Roman, nor an empire.' Voltaire's famous comment of 1769, less than 40 years before the Holy Roman Empire crumbled in the Napoleonic wars, was a trenchant epitaph on a 1000-year institution. It might have been more accurate to say that the empire was all three – but never at the same time.

Charlemagne, the first and in many ways the greatest of the emperors, was never crowned Holy Roman Emperor. When Pope Leo III (r. 795–816) named him as *Augustus et imperator*, or Majestic Emperor, he was using the language and the terminology of the Romans, but making no explicit connection between the Roman empire and the one that Charlemagne had carved out for himself.

At the time, with the Byzantine emperors insisting that they and they alone were the true heirs of the Caesars, this was a subtle way of handling a delicate problem. It was only after a long period of diplomacy and a series of battles that they accepted Charlemagne's personal title of emperor in 812, and they were unwilling to extend that courtesy to his successors.

The name changes over the next thousand years often mirrored the political realities of the shifting relationship between popes, emperors and German princes. During the 11th and 12th centuries for instance, with the Hohenstaufens stressing their independence from Rome, it was known as the Holy Empire. It was not until another hundred years had gone by, in the year 1254, that the term Sacrum Romanum Imperium, or Holy Roman Empire, was used for the first time.

Two hundred years later, with the empire now firmly grounded in its Germanic heartland, it became Sacrum Romanum Imperium Nationis Germanicae, or Holy Roman Empire of the German People. In the 16th century, the power of the German princes who, at least in theory, determined the succession was implicitly acknowledged in the imperial title Imperator Electus, or Chosen Emperor, which was bestowed on Emperor Maximilian I (r. 1508–19).

By the final days of the empire at the beginning of the 19th century, the title – and the dignities that went with it – were all that was left.

Even then, the imperial title survived for a few decades, bestowed by the reigning pope on a succession of minor Italian notables, until in 924 it was suppressed by a group of powerful Roman families. The empire that Charlemagne had created seemed to have vanished in name as well as in fact.

A NEW EMPIRE

Further north, though, the Frankish tradition of a military empire survived. It depended neither on succession from Charlemagne nor on papal approval, but on the emergence of a leader strong enough to dominate the different factions, tribes and nations. That leader was Otto I (r.936–73), who succeeded in 936 to the eastern part of the empire which lay beyond the Rhine. From the start, he stamped his authority on the dissenting nobles in a series of battles and also strengthened the borders of his territory, which had been ravaged by Slavs and Magyar tribesmen. In 951, allegedly invited by the widowed Queen Adelaide (931–99), he marched into Italy to protect her against an attempt to take her throne, and promptly married her. He named himself the new ruler of Italy, and installed a new king of the Lombards, Berengar (d.966), as his vassal.

It was the Battle of Lechfeld, near Augsburg, in 955 that cemented Otto's reputation, and justified the claims he made to be the true inheritor of the spirit of Charlemagne. Hordes of Magyars from Hungary had stormed across Bavaria and Franconia, pillaging towns and villages as far as Burgundy, and Otto finally caught up with them on the banks of the River Lech. He was heavily outnumbered – contemporary estimates put his forces at around 10,000, facing some 50,000 Magyar horsemen – but he conquered them with a disciplined cavalry charge. He then spent several days tracking down survivors to be either executed or have their ears and noses cut off before being sent home as a warning. This bloody victory, in which some 30,000 Magyars were said to have died, effectively ended the threat to Europe from the east for four centuries. The German nobles in Otto's army raised him on their shields in triumph to declare him the new emperor by right of conquest in the traditional Germanic fashion.

ABOVE *Otto I, a strong and violent leader who became emperor by right of conquest.*

CONFLICT WITH ROME AND CONSTANTINOPLE

Otto was, in effect, ruler of a confederation of the ancient Germanic tribes of the Franks, Saxons, Alemanns and Bavarians. One strategy he employed to maintain his authority across his lands was to install bishops and church officers, imitating Charlemagne's fervour for spreading Christianity. Once again, as in the days of Charlemagne, the empire was synonymous with Christianity. Otto, however, was still not emperor in the eyes of the pope. Seven years later, however, in 962, Pope John XII (r. 955–64) needed help when Otto's protégé, Berengar, threatened to seize power in Rome. Otto returned to Italy to take up Charlemagne's former role as defender of the papacy; once again, just as Pope Leo III had crowned Charlemagne in order to cement their alliance, John accepted the reality of power and placed the imperial crown on Otto's head. He needed the protection of the most powerful man in Europe, and crowning him emperor seemed the best way to guarantee it.

But the balance of power between pope and emperor had shifted. Only a few months later Otto summarily dismissed John, whom he believed to be plotting against him, and replaced him with a pope of his own choosing, Leo VIII (r. 963–5). For more than 100 years, that relationship continued, with Otto's successors deposing and nominating popes as they chose, to fit in with their political aims: contemporary religious paintings show the emperor, not the pope, as God's representative on earth.

But the empire Otto controlled was greatly reduced. He made no effort to challenge the division of Charlemagne's territory, and the West Frankish lands – as they were called – remained separate from his possessions, which extended no further than present-day Germany and Italy. Nonetheless, the rivalry with Constantinople that dated back to Charlemagne's original investiture continued. The Byzantines, stronger and more confident, threatened to take back parts of Italy they had lost, and Otto sent his troops south down the Italian Peninsula into the land the Byzantines already occupied, as a demonstration of his determination to defend Rome. In a parallel diplomatic strategy, he arranged for Otto II (r. 967–83), his son by Adelaide of Italy (931–99), to marry the Byzantine princess Theophano (c.956–91).

Despite this union, relations between the two empires continued to be difficult. Otto II, who ruled jointly with his father from 967 and took over as sole emperor when his father died in 973, had himself proclaimed Roman emperor in a direct challenge to the Byzantine rulers. A few years later, in 1024, the empire was formally declared to be the Roman empire, and each new emperor given the title of 'king of the Romans' before his investiture.

AN ARTISTIC RENAISSANCE

The relative peace that Otto I brought created the cultural highpoint of the empire in Germany, manifested in the creation of magnificent buildings such as the abbey church of St Michael at Hildesheim (founded in 1001), or the cathedrals at Magdeburg (where Otto I was buried) and at Augsburg. This artistic flowering, often known as the Ottonian Renaissance, demonstrates the closeness with which the empire was allied to Christianity.

The succession was largely arranged by each reigning emperor, who would nominate the next emperor. Each one considered himself to be anointed by God as religious as well as temporal leader of the empire, but at the same time the choice of emperor had to be confirmed by an election among the leaders of the Germanic tribes. After Otto's death, Henry II (r. 973–1024) managed to secure the succession only through his military power, and when he died without children 22 years later, it was only after a long period of debate that Conrad II (r. 1024–39) was approved as emperor by the tribal leaders.

Conrad's accession replaced the old Ottonian dynasty of emperors with the Salian dynasty. At the same time, the empire began to be referred to in official documents as Regnum Teutonicum, or the German kingdom – an implicit recognition that the old tribal distinctions were breaking down. The new German aristocracy was asserting its dominance over the pope, the primacy of the German lands over Rome. The empire might represent the power of Christianity on earth but only through the swords of the tribal leaders.

ABOVE *Detail showing Emperor Conrad II. After Henry II died without heirs, Conrad II became emperor after agreement between the tribal leaders.*

THE INVESTITURE CONTROVERSY

Even while the tribal leaders were demonstrating their authority, however, the situation in the empire and in Europe as a whole was gradually changing again. From about 1020 onwards, Norman mercenaries had been arriving in Sicily and southern Italy, to the considerable alarm of the popes in Rome. In 1053, they defeated a papal army at the Battle of Civitate near Foggia in southern Italy, and took Pope Leo IX (r. 1049–54) prisoner. Nine years later Pope Nicholas II (r. 1059–61) reached an agreement with the Normans whereby they would accept his spiritual overlordship, and also become his military allies.

OPPOSITE *The cathedral of Augsburg, begun in 994, is part of the cultural heritage of the Holy Roman Empire in Germany.*

With this support, Nicholas was able to maintain his distance both from the Germans and the Byzantines, giving the papacy a new independence which caused a lasting rift between pope and emperor. The specific issue which divided them, known as the Investiture Controversy, was ostensibly a disagreement about who should have the power to create bishoprics and appoint bishops and abbots, but it involved a much more radical clash over whether the pope or the emperor wielded supreme power. It was a return to the unsettled argument remaining from Charlemagne's day about the respective roles of the empire and the church.

This argument led Pope Gregory VII (1073–85) to announce in 1077 the excommunication and deposing of King Henry IV of Germany, the future emperor. Henry (r. 1084–1105/6), who had been the German king since the age of six in 1054, travelled to the northern Italian town of Canossa. There he waited for three days outside the castle where Gregory was in residence before the pope agreed to accept his repentance and rescind the sentence of excommunication. Initially it seemed that the dispute over supremacy had been won by the church, but the tension continued. Gregory announced Henry's excommunication again just three years later, and also formally banned all temporal rulers from making church appointments. This time Henry responded by declaring his own nominee for a new pope, and by marching his troops into Rome to enforce his decision. Gregory was forced to flee, and died in exile, while Henry was crowned emperor in 1084 by his own nominee as pope.

A determined attempt was made to settle the issue in 1122, in a compromise agreement signed at Worms, in southwest Germany. However, arguments continued to resurface well into the 14th century. A series of 'anti-popes' with imperial backing provided religious opposition to the popes and lent the imperial cause a veneer of religious respectability.

THE HOHENSTAUFEN EMPERORS

The election of Conrad III (r. 1138–52) as emperor by the German princes started a new imperial dynasty, the Hohenstaufens. Conrad strengthened the empire both by military conquests in the east – where the Poles and central European tribes had established their effective independence over the previous decades – and also by diplomacy in the west, with the accession of Burgundy to the empire on the death of the childless King Rudolf III (r. 993–1032).

Under Conrad III and his successor, Frederick I Barbarossa, or 'Redbeard' (r. 1155–90), the empire began once more to emphasize its independence from the papacy.

Barbarossa stressed his Frankish antecedents and his right to power by conquest, as distinct from reliance on the approval of the pope. His aim was to secure the

RIGHT *Engraving of Frederick I's entry into Milan in 1158, by Matthäus Merian the Elder (1593–1650). This capture marked the beginning of his long struggle with Pope Alexander III.*

loyalty of the German princes, but there had also been a deep-seated transformation in the nature of the empire itself. Growing economic power in Germany and restlessness among the Italian cities caused Barbarossa to focus on his possessions north of the Alps. At the Battle of Legnano in 1176, the Italian cities, united in the Lombard League and backed by Pope Alexander III (r. 1159–81), forced the emperor to grant them a degree of local autonomy and accept the pope's right to rule over the Papal States.

ibilis tenebrosus demone plenus, palam et secure loquitur. et utalitus ent [manuscript text, partially legible]

en te disperdam satorem magnum de babilone tenentem fal[c] [manuscript text, partially legible]

DIVISION WITHIN THE EMPIRE

Frederick's son, Henry VI (r. 1191–7), was more successful through marriage than his father had been through battle and warfare. His wife was Constance I (1154–98) whose father, the Norman king Roger II of Sicily (r. 1130–54), had died. She brought with her to their wedding in 1186 the right for Henry, as her husband, to be crowned king of Sicily, thus bringing much of Italy back into the empire, at least temporarily.

Henry's death at the age of 32, as he prepared to go on a crusade to the Holy Land, left the succession to his three-year-old son Frederick. Henry had already insisted that the German princes should formally elect the child as the future emperor, but Constance's actions in bringing him back to Sicily and then appointing the pope as his guardian drove them to seek another emperor to replace him. The Germanic character of the empire was more important than the principle of dynastic succession. One group voted for the baby's uncle, Philip of Swabia, and another for Otto of Brunswick, a grandson of Henry II of England (r. 1154–89), who had been brought up at the court of his uncle, Richard I, 'the Lionheart' (r. 1189–99), in England. This three-way division of loyalties between Philip, Otto and the young Frederick almost brought about the final dissolution of the empire.

In Germany, Philip seemed initially to have the support of the princes, and he was recognized by the pope as king (r. 1198–1208), though not as emperor. When he was murdered, however, in an argument over his daughter's marriage, Otto of Brunswick was crowned first king (r. 1208–15), and then, in 1209, Emperor Otto IV – apparently ending the aspirations of Frederick (r. 1220–50), who was then 15 years old.

But Otto had agreed not to try to take Frederick's Sicilian possessions, and when he marched his troops into southern Italy, he lost the support both of the princes at home and the pope in Rome. Frederick, seizing his chance, led an army into southern Germany, while his ally, Philip II of France (r. 1180–1223), overwhelmingly defeated Otto and his forces at Bouvines in Flanders on 22 July, 1214. Frederick was free to resume his rule as emperor.

A few decades later, in 1241, a huge stroke of luck saved the empire from even greater destruction, when the Mongol armies which had burned, sacked and plundered their way west from the steppes of Asia suddenly stopped their advance just as they were crossing the Danube. There was no army in Europe that could have defeated them – but news from Mongolia of the death of the 'Great Khan', Ogedei (r. 1229–41), had made them turn around and go home. (See The Mongol Empire, pages 134–145.)

BELOW *Map showing the kingdoms, duchies and marches making up the Holy Roman Empire in c.1175, during the reign of Frederick I Barbarossa.*

Frederick's persistent attempts to reunite Italy and the empire north of the Alps foundered with his failure to crush the independent-minded cities of the reformed Lombard League. There were also continuing clashes with the papacy, which culminated in Frederick's excommunication in 1239.

While he concentrated on his Italian possessions and his efforts to subdue the Lombard League, Frederick had granted a significant degree of independence to the German princes: now, his attempts to rouse them against the pope met with little success. When he died suddenly in 1250, the emperor's authority was increasingly being called into question, and the princes had gained new powers that they would never relinquish.

HOLY ROMAN EMPERORS

Carolingian Dynasty
800 – 814 Charlemagne
814 – 40 Louis I (the Pious)
840 – 55 Lothair I
855 – 75 Louis II
875 – 7 Charles II (the Bald)
881 – 7 Charles III (the Fat)
887 – 99 Arnulf
899 – 911 Louis III
911 – 18 Conrad I
919 – 36 Henry I (the
    Fowler)

Ottonian Dynasty
936 – 73 Otto I (the Great)
967 – 83 Otto II
983 – 1002 Otto III
1002 – 24 Henry II

Salian Dynasty
1024 – 39 Conrad II
1039 – 56 Henry III
1056 – 1106 Henry IV
1077 – 1080 Rudolf
1106 – 25 Henry V
1125 – 37 Lothair II

Hohenstaufen Dynasty
1138 – 52 Conrad III
1152 – 90 Frederick I
    Barbarossa
1191 – 7 Henry VI
1198 – 1208 Philip
1198 – 1218 Otto IV
1220 – 50 Frederick II

THE EMPIRE'S LONG DECLINE

The medieval empire is generally considered to have died with Frederick, but the papacy did not inherit the powers that the emperor had lost. In clashing openly with the popes, the Hohenstaufens had also lost the military and political support of the temporal rulers on whom they depended. For nearly 30 years there was no universally acknowledged emperor, and the princes took the opportunity of entrenching their independent power. Soon after Frederick's death they established a formal college of electors who would in theory wield unchallenged power over the succession. From the 14th century onwards, only four emperors were formally crowned by the pope.

The power of the emperor was also limited by international pressures. The French were determined not to see the re-emergence of a powerful and ambitious emperor in Germany. Further south, neither the papacy nor the cities of northern Italy would tolerate the return of imperial power south of the Alps. In 1355 emperor Charles IV (r. 1355–78), one of the few emperors to be crowned by the pope, had to agree to abandon all claim to Italy, and to enter and leave Rome only on the day of his coronation. Whatever power the Holy Roman Empire still exerted had shrunk back to its German heartland and, by the mid-15th century, this was reflected in a new official name: Sacrum Romanum Imperium Nationis Germanicae, or Holy Roman Empire of the German Nation. Its claims were as far-reaching as before, but they extended no further than Germany itself.

Despite occasional attempts by individual emperors to regain the power of the past, talk of the leadership of Christendom was increasingly hollow. Elections became a formality – for almost all of that time, the supposedly elective imperial crown was actually inherited by one member of the Austrian Habsburg family after another. By now, the Holy Roman Empire was little more than the foundation on which a unified Germany would eventually be built.

A LAST ATTEMPT TO RE-ESTABLISH THE EMPIRE

With Charles V (r. 1519–56), who succeeded his grandfather Emperor Maximilian I (r. 1508–19), there was a final flurry of the old grandeur. He tried to re-establish international rule, bringing together his imperial possessions with the territories in Spain, Italy and the Netherlands that he had inherited as king of Spain. (See The Trading Empires of Spain and Portugal, pages 178–187.) His lands stretched from Spain to Austria, and from the Netherlands to the kingdom of Naples (with the exception of

France). But with Charles enjoying very little of the military or political power that the earlier emperors had wielded, there was little chance that the empire would revive. The Reformation destroyed much of his authority in Germany, leaving him as leader of the Catholic faction, facing the opposition of the Protestant princes. On his abdication in 1556 his lands were divided, with his son Philip (r. 1556–98) inheriting the Spanish possessions, while his brother Ferdinand I (r. 1558–64) succeeded to the imperial title in Germany.

In the end, after 250 years of decline, the death blow to the empire was dealt neither by the pope nor the German aristocracy but by another, more powerful emperor. Napoleon (r. 1804–15), having already seized Lombardy and the left bank of the Rhine, decreed in 1805 that the 1000-year-old empire was dissolved.

The Umayyad empire was the first of two great Arab empires that dominated the Middle East for 600 years. It grew out of the sudden Arab expansion which started within a year of the death of the prophet Muhammad in 632, and lasted until it was destroyed in the 'Abbasid revolution of 750. The empire was constantly plagued by internal fighting, causing a religious split which survives today in the rival sects of Shi'a and Sunni Islam. The conversion to Islam of many of the empire's conquered peoples brought another challenge, as non-Arab Muslims began to demand the same rights and privileges as their rulers, providing widespread support for the uprising that eventually toppled the dynasty.

THE UMAYYAD EMPIRE
633 – 750

NEITHER THE BYZANTINES NOR THE PERSIANS, battle-weary and exhausted after a series of wars and frontier skirmishes in the early seventh century, had any idea of the storm that was about to break over them out of the desert. Nor, almost certainly, had the Arabs themselves: their immediate priority was simply to reassert their authority over the tribes of Arabia after the death of the prophet Muhammad (570–632). His successor as ruler, Abu Bakr (r. 632–4), was given the title *Khalifa* or deputy, but there was no suggestion that the caliphate which he founded would eventually extend its power throughout the Middle East and North Africa, and even into Europe.

An army from Muhammad's city of Medina, commanded by Abu Bakr's general, Khalid ibn al-Walid (592–642), crushed tribal resistance at the Battle of Aqraba, on Arabia's Nejd Plateau in 633; the slaughter at this site later earned it the name 'Garden of Death'. Then they began to launch raiding parties further north, where the various city-states had come under the loose authority of the Byzantine empire. Within a few months, having encountered little effective resistance, Khalid was looting the city of Damascus. When the Byzantine emperor Heraclius (r. 610–41) marched against them with well over twice as many soldiers as Khalid commanded, the Arabs abandoned the city and faced him in 636 at the Yarmuk river, a tributary of the River Jordan.

LEFT *Muhammad's grandson Husayn ibn Ali on horseback at the Battle of Karbala in 680, where he was killed by Umayyad forces. Detail from an early 20th-century painting by Abbas Al-Musavi.*

TIMELINE

632 Death of Muhammad

633 Khalid ibn al-Walid defeats tribes at the Battle of Aqraba

636 Arabs defeat Byzantines at the Battle of Yarmuk river; Persians are defeated at the Battle of Qadisiyah

656 Assassination of Uthman

656–61 First *Fitna*

674–8 First siege of Constantinople

680 Battle of Karbala

683 Second *Fitna*

684 Battle of Marj Rahit; start of Marwanid dynasty

711 Arab forces land in Spain

717–18 Second siege of Constantinople

732 Battle of Poitiers halts Arab expansion in France

744 Third *Fitna*; Marwan II seizes power and moves the capital to Harran

747 'Abbasid Hashimiyya revolt

749 Abu-al-Abbas al Saffar recognized as caliph in Kufa

750 Umayyads defeated at the Battle of the River Zab

755 Exiled Umayyad leader Abd ar-Rahman defeats pro 'Abassid governor of al-Andalus and later establishes a new Umayyad dynasty in Spain

In the ensuing six-day battle, the Byzantines were routed by the Muslim cavalry in a crushing victory that left the whole of Syria and Palestine at their mercy. Only the two heavily fortified cities of Caesarea and Jerusalem remained as Byzantine strongholds. The Battle of Yarmuk river is generally considered one of the most significant in the history of warfare, ushering in centuries of conflict between the Christian states of Europe and the Muslim forces of Arabia. A year after the battle, the caliph Umar (r. 634–44), who had succeeded Abu Bakr two years earlier, visited Syria to decide how the newly won lands were to be governed. By the end of his reign, Arab power would extend over the whole of Arabia, part of the Persian empire, and the Syrian and Egyptian provinces of the Byzantine empire.

CONQUEST OF THE FERTILE CRESCENT AND EGYPT

At the same time, the Arabs launched raids into Iraq, although the Persian army of Emperor Yazdagird III (r. 632–51) halted their advance briefly at the Euphrates river in 634 at the Battle of the Bridge, when the Muslim cavalry was put to flight by the appearance of the Persian war elephants. But two years later, at Qadisiyah on the Euphrates, a new Arab force defeated the Persians and swept on to the capital of Ctesiphon, pushing north to join up with the victorious armies in Syria.

The conquest of Egypt followed, with the general 'Amr ibn al-As (d.633) – angry, according to some accounts, not to have been promoted in Syria – leading an exploratory raid on the settlement of Al Arish in 639. Surprised by the lack of resistance, he continued deep into Egypt, capturing the fortress of Babylon near Cairo in 640. By this time, reinforcements had arrived from Medina, changing the raid into a concerted attempt at conquest, and 'Amr defeated the Byzantine forces at the Battle of Heliopolis later the same year, going on to take the city of Alexandria after a year-long siege.

In all their early conquests, the Arabs exploited the desert in much the same way that later empires would use sea power. They were at home in terrain that was impassable to their enemies. One reason for choosing the Yarmuk river for their first decisive confrontation in Syria was that it offered the possibility of a quick retreat into the desert, where the Byzantines would be unable to follow them.

A WELL-DEFENDED TRADING NETWORK

As they conquered new provinces, they created strongholds in towns such as Damascus on the desert fringes, where they established garrisons and administrative centres and built up the trading network on which the local

ικολ|τοιωχε|ρόυ;ιμα| χμαρ̃ύτο.ω|καταστ.α̃.αρ|τωρ̃ε̃ικοστωε̃μ̃πε̃χλαδ̃ων· καὶ μετα̃νίκ̃

economies relied. By controlling these cities, even though they were heavily outnumbered throughout the provinces as a whole, the Arabs could maintain their military grip.

Their rule was also facilitated by a relaxed policy towards their subject peoples. Non-Arabs and non-Muslims – broadly the same thing in the early days of the conquests – faced discriminatory taxation, but private property was usually respected, and local customs and religions were generally permitted by the law. For many people, Muslim rule was much easier to bear than that of the Byzantines had been.

The death of the caliph Umar in 644, allegedly murdered by a Persian slave, marks the end of this initial staggering expansion of Arab power. In ten years, the Arab tribes which Muhammad had welded into a unified religious society had conquered most of the surrounding lands. To the east were the highlands of Iran, to the west, the waters of the Mediterranean, and in the north, the mountains of Asia Minor. The new caliph, Uthman ibn Affan (r. 644–56), lacked the charisma and military capabilities of his predecessors, and central authority, never very strong, began to break down in internal conflict. Uthman was murdered in 656, and the empire essentially split into two rival parts. One was centred on Medina in the south, where Muhammad's cousin and son-in-law 'Ali (r. 656–61) was acclaimed as the new caliph; the other was in Damascus in the north, where Mu'awiya (r. 661–80), appointed governor by Umar, was in unchallenged control of a disciplined and battle-hardened army.

ABOVE *The Battle of Yarmuk river in 636 sparked centuries of intermittent warfare between the expanding Arab empires and the shrinking Byzantine empire. Yet for all their remarkable military successes, Umayyad attempts to take Constantinople in 674–8 and 716–17 failed. This 11th-century illumination, from the chronicle of John Scylitzes, shows a clash between Arab and Byzantine cavalry forces.*

This civil war is referred to in Muslim history as the First *Fitna*. Battles between the two sides were largely inconclusive, with Mu'awiya refusing to accept 'Ali's authority, and it was only the murder of 'Ali in 661 that ended the fighting. The rift in the Muslim world remained, the centre of gravity of the empire irrevocably shifting away from Medina: Mu'awiya, from a branch of the family known as the Sufyanid, was the new caliph, and Syria was the new seat of government.

KING OR CALIPH?

Abu Bakr and the three succeeding Arab rulers are often known as the 'Rightly Guided Caliphs'. By contrast, later Arab historians declared that Mu'awiya and his successors, known as the Umayyad from the name of Mu'awiya's great-grandfather Umayya ibn Abd Shams, were kings rather than caliphs, pointing to the move away from the old Islamic theocracy which took place during their rule as evidence that they were not true deputies of the prophet Muhammad. Others describe the Umayyad as the first dynasty of the Muslim caliphate, as they were the first rulers to enforce a dynastic succession.

The new ruler had to reassert the central power of the Arab empire, which had been badly shaken by the internal strife that had preceded his succession. He also had to face continuing opposition from those who believed that only members of Muhammad's own clan, the Hashimi, or descendants of 'Ali, should be allowed to rule. Mu'awiya had won power, but he had to govern the independent-minded tribes by winning the consent of tribal councils known as the wufud and consulting with the shura, an assembly of sheikhs. The eventual succession of his son Yazid (r. 680–3) was only announced after Mu'awiya had first agreed it with the shura and then confirmed the choice with the wufud.

A PERIOD OF EXPANSION

Even his control of the army in Syria was not enough to enable Mu'awiya to force his decisions through without consultation and diplomacy at home. But abroad he returned to a policy of armed aggression as he sought to push the boundaries of his empire further east and west. There was no return to the explosive expansion of the early years, but under Mu'awiya the empire embarked upon a period of steady growth that would extend its power into Herat, Bukhara and Kabul in Central Asia, and begin a gradual westward progression out of Egypt and along the northern coast of Africa.

Yet Mu'awiya's reign saw continual fighting with the Byzantine empire. In 655, when his rule extended no further than Syria, his newly formed navy triumphed in the Battle of the Masts off the southern coast of Asia Minor, a victory that established the Arabs as a sea power in the Mediterranean. After he became caliph, his forces continued to nibble away at the Byzantine possessions in the Mediterranean, taking control of Rhodes and Crete. When they tried to take the battle to Constantinople itself, however, they were beaten back. There were repeated unsuccessful efforts to blockade the city by sea during the 670s, but although the Arabs managed to establish a bridgehead south of the city, they never breached the walls. At sea, they had no answer to the Byzantine deployment of so-called 'Greek fire', which hurled flaming chemicals into their ships. The campaign was abandoned when Mu'awiya died in 680.

ABOVE *Portrait of the caliph Mu'awiya on a seventh-century Sassanian-style coin. His relocation of the Arab capital to Damascus in 661 caused Arabia to decline steadily in political significance, though the holiest sites of Islam were located there.*

DISSENT AND CIVIL WAR

It is a mark of Mu'awiya's achievements that his son Yazid was able to succeed to the throne without any renewal of the civil wars that had blighted the early part of his father's reign. A policy of careful diplomacy at home, religious tolerance – there were Christian officials in Mu'awiya's own court – and aggressive expansion abroad seemed for a time to have effectively removed the threat to the central government of the empire.

That was not to say that there was no opposition – less than six months after Mu'awiya's death, 'Ali's son Husayn (626–80) travelled into Iraq, where he hoped to gather support for a revolt against Yazid and the Umayyad dynasty. Husayn and his followers believed the Umayyad had illegally seized power and betrayed the Islamic religion, but they were slaughtered by the Umayyad army in 680 at Karbala, near a tributary of the Euphrates. The battle resonated for centuries – the death of Husayn remained a rallying cry for opposition throughout the Umayyad reign, and is still commemorated each year by Shi'a Muslims, whose name is a contraction of the phrase *shi'at-'Ali* ('party of 'Ali').

Yazid's death only three years later was followed within months by that of his infant son Mu'awiya II and the outbreak of another round of savage infighting, known as the Second *Fitna*. The Battle of Marj Rahit (684), close to Damascus, resulted in the victory of Marwan (r. 684–5), a member of a different branch of the Umayyad dynasty, who was already in his sixties. He was proclaimed caliph in 684, ending the rule of the Sufyanid branch of the dynasty, but his power was effectively limited to the northern areas of Syria and Egypt. Marwan immediately set about eliminating possible rivals to his son Abd al-Malik (r. 685–705) for the succession, and when he died after just a year, it was left to the 39-year-old Abd al-Malik to reimpose firm Umayyad control over the empire as a whole.

THE MARWANID DYNASTY

Abd al-Malik sent his army into Basra, at the northern tip of the Arabian Gulf, where they began the long process of rooting out the surviving supporters of the House of 'Ali. Having exerted their authority over the city, they marched on into the Hejaz, where they defeated and killed another claimant to the throne, Ibn al-Zubayr (624–92), who had refused to accept either Yazid or Marwan as caliph and had gathered supporters to back his own claim. Within three years, the new ruler had won general acceptance of his authority.

Abd al-Malik resumed the empire's expansion, with his armies pushing westwards through North Africa. Carthage was seized from the Byzantines in 695, and then razed to the ground three years later after a Byzantine naval force had briefly recaptured it. To the north, he advanced into Turkestan, while in Iraq he continued the campaign against opponents to his rule. Most significantly, though, he rebuilt the internal organization of the empire: new coins were introduced as a sign of his authority, Arabic was brought in as the single language of administration, and the taxation system was reorganized. Abd al-Malik also started a programme of mosque building with the construction of the Dome of the Rock, built on the site of the Jewish Temple in Jerusalem; then, under his son, came a mosque in Damascus, followed by more at Aleppo, Medina and Kairouan in North Africa.

By the time his son succeeded to the caliphate as al-Walid I (r. 705–15), Umayyad power was reaching its zenith. Al-Walid's troops moved east beyond the River Oxus, taking control of the ancient trading cities of Bukhara and Samarkand, and also moving south into the Indian province of Sind. His most famous conquest, however, came when the North African general Tariq ibn Ziyad (d. c.720) invaded Spain in 711, thus initiating 700 years of Muslim rule there. The huge rock where they landed was named in his honour as Jebel Tariq – Gibraltar. The Arab forces defeated Roderic (r. 710–11), the king of the ruling Visigoths, at the Battle of Guadalete, ending effective resistance to the invaders. Within five years, most of the Iberian Peninsula was under Arab control. Their expansion continued until the Franks defeated the Arab army at the Battle of Poitiers in 732.

LOOMING FINANCIAL CRISIS

In his brief term as caliph, Al-Walid's son Sulayman (r. 715–17) made a determined effort to crush the Byzantine empire, with 80,000 men besieging Constantinople for a year. The failure of this campaign not only damaged Umayyad prestige but also left the dynasty fatally weakened. On his deathbed in 717, he named the governor of the Hejaz, Umar ibn Abd al-Aziz (r. 717–20), as his successor, leaving him with the near-impossible task of rescuing the empire's tottering economy.

The disaster at Constantinople precipitated the financial crisis, but the reasons for it were deep-seated. The Arab empire had started as a confident and aggressive theocracy; from the beginning, laws and taxes had favoured its Muslim rulers, which in the early days had meant the Arabs themselves. They paid a personal religious tithe, but they were not liable for taxes on their lands, and they established large and profitable estates. Unsurprisingly, adherents of other faiths, known as *dhimmi*, converted to Islam in large numbers to share in these benefits. Where they succeeded, they drastically reduced the revenue to the Umayyad coffers, and where they failed, they built up a reservoir of resentment that found its expression in support for the followers of 'Ali and his descendants.

Umar's twin priorities were to try to ease discontent among non-Arab Muslims – the *mawali* – and to improve his finances. Umar eased the tax burden on the *mawali* and raised the rate of pay for Arab soldiers. A pious and devout Muslim, and the only Umayyad caliph to win the respect of the later 'Abbasid dynasty

BELOW *The Umayyad mosque in Damascus, Syria was built between 706 and 715, during the caliphate of al-Walid I. One of the most important cultural developments of the Umayyad period was the construction of the first mosques as centres of Islamic worship. Mosques were a statement of the power and authority not just of the Arabs as rulers of the empire, but of Abd al-Malik himself and his successors.*

THE UMAYYAD IN SPAIN

The defeat at the River Zab in 750 did not completely end Umayyad power in the Arab empire. Many of the family were killed in an 'Abbasid blood-letting that followed their defeat, but Abd ar-Rahman (fl.750–88) escaped to Spain (al-Andalus), where in 755 he defeated the pro-'Abbasid governor. Over the next few years, he crushed armies sent against him by Charlemagne (r. 771–814) from Europe and by the 'Abbasids from Syria, and put down a series of rebellions by Muslim Spaniards, Berbers from North Africa and various Arab factions, to establish a new Umayyad dynasty that would last for nearly 300 years.

Islamic calligraphy adorns stonework on the magnificent Alhambra palace and fortress complex in Granada.

Immigration by Berbers from North Africa, together with Christians, Jews and Muslim converts among the Spanish population, helped to create a distinctive and independent state in Spain which established its own trade and diplomatic relations with Constantinople and the east. It was only in the 11th century that Umayyad power faded, with their Spanish possessions broken up into tiny statelets ruled by independent princes. But the Christian recapture (*reconquista*) of the Arab lands was a long, slow process – in 1085 the Arabs were driven out of Toledo, in 1236 they lost Córdoba and in 1248, Seville. It was only in 1492 that the explorer Christopher Columbus (1451–1506), about to sail across the Atlantic, witnessed the last Arab soldiers forced out of Granada. Within a few years, first Jews and then Muslims were expelled from Spain, marking the end of the period of Muslim power.

Behind them, though, they left a language and a heritage that still survive. The Moorish *wadi al-kabir*, or 'big river valley', is recalled in the name of the country's fourth-longest river, the Guadalquivir; the Arabic *al gharb*, or the west, has become the Algarve region of Portugal; and the Arabic word for a water source, *al magridh*, is the derivation of the name of Spain's capital, Madrid. The Great Mosque of Córdoba and the Alhambra of Granada are only two out of scores of magnificent Umayyad buildings that remain as testament to the glories of Arab Spain.

and of many of the Shi'a opposition of his own time, he also banned non-Muslims from serving in his administration. But the policies were mutually incompatible – by reducing income, increasing spending and excluding talented and experienced *dhimmi* from government service, he left an economy teetering on the edge of chaos. At the same time, the empire was dividing into two large factions – one in the north and one in the south – which hated and distrusted each other.

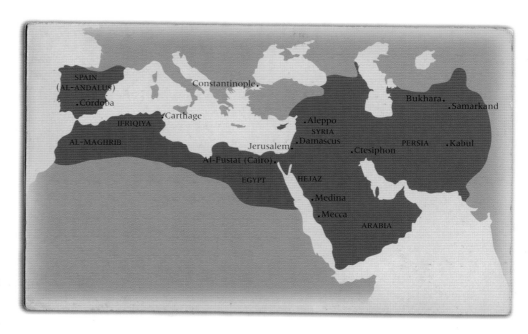

ABOVE *Rapid expansion under the Umayyad dynasty saw Arab territories spread through North Africa as far as Spain (al-Andalus), while in the east, the region under their control extended beyond Samarkand and Kabul.*

Umar died in 720, and his successors Yazid II (r. 720–4) and Hisham (r. 724–43) wrestled unsuccessfully with the problem. Arab historians describe Hisham as a miserly and rapacious ruler whose officials were ordered to wring every last penny out of the taxpayers in their provinces – yet it is hard to see what other policy he could have followed. Hisham also worked hard for a *rapprochement* between the northern and southern factions, bringing Arabs from each into his government.

For a while the policies worked, and Hisham managed to maintain order across the empire. But with his death, the internal fighting between the different sects and families intensified in the third and final *Fitna*, so that violent opposition spread right into the Syrian heartland of Umayyad power. Elsewhere in the empire – in the Arabian Peninsula, in the eastern lands stretching towards Central Asia and most of all in Iraq – Hisham's successors were rejected. It was a branch of the party of 'Ali, murdered more than 80 years before, who dealt the decisive blow to the dynasty, finally avenging the massacre of Karbala.

THE 'ABBASID SUCCEED THE UMAYYAD

The 'Abbasid Hashimiyya revolution began in 747 in the Shi'a strongholds of Kufa and Khurasan in Iraq. In 750 the combined Arab and Persian forces of the revolt's military leader Abu Muslim (d.755) defeated the Umayyad army at the Battle of the River Zab, a tributary of the Tigris in Iraq. The last Umayyad caliph, Marwan II (r. 744–50), was one of very few survivors to escape from the battlefield, but he was captured and killed shortly afterwards in Egypt.

Abu Muslim's support for the 'Abbasid was steadfast, and Abu al-'Abbas (r. 749–54) was proclaimed as the new caliph, with the title al-Saffah. The new dynasty would rule the eastern half of the Arab empire for the next 500 years.

Unlike the Umayyad, the 'Abbasid claimed direct descent from the family of Muhammad, and the emphasis of the rebellion that brought them to power in 750 was on the unity of Islam rather than Arab supremacy. The 'Abbasid heartland was in the traditionally Persian lands stretching east from southern Iraq and, as a result, the empire acquired a distinctly Persian flavour. Its hold on the more remote provinces was fragile, and by the time the Mongol invasion destroyed the 'Abbasid caliphate, its power was an empty shell. Yet its cultural achievements were considerable, and the grandeur of the eighth-century court of Harun al-Rashid at Baghdad became a byword for sophistication throughout the known world.

THE 'ABBASID EMPIRE
750–1258

THE NEW 'ABBASID DYNASTY MARKED ITS ACCESSION TO POWER with a furious blood-letting as the new caliph set about making himself secure and earning his nickname al-Saffah – 'the Slaughterer'. First, the surviving members of the Umayyad family who had ruled the empire were wiped out. Next, members of the 'Abbasid family who had grown too popular were put to the sword; revolts by Shi'a Muslims who had supported the revolution were savagely put down; soon afterwards, Abu Muslim (d.755) – the general who had done more than anyone else to bring about the defeat of the Umayyad – was summoned to Baghdad, where he too was murdered. The new leaders would tolerate no potential rivals.

Al-Saffah (r. 750–4) lived for only five years after the seizure of power before he was succeeded by his brother, al-Mansur (r. 754–75), and the stern response to any potential opposition continued. The new caliph's 21-year rule set the tone of the dynasty that would remain the ruling house of the Arab world for the next 500 years. Those who followed him might wield more or less real power, but each one would trace his descent back to al-Mansur himself.

LEFT *This 19th-century painting by the German artist Julius Köckert (1827–1918) shows the 'Abbasid caliph Harun al-Rashid receiving envoys from the Holy Roman emperor Charlemagne.*

A NEW CAPITAL AND A NEW STYLE OF GOVERNMENT

The power of the old Arab aristocracy had vanished with the slaughter of the Umayyad family. The *mawali,* or non-Arab Muslims, many of whom were Persian by birth, had been important supporters of the uprising (see The Umayyad Empire, pages 112–121) and were in a strong position. They had been considered inferior under the Umayyad, but over the next few decades they gradually acquired genuine equality. Where the Umayyad had emphasized the aristocratic, soldierly virtues of an Arab warrior class, the 'Abbasid oversaw the development of a wealthy and influential merchant class drawn from Arabs and non-Arabs alike.

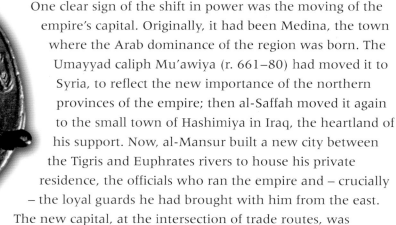

One clear sign of the shift in power was the moving of the empire's capital. Originally, it had been Medina, the town where the Arab dominance of the region was born. The Umayyad caliph Mu'awiya (r. 661–80) had moved it to Syria, to reflect the new importance of the northern provinces of the empire; then al-Saffah moved it again to the small town of Hashimiya in Iraq, the heartland of his support. Now, al-Mansur built a new city between the Tigris and Euphrates rivers to house his private residence, the officials who ran the empire and – crucially – the loyal guards he had brought with him from the east. The new capital, at the intersection of trade routes, was officially named Medinat al-salaam, or City of Peace. It was more often known by the name of the Persian village that had occupied the site previously – Baghdad.

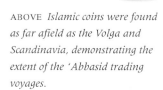

ABOVE *Islamic coins were found as far afield as the Volga and Scandinavia, demonstrating the extent of the 'Abbasid trading voyages.*

With the new capital came a new style of hierarchical government, partly based on the traditions of Persian rulers, and partly a result of the difficulties of ruling over the vast empire from the eastern city of Baghdad. While the early caliphs had been approachable by any fellow member of their tribe, the 'Abbasid rulers were approached through a succession of court officials – and then only with great ceremony and deference. Where the Umayyad had ruled by cajoling and persuading sheikhs and tribal elders, the 'Abbasid caliphs enjoyed unlimited power within their own courts.

Their control, however, extended in reality no further than the cities and the areas immediately around them. Outside the capital, the regional governors wielded increasing power of their own. The sheer extent of the empire meant that 'Abbasid power had to be directed through a huge bureaucracy, with a series of diwans, or ministries, all reporting back ultimately to the wazir, or vizier, whose role as chief executive under the caliph brought him immense personal wealth and power.

REVOLTS AND INDEPENDENCE MOVEMENTS

With the capital moved east to Baghdad, it was not practical to maintain tight control over all the possessions of North Africa – and the focus of the empire was now on the profitable trade routes to the east.

In a military sense, the empire was becoming more inward-looking. The attention of succeeding caliphs was directed primarily towards putting down revolts by different religious sects closer to home. In particular, the ghost of the murdered general Abu Muslim returned periodically to haunt the 'Abbasid – in one early revolt, Abu Muslim's supporters, claiming he was still alive, captured several towns scattered across western Persia before being crushed by al-Mansur's troops. A Persian rebel leader named Babak Khorramdin (c.798–838) disrupted trade routes and constantly threatened to create a dangerous alliance with the Byzantines until he was finally defeated in 837.

In another insurrection, thousands of black African slaves who worked in the salt flats around Basra captured several cities in the region, briefly sacked Basra and came within 20 miles (32 km) of Baghdad itself. Known as the Zanj, they established their own rebel city-state in the salt flats, which lasted for more than ten years before the armies of the ruling caliph, Al Mu'tamid (r. 870–92), crushed them and destroyed their city.

AN EXTENSIVE TRADING EMPIRE

But if the Arabs had ceased to look for foreign military conquests, they were developing a vast and profitable trading network. Peace with their neighbours, the 'Abbasid discovered, could be infinitely more profitable than war. From the Persian Gulf and from the Red Sea, Arab trading ships brought silks, spices, aromatics, fine crockery and other wonders from the East Indies and China, both for use within the empire and for re-export to Europe. From India came exotic animals and skins such as tigers and elephants, along with rare types of wood, rubies and precious stones. Trade with the Byzantines brought gold, brocades and carved marble; furs, swords, armour, sheep and cattle came from Russia and the Baltic. Thousands of Islamic coins have been found in Sweden and along the Volga dating from between the seventh and 11th centuries, confirming that wide-ranging trading voyages took place.

There were also, of course, the ancient overland routes to the east – camel trails that snaked through Central Asia to India and China to meet in the busy metropolis of Baghdad. When the fifth caliph, Harun al-Rashid (r. 786–809), came to power in 786, unprecedented wealth

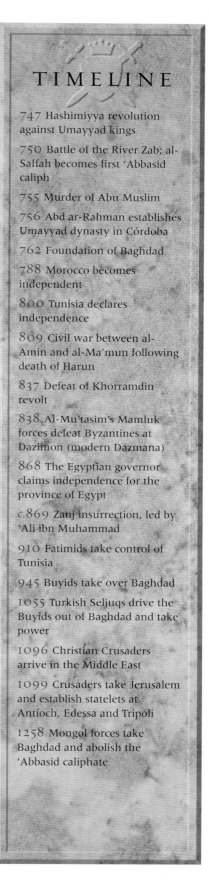

TIMELINE

747 Hashimiyya revolution against Umayyad kings

750 Battle of the River Zab; al-Saffah becomes first 'Abbasid caliph

755 Murder of Abu Muslim

756 Abd ar-Rahman establishes Umayyad dynasty in Córdoba

762 Foundation of Baghdad

788 Morocco becomes independent

800 Tunisia declares independence

809 Civil war between al-Amin and al-Ma'mun following death of Harun

837 Defeat of Khorramdin revolt

838 Al-Mu'tasim's Mamluk forces defeat Byzantines at Dazimon (modern Dazmana)

868 The Egyptian governor claims independence for the province of Egypt

c.869 Zanj insurrection, led by 'Ali ibn Muhammad

910 Fatimids take control of Tunisia

945 Buyids take over Baghdad

1055 Turkish Seljuqs drive the Buyids out of Baghdad and take power

1096 Christian Crusaders arrive in the Middle East

1099 Crusaders take Jerusalem and establish statelets at Antioch, Edessa and Tripoli

1258 Mongol forces take Baghdad and abolish the 'Abbasid caliphate

HARUN AL-RASHID

The caliphate of Harun al-Rashid (r. 786–809) is often considered to have marked the zenith of the wealth, power and culture of the 'Abbasid dynasty. The opulence of his court in Baghdad is a recurrent theme of the tales of the *Thousand and One Nights*, which are believed to have been gathered together during the century following his reign. He exchanged gifts with the Frankish emperor Charlemagne (r. 768–814) in the west and with Chinese emperors in the east.

But, like his predecessors, Harun was also capable of ruthlessness. His court included an official executioner – named Masrur in the stories – and when he doubted the loyalty of an old friend,

Harun al-Rashid's court was renowned for its style and grandeur. This 17th-century Persian miniature painting shows a scene from the Thousand and One Nights.

Ja'far the Barmakid, he had no hesitation in executing him and having the rest of his family imprisoned. The Barmakids, who had served the 'Abbasid as viziers on several occasions, were a noble Persian family, and it is likely that their fall from grace was connected with the growing rivalries between the western part of the empire, dominated by Arabs, and the Persian-dominated east.

That split also led Harun to divide his empire between his two sons at his death – a decision that led to several years of civil war and contributed to the continuing decline of 'Abbasid power.

was flooding into the new city from all over the world. This was the peak of the 'Abbasid dynasty – notwithstanding the unravelling of the empire in North Africa, control of the trade routes brought Harun luxury that became legendary far beyond the borders of his empire.

CRUMBLING POWER

After Harun's death in 809, however, 'Abbasid power began to fall apart at home as well. The caliph's two sons, al-Amin (r. 809–13) and al-Ma'mun (r. 813–33), fought over the succession. Their individual power bases reflected the split that had developed in the empire, with al-Amin drawing his support from the capital and the surrounding region, while al-Ma'mun had the backing of the eastern provinces and Persia. Al-Amin was finally defeated and executed after a siege of Baghdad which lasted more than a year, but the conflict had encouraged local dynasties in Persia to struggle for their independence.

And in Baghdad itself, the 'Abbasid were no longer secure. Even the income from the trade routes could not support the luxury of the court. To increase their revenues, the caliphs began to demand fixed payments from provincial governors, and allowed them to raise taxes themselves to cover the cost – a policy that greatly increased their independence of the central government. Then al-Ma'mun's successor, his brother al-Mu'tasim (r. 833–42), saw a simple way to increase his military power by importing large numbers of slaves from Turkey – the Mamluks, or 'owned' soldiers.

It was a policy that paid quick dividends. Al-Mu'tasim first put down Babak Khorramdin's 20-year-old rebellion in Persia and then sent his Mamluks into battle against the Byzantine emperor Theophilus (r. 829–42) in Asia Minor, winning a crushing victory over him as well. In the longer term, though, the employment of the Mamluks was a disaster for the dynasty: over the next few

BELOW *A 13th-century Arab manuscript illumination depicting a merchant's sailing dhow. 'Abbasid ships developed a far-reaching trading empire, from Russia and the Baltic to the East Indies and China, bringing luxury and wealth to the caliph's court.*

decades they gradually increased their power until they were able to push the ruling caliph aside at will.

In 945, another threat emerged with the arrival of the Buyids, a military dynasty from the Caspian Sea, who had extended their power into neighbouring provinces and now seized control of Baghdad itself. They took the Persian title of shahanshah, or 'King of Kings', for themselves but left the caliph as Islamic leader and still, in theory, ruler of the empire.

Even the claim to religious supremacy was bitterly challenged. There had been constant revolts by various Islamic sects throughout the 'Abbasid dynasty that had been put down with more or less brutality, but now a new group, the Fatimid – claiming descent from Fatima, Muhammad's daughter and 'Ali's wife – proclaimed themselves to be the true caliphs. They had taken control of Tunisia in 910 and gradually moved eastwards, until by 969 they controlled Egypt and the revenues of the fertile Nile Valley.

THE DEATH BLOW

By the 11th century, Arab power faced a wave of attacks from all sides. In Europe, Christian forces began to advance into Muslim Spain, and the island of Sicily, which had been seized by Tunisian Arabs in 827, was conquered by Norman soldiers. By the end of the century the first Christian Crusaders were threatening the very heartland of the Arabs.

From Central Asia, waves of Turkish invaders, the Seljuks, were pouring into Persia, and in 1055 an army headed by Tughrul Bey drove the Buyids out of Baghdad and took power for themselves. The Turks had accepted Islam, and allowed the caliph to continue as titular head of state, while

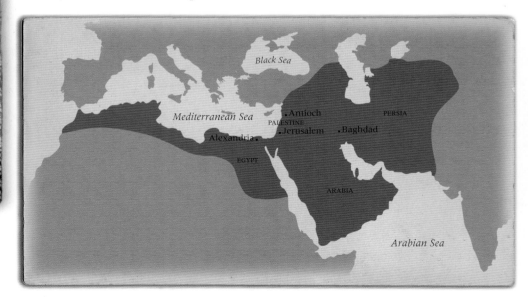

Tughrul Bey assumed the title of 'Sultan of East and West'. For the next 50 years or so the Seljuks ruled over Iran, Iraq and most of Syria, and conquered parts of Asia Minor that had been held by the Byzantines, but by the time the Crusaders arrived in the Middle East in 1096, their rule had fragmented among a number of semi-independent Seljuq chiefs.

The disunity of the Arabs allowed the Crusaders to take Jerusalem and establish a chain of statelets based on the cities of Antioch, Edessa, Tripoli and Jerusalem. However, it was left to the Mongol prince Hülegü (r. 1256–65) to deal the death blow to an empire that had been moribund for 300 years. In 1258, like other war leaders before him, he led his troops into Baghdad – but unlike the others, he did not permit the defeated caliphs to continue their pretended authority. Hulegu burned the city, slaughtered its inhabitants, executed al-Musta'sim, and declared the 'Abbasid caliphate abolished.

THE ISLAMIC LEGACY

When the first caliphs had taken their power into Syria, Palestine, Egypt and Persia, the word 'Arab' had described a native of the Arabian Peninsula. The Umayyad had maintained that distinction as long as they could, but under the 'Abbasid, Islamic and Arab life had embraced the different peoples and races of the empire. The Arab empire had metamorphosed into an Islamic world, which has continued for centuries.

ABOVE *An uneasy impasse was reached in the Holy Land – while the Muslims were too disunited to drive the invaders out, the Crusaders lacked the manpower and logistical support to make serious inroads into what was left of the 'Abbasid empire. This 11th-century illustration from a Fatimid manuscript shows warriors on horseback.*

FAR LEFT *Map showing the 'Abbasid empire at its height in 763, when Baghdad was founded as its capital.*

The Chola people are mentioned in carvings from the third century BC, and the Greek geographer Ptolemy, writing a century later, referred to important trading ports that exported spices, sandalwood and pearls from the coast of Andhra Pradesh, where the Cholas lived. The Cholas were a Tamil people, whose power lasted from the tenth century to the 13th, stretching through southern India as far north as the Godavari River in Andhra Pradesh, and to Sri Lanka in the south. At its peak, the empire also included the Maldive and Laccadive islands, stretches of coastline on the eastern side of the Bay of Bengal and parts of western Borneo.

THE CHOLA EMPIRE
c.985 – 1279

IN THE FIRST YEARS OF THE ELEVENTH CENTURY, KING RAJARAJA (r. 985–1014) led his troops against the Pandya people, another Tamil nation in the south of India. It was partly a revenge attack, since the Pandyas had previously defeated his father in battle, ending an earlier attempt to establish a Chola empire across southern India. This time the Cholas' conquest was more firmly based: over several years, Rajaraja conquered the Pandyas and the neighbouring Chera before mounting a seaborne invasion of Sri Lanka.

DEDICATED TO DESTRUCTION

His powerful army rampaged through the northern Sri Lanka countryside and destroyed Anuradhapura, the ancient capital of the Sinhalas, before returning to the mainland, where Rajaraja, a devout Hindu, supervised the start of the building of the Thanjavur temple, which was dedicated to Shiva, the god of destruction.

Shortly afterwards, he took his army north from his capital, Uraiyur, to seize more territory across the modern Indian state of Karnataka. Rajaraja was taking advantage both of his own wealth – founded largely on the prosperous trade routes which led to China and the Far East from Chola ports on the East Indian coast – and also of the political confusion that was tearing apart much of southern India. Various local kings

LEFT *The Chola dynasty left behind magnificent Hindu temples, such as the Brihadeeswarar Temple at Thanjavur in the Indian state of Tamil Nadu, with its exquisitely carved stonework.*

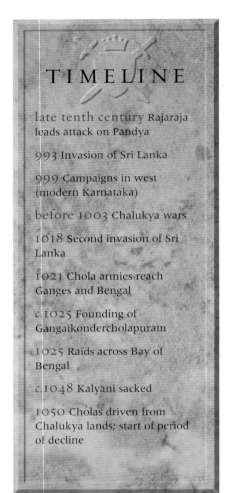

BELOW *The Chola dynasty ruled southern India in the 13th century.*

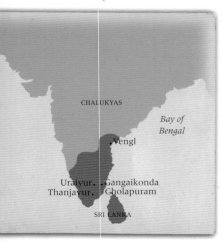

were fighting with each other, making and breaking alliances, and giving the militarily powerful Rajaraja the opportunity to extend his kingdom. Ancient inscriptions describe how Rajaraja pushed the boundaries of the empire as far as the River Tungabadhra, to the north of modern Madras.

ADMINISTRATION AND SUCCESSION

The king had already created the most powerful standing army in the region and now concentrated on the development and administration of the lands he had conquered. He also established a tax-gathering system that required individual villages to gather revenue from landowners on his behalf, and also to supply labour for the massive programme of public works and temple building that he undertook. But perhaps his greatest achievement was the creation of an efficient naval force, based partly on his experience of the seaborne conquest of Sri Lanka.

During the last years of his reign Rajaraja appointed his son, Rajendra Chola I (r. 1012– 44), who had already commanded his forces in several major battles, to rule alongside him, helping to ensure a smooth transfer of power when the king died in 1014. Rajendra started his reign with fresh campaigns against the Chalukyas around the area of modern Hyderabad, crossing the Tungabadhra and securing the northwestern borders of the empire.

In 1018 he mounted a massive naval expedition to Sri Lanka, intent on building on his father's earlier victories and extending Chola rule over the whole island. Neither this campaign nor a later one in Kerala brought peace to the country. Sri Lanka continued to be torn apart in sporadic outbreaks of warfare for decades, but Rajendra's invasion brought the whole island at least nominally under Chola rule.

A fresh expedition in around 1021 saw a Chola army travelling north as far as the Ganges and Bengal, winning a series of battles against various kings and demonstrating Rajendra's military might. To mark his successes in the north, Rajendra took the title of Gangaikonder, or Conqueror of the Ganges, and founded a new city, Gangaikonda Cholapuram, which was to replace Uraiyur as the Cholas' capital city. It contained another great temple to Shiva, which still survives. The Cholas were now unchallenged rulers of much of southern India, but although the Ganges expedition led to huge amounts of prestige, wealth and plunder, there was no attempt to maintain their power this far north.

BEYOND THE SEAS

Rajendra's greatest priority was protecting and developing the eastern trade routes that held one important key to his empire's prosperity. The ports of the eastern coast and the Malabar coast to the west gave the Cholas control over the transit of Arab vessels travelling back from China and the countries of Southeast Asia with valuable cargoes of spices bound eventually for Europe. They also had a highly developed merchant fleet of their own.

In 1025, after a programme of shipbuilding to strengthen the navy his father had created, Rajendra launched a series of raids across the Bay of Bengal into present day Burma (Myanmar), Sumatra and the Malay Peninsula. Several cities were sacked and burned, and the powerful ruler of the Srivijaya kingdom was taken into captivity, along with much of his treasure. But again, there was no serious attempt to colonize the lands that were conquered, and the captured king was later restored to his throne after agreeing to pay regular tribute. Rather than looking for new territories, Rajendra was mounting a concerted campaign to extend Chola influence beyond the Indian subcontinent and protect the activities of his merchants. A string of subordinate rulers down the western seaboard of the Bay of Bengal and extending into western Borneo who acknowledged Chola supremacy guaranteed the continued operation of the profitable trading routes.

Rajendra reigned for another 19 years, during which the Cholas' power and prestige were at their height. Local rulers were generally allowed to remain on their thrones as long as they acknowledged Chola supremacy, and Rajendra himself concentrated on the administration of what had become one of the most extensive empires ever seen on the Indian subcontinent.

CHOLA POWER WEAKENS

But the weaknesses of the empire were already evident. Rajendra's sons had to lead a series of campaigns against uprisings and incursions in the north and west of the empire, and also in Sri Lanka. The Chola forces, mighty as they were, were overstretched. In 1044 the king was succeeded by his son, Rajadhiraja (r. 1018–54) who had been co-ruler since 1018, but the unrest went on. Over the next few decades, Chola power was gradually weakened. Although the Chola dynasty continued, by the 13th century the Pandya people who lived further south – and who had at one time been conquered by Rajaraja – had absorbed what was left of the once mighty empire into their own kingdom. Kings who had once owed an uneasy allegiance to the Cholas now ruled over their lands.

MAIN CHOLA RULERS

985 – 1014 Rajaraja Chola I

1012 – 44 Rajendra Chola I
(co-rule with Rajaraja to 1014)

1018 – 54 Rajadhiraja Chola
(co-rule with Rajendra to 1044)

1054 – 63 Rajendra Chola II

1063 – 70 Virarajendra Chola

1070 – 1120 Kulothunga Chola

1178 – 1218 Kulothunga Chola III

1246 – 79 Rajendra Chola III

ABOVE *The sculptures of Hindu deities that were produced during the reigns of Rajaraja and Rajendra, such as this bronze of Rama, are often considered to be among the finest Indian works of art.*

The Mongols ruled over the largest land empire in history. At its peak it covered over 12 million square miles (31 million sq km) from the Pacific Ocean to the shores of the Danube, and counted more than 100 million people as its subjects. The empire is always associated with the name of Genghis Khan, the great military leader who first led his tribesmen out of their homeland on the steppes of Mongolia, but it continued to increase in size for at least a generation after his death.

THE MONGOL EMPIRE
1206 – 94

WHEN TEMUJIN, THE FUTURE GENGHIS KHAN (r. 1206–27), was born into one of the nomadic tribes of the steppes some time during the 1160s, he was heir to a family history of some stature, but little else. His father, Yesugei, was leader of his clan and a descendant of a khan of the former Mongol kingdom, but the Mongols themselves were in disarray, defeated by the neighbouring Tartars and riven by infighting. When Yesugei died, allegedly poisoned by the Tartars, the nine-year-old Temujin and his family were deserted by the clan.

According to *The Secret History of the Mongols*, an account written for the royal family some time after Genghis' death, he returned to the clan after years of hardship and poverty, and won enough support to be named khan, or chief, of his tribe by the time he had reached his late twenties. Much of *The Secret History* is undoubtedly fanciful myth-making of the kind that gathers around great leaders, but it is clear that some time around 1206, after a series of battles among the tribes, he took the title Genghis Khan – meaning 'the Mightiest Ruler' – as leader of all the tribes of Mongolia.

It seems likely that the Mongols' early victories were simply raids in search of plunder rather than deliberate attempts to establish their domination of the lands around them. As nomads who roamed the steppes, they were already a tough, warlike people, and instinctive horsemen from childhood. Their archers were renowned for their terrifying ability to fire off deadly accurate volleys of arrows from their short composite bows while galloping on horseback. Over the following decades, they

LEFT *A Chinese portrait (1786) of Genghis Khan. After just three decades, the empire he founded had conquered central Asia and was threatening Europe.*

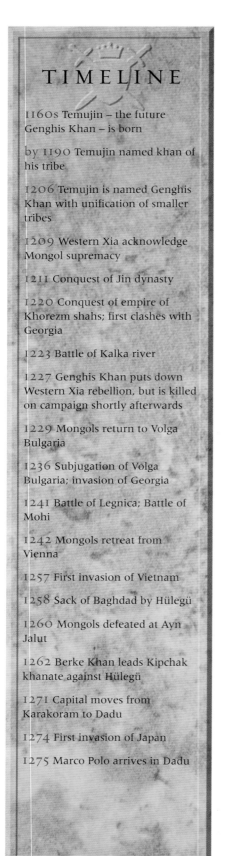

developed new skills in siege warfare and the use of gunpowder, but at this early stage, they were essentially an army of highly mobile raiders from the steppes.

Their first concerted attacks were against the Tangut empire of the Western Xia in northern China, which had been weakened by corruption and dissent among its rulers and by years of conflict with the neighbouring Jin dynasty. After several years of ravaging the lands of the Western Xia, Genghis Khan accepted tribute from the empire's battered leaders. He led his forces on towards the Jin people, who retreated in the face of their attacks, allowing the Mongols to sack and plunder their cities, including the capital, Yanjing (modern Beijing). The expansion of the Mongols had begun.

THE DESTRUCTION OF KHOREZM

Raids on the Jin continued for decades, but in 1219 they were given a respite by events further west. The Mongols had sent a trading caravan to the city of Utrar in modern-day Kazakhstan, with the apparent intention of establishing trading links with the shahdom of Khorezm, which stretched from the Aral Sea to the Persian Gulf. The merchants were arrested and executed, perhaps as a deliberate provocation of the Mongols, since the shah of Khorezm, Ala ad-din Muhammad (r. 1200–20), had ambitions to extend his empire eastwards – in any event, he certainly underestimated the Mongols' power.

Genghis Khan's initial response might have encouraged him: with his armies engaged in the plundering of northern China, he decided to seek a diplomatic solution, and sent a group of envoys to demand simply that the governor of Utrar should be punished and the goods that had been seized from the caravan returned. Muhammad contemptuously beheaded the envoys and dared the Mongols to do their worst.

This was a fateful mistake. Pulling back his armies from China, Genghis spent several months preparing for a long campaign in the west, and then set off with a force estimated at between 80,000 and 120,000 men, taking with them Chinese siege engines, battering rams and gunpowder. Part of this formidable force took the heavily defended city of Utrar after a lengthy siege and slaughtered the inhabitants. The Persian historian Juvaini said the vengeance taken for the murdered Mongol merchants was so great that *'in retribution for every hair on their heads it seemed that a hundred thousand heads rolled in the dust'*. One story claims that the governor of the town was taken alive and brought before Genghis, who ordered that molten gold should be poured down his throat.

But Genghis Khan's revenge was not yet complete. Further south, another section of the Mongol force had defeated Muhammad's army, forcing him to flee for his life through his own kingdom. As the ancient city of Bukhara, dating back to around 500 BC, was sacked and burned in 1220, Genghis is said to have made his famous boast to the cowering inhabitants that he was the wrath of God personified. It must have seemed like it – and the wrath of God swept on, leaving the smoking ruins of Bukhara and leading his forces on to Samarkand. When that city fell after five days, every one of the defenders was slaughtered, including those who had accepted Genghis' promise of safe conduct and had surrendered.

Stories of Mongol savagery spread like wildfire through the terrified population. When the city of Urgench was taken, it was said that the Mongols diverted the course of the Oxus river to wipe its ruins off the map completely; in Nishapur, every living creature, including the cats and dogs, was slaughtered. Wherever the Mongols went, workers who could be useful were sent back to Mongolia, young women and children were given to the soldiers as slaves and virtually everyone else was killed. After two years of butchery, the empire of Khorezm had been destroyed forever, and the legends of the overwhelming power and cruelty of the Mongol armies had been born.

THE DEATH OF GENGHIS KHAN

The Mongol armies, split into two separate forces, spent the next three years roaming through Central Asia and northern India, pillaging and burning towns and cities at will. One force pushed into Armenia and through the Caucasus to southern Russia, meeting the armies of Mstislav Mstislavich the Bold of Kievan

ABOVE *Mongol incursions into the Indian subcontinent began in 1221, with an attack on the city of Multan, and continued until 1327. The fearsome war elephants of the Delhi sultanate were outmanoeuvered by the highly mobile Mongol horsemen.*

THE MONGOL LIFESTYLE

The Mongols were seen in the West as wild, undisciplined and terrifying warriors whose life away from the battlefield consisted of aimless tribal wandering across the apparently limitless steppes. In fact, their nomadic lifestyle was one of order and routine.

Each clan travelled annually in the spring from the sheltered valleys to a particular area of the high plateau, where they grazed their flocks. Their circular tents, or yurts, made of greased felt stretched over collapsible wooden frames, were carried with the women and children on wagons drawn by oxen. The Venetian adventurer Marco Polo (1254–1324), writing at the end of the 13th century, described how they drove oxen and camels alongside their flocks, pulling two-wheeled carts with all their possessions

This detail from a 16th-century Mughal manuscript shows Genghis Khan returning to his home camp from the land of the Tajiks.

covered under yards of thick black felt.

Life inside the tents was rigorously organized, with the entrances always facing south, the men's quarters on the left and the women's on the right. The northern end of the tent, furthest from the entrance, was reserved for the leader of the family. He sat with carved images of the spirits, which, according to Marco Polo, were given offerings before each meal. Despite their fierce reputation on the battlefield, inside their tents, the Mongols appear to have observed a strict etiquette.

Crucially, they relied on trade for such essentials as grain, rice and metal for their weapons – a fact that was probably instrumental in encouraging them to leave the steppes and attempt to extend their power further afield.

Rus (d.1228) at the Battle of the Kalka river (1223). The Mongols were outnumbered by around two to one – despite the legends about vast Mongol hordes which swept across Europe, their armies often fought with far fewer men than their adversaries – but their high-speed tactics, pulling the Russian troops this way and that and killing them from a distance, harried Prince Mstislav's heavily armed soldiers until those who were still alive were glad to escape, leaving 90 percent of their men dead or dying on the battlefield. After the battle, six of the Russian princes were reputed to have been executed by being crushed to death under wooden boards on which the Mongol generals sat to eat their meals. The Mongols' idea of mercy was to allow the princes to die a noble death without shedding their blood.

Genghis himself, meanwhile, was leading the other Mongol force through Afghanistan, Pakistan and India on his way back east, plundering as he went. In China, the Tanguts of the Western Xia and their old enemies in the Jin dynasty had formed an alliance against the Mongols, and in 1226 he launched another invasion, sacking city after city as he rode through northern China. One year later the Tanguts surrendered again, and the emperor and his entire imperial family were put to death.

It was Genghis' last victory. Exactly how he died is not known, but his body was carried back to Mongolia and buried in secret. Ancient chronicles tell different stories of the ways in which his loyal soldiers took pains to see that his grave could never be discovered. Some say that they diverted a river to cover the site, much as they did at Urgench, others that a forest of trees was planted over his body, and others that the soldiers simply killed everyone they saw as the funeral procession made its way towards Mongolia, so that nobody would have any clue where they were going. To this day, although Genghis Khan is revered in Mongolia as the father of the Mongol nation, and although archaeological expeditions occasionally claim to have found the site of his tomb, its actual whereabouts remains a mystery.

GENGHIS KHAN'S ACHIEVEMENTS

Genghis Khan's most obvious achievements were military. How could a band of nomads, however accomplished they were as horsemen and archers, defeat organized armies and batter their way into strongly defended cities and fortresses?

One answer is that the Mongol armies gathered not only manpower but also knowledge, expertise and skilled help from the countries they ravaged. In northern China, where the empires they ripped apart were already weakened by internal dissent, they had come into contact with the latest theories of siege warfare and gained expertise in handling rockets, gunpowder and smoke bombs that was far in advance of the rest of the world. The Chinese engineers and weaponry which they carried west enabled them to turn this technology on the walls and fortified gateways of the cities of Khorezm.

Their enemies were often incompetent. Shah Muhammad, for example, never gathered all his forces together to challenge the Mongols in a single decisive

ABOVE *Genghis Khan's army storming a Tangut fortress in northwestern China in 1226, in the campaign that immediately preceded the Mongol leader's death.*

battle, but seems to have relied on pockets of resistance spread around his walled cities. There is no doubt that he greatly underestimated the military skills of his opponents. None of this detracts from the brilliance of Genghis Khan as a commander or from the quality of the Mongols as soldiers. The Mongols may seem to have appeared from nowhere, but their campaigns were always carefully planned, and relied on detailed reconnaissance of the land before they launched a full-scale attack.

A REPUTATION FOR MAGIC AND CRUELTY

In addition to the devastating and high-speed thrusts of their horse-riding archers and the mass of well-drilled foot soldiers with lances, they possessed an unrivalled ability to cover vast distances of the most hostile terrain. When Genghis attacked Bukhara, for instance, he approached it through the fabled Kyzyl Kum, the Red Desert, which was supposedly impassable. Genghis not only found a way through it, but did so at the head of thousands of men. This ability to strike suddenly and unexpectedly, to appear with his armies as if from nowhere, caused people to impute supernatural powers to him. The contemporary Persian chronicler Minhaj al Siraj Juzjani, for example, wrote that he was *'adept at magic and deception, and some of the devils were his friends'*.

ABOVE *Ögedei Khan with his sons Küyük and Kadan. On the news of Ögedei's death in 1241, the rampaging Mongol armies suddenly withdrew from Europe, never to return.*

It all added to his reputation: 1000 years ahead of his time, he knew the value of a strategy of 'shock and awe'. The rumour of an approaching Mongol army was enough to throw the population of a town into panic. Crowds of refugees would choke the streets and gateways of the towns as the Mongols approached, leaving hundreds of prisoners to be pushed in front of the advancing armies as a human shield.

The other significant advantage that Genghis enjoyed was in the organization of his army and of Mongol society. The Mongols had laws and traditions that stretched back for centuries – laws and traditions which he codified and set out in his *Yassa* or decrees. No written record survives, but it seems clear that death was the penalty for the smallest infringement, and that whole families might be wiped out in punishment for serious crimes. There was a legend, no doubt exaggerated, that a woman could travel in safety anywhere along the roads within the Mongol lands.

ÖGEDEI KHAN — THE EMPIRE CONTINUES TO EXPAND

Many of these qualities began to decline in the years after Genghis' death, but the empire had developed its own momentum. Before he died, he had decreed that his lands would be split between his four sons, but named his third son, Ögedei (r. 1229–41), as his successor and overall leader, or 'Great Khan' – a decision which was confirmed by an assembly of Mongol chiefs.

Ögedei's Mongol armies pushed deeper into Persia, and over the next ten years they followed up the earlier battles in Central Asia by driving relentlessly north towards Russia, with full-scale invasions of Volga Bulgaria in 1229, Georgia in 1236 and Kievan Rus in 1237 – the only successful winter invasion of Russia in history. Then, in 1241, they turned to Europe.

Forces led by Genghis' grandson Batu Khan, with troops commanded on the battlefield by the grizzled old general Subutai (1176–1248), who had served under Genghis himself in Mongolia, northern China and Khorezm, moved westwards through the Carpathian Mountains into Poland and Hungary. A diversionary attack brought combined Polish and German troops into the battlefield at Legnica in 1241 – to be destroyed, as so many armies had been before them, by repeated feints and hit-and-run dashes by the mobile archers, who shot and killed the cumbersome horses of the European knights. By the end of the day, although the Mongols had suffered heavy losses themselves, they had cleared the way through Poland.

Two days later, on 11 April, 1241, the main Mongol force annihilated the army of King Bela IV (r. 1235–70) at Mohi in Hungary, and occupied the city of Pest. As the Mongols ravaged the countryside, there was panic throughout the region,

BELOW *The Mongols defeat the combined armies of eastern Europe at the Battle of Legnica in 1241. A favourite Mongol tactic was the feigned retreat, used to lure rash pursuers into ambushes on unfavourable terrain, where they could then be picked off at will.*

with those who could fleeing into the fortified towns and stone castles which dotted the landscape. By December, the first Mongols were crossing the frozen Danube, moving inexorably towards Vienna.

There seemed to be nothing to prevent Subutai from pressing on to Germany, Italy and the rest of Europe. But suddenly, inexplicably, the Mongol armies stopped advancing. For a few days, they paused. And then, as if in answer to the fervent prayers of the people of Austria, they began to withdraw. The reason for their abrupt departure was that Ögedei had died suddenly in the Mongol capital he had founded at Karakorum, far away on the Mongolian steppes. Batu Khan, Subutai and other Mongol leaders had to return to play their part in the selection of a successor, and to see that their own interests were protected in the political wrangling and horse-trading that was sure to follow. To the terrified Europeans, it seemed like a miracle. The Mongols would never venture so far west again.

INTO THE CALIPHATE

Ögedei's successor, Küyük Khan (r. 1246–8), lived long enough to send a contemptuous reply to a message from Pope Innocent IV (r. 1243–54) which demanded that he end the Mongol attacks on Europe, convert to Christianity and acknowledge the pope as his master. It was a staggering misreading of the situation, and Küyük took great pains to see that the papal emissaries carried back his reply accurately. God, he said, wanted the Mongols to extend their rule over the whole world. It was the pope, not the Great Khan, who should submit.

BELOW *One of the cities of the former Sassanian empire in Persia overrun by the Mongols during their conquests was Takht-e Suleyman in modern Azerbaijan.*

By the time this message reached Rome, however, Küyük was dead too, almost certainly murdered in continuing family disputes over the succession. His replacement, Möngke Khan (r. 1251–9), was, like him, a grandson of the great Genghis, and seemed concerned to build on his grandfather's efforts to develop a code of law that would apply throughout his lands. Over the next few years, he

embarked on a programme of reforms aimed at limiting the powers of his military chiefs and bringing security to the all-important Silk Road, along which trade flowed between China and the West.

The military campaigning began again: Möngke, just as much as Küyük, Ögedei and Genghis himself, believed that the Mongols' destiny was to rule the entire world. In the east, he led a new invasion of China, and sent his brother Hülegü (1217–65) with a large force headed for Baghdad, the capital of the Arab caliphate. Unless the Muslims accepted Mongol rule, the city would be destroyed.

Hülegü approached down both banks of the Tigris and settled down for a lengthy siege – but within two weeks, he was in control of Baghdad. The devastation that followed in this centre of Arab culture and civilization was comparable to the sack of Constantinople by the Fourth Crusade 54 years before. Tens, or possibly hundreds, of thousands of civilians were slaughtered; the Grand Library – the so-called House of Learning, where many old texts from Constantinople had been preserved and translated by Arab scholars – was plundered. Priceless books and ancient manuscripts were hurled into the river, and mosques, palaces and other great buildings burned. The 'Abbasid caliphate was destroyed, and for several centuries Baghdad remained a ruined city.

Word of the savagery on the streets of Baghdad spread rapidly, and by the time the Mongols arrived at Damascus no one had any stomach for resistance. The city was spared and the army rode on, apparently invincible, towards Egypt. Hülegü himself had returned to Mongolia with most of his army, after hearing of the death of Möngke in China, but he had left more than 20,000 soldiers behind – more than enough, he calculated, to continue his conquests in his absence. But Hülegü had underestimated the fighting qualities of the Mamluks, tough

tribesmen of Turkish origin who had been employed as mercenaries in Egypt and had seized power for themselves about ten years earlier.

They executed the Mongol envoys who came to demand their surrender, displaying their heads on spikes over the gates of Cairo, and sent their forces out to challenge the Mongol power. The two sides met in September 1260 at Ayn Jalut, near Nazareth in the Holy Land. For the first time, the weakened Mongols faced opponents who were as skilful and daring as they were on horseback. The Mamelukes copied the Mongols' tactic of feigned retreat and destroyed them with a series of determined cavalry charges. The commander Hülegü had left in charge was captured and executed, and the remnants of his army butchered. It was one of the most significant battles in history and the most serious reverse the Mongols had suffered. It set a permanent limit to their empire.

COLLAPSE OF THE EMPIRE

The Battle of Ayn Jalut also marks the start of the final break-up of the Mongol empire, as different leaders began to adopt Islam. Berke Khan (r. 1257–66), who ruled the Kipchak khanate in Russia, had already become a Muslim, and attacked Hülegü when he returned from Mongolia in 1262, drawing him into the first of the final series of civil wars that would eventually destroy the empire.

In the east, Möngke's brother, Kublai (r. 1260–94), was eventually named as his successor and is generally considered as the last of the Great Khans. His own base had always been in China, and in 1271 he formally moved the capital of the empire from Ögedei's city of Karakorum to Dadu, modern Beijing – later renamed Cambuluc, or 'the great residence of the khan'. Marco Polo is said to have arrived there in the late 1290s and marvelled at its wealth and sophistication.

BELOW *Map showing the extent of the Mongol empire by 1260.*

It is largely thanks to the Venetian adventurer that Kublai Khan is as well known in Europe today as his grandfather, Genghis – Samuel Taylor Coleridge (1772–

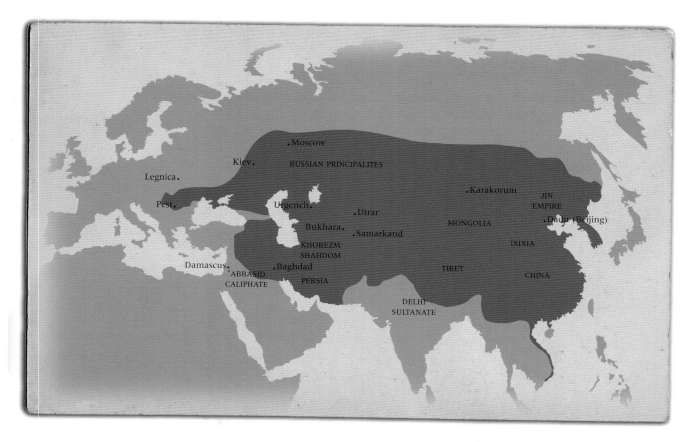

1834) had been reading a 17th-century reworking of Polo's diaries when he wrote about the summer capital of the empire, Shangdu:

'In Xanadu did Kubla Khan
A stately pleasure dome decree…'

The description owed more to the distortions of hundreds of years and Coleridge's own consumption of opium than it did to reality, but it does reflect Kublai Khan's passion for building and restoring the great monuments to Chinese culture. He also pushed the empire further south, with a successful campaign against the Song dynasty in southern China, Yunnan and Korea. However, abortive invasions of Japan and Vietnam mirrored the defeat of Ayn Jalut in the west, revealing that the Mongol forces were not indestructible. The empire had already started to fragment when Kublai Khan came to power, but by the time of his death in 1294 the process was clearly irreversible. Civil wars and regional conflicts broke out across the territory that the khans had once ruled so sternly, and the ancient Silk Road became impassable to merchants.

The weakest moments of the 88-year empire followed the death of an emperor. There was no fixed line of succession, and the rivalry and fighting that accompanied each election to the post paralyzed the empire for years at a time. Arguments over the succession brought the Mongol armies back from the frontiers of Europe and were largely responsible for the crucial defeat at Ayn Jalut.

THE MONGOL LEGACY

Today, Genghis Khan – a byword for cruelty in the West – is remembered with pride in Mongolia as the unifier of the various tribes and the founder of the Mongol nation. The communications that were made possible by Mongol authority along the Silk Road brought knowledge and technology to the West, as well as silks and spices – gunpowder, paper and the compass are just three of many inventions believed to have reached Europe by that route. According to some theories, the Black Death that wiped out around one-third of Europe's population in the 14th century may also have travelled overland in the same way.

Modern historians suggest that the Mongol armies and the famines that followed their pillaging and destruction may have killed as many as 30 million people. Later conquerors drew on the name and reputation of the Mongols to glorify their own conquests: the Timurid empire of central Asia and the Mughal empire that held sway over much of India, Pakistan and Afghanistan consciously invoked Mongol ancestry. The 'wrath of God' cast a long shadow.

ABOVE *In the 14th century, the central European warlord Timur the Lame, or Tamerlaine (r. 1369–1405), claimed direct descent from Genghis Khan in launching his own brutal campaign of conquest.*

The Ottoman empire, which at its height stretched from the Balkans to Central Asia, threatened briefly to overwhelm European civilization. The seizure of Constantinople in 1453 by the Ottoman Turks is one of the landmark dates of European history. A hundred years later, the court of Suleyman the Magnificent was a match for any royal house in Europe, and the 1529 siege of Vienna sent shock waves through the continent. But the empire's failure to modernize its administration and armed forces and a succession of incompetent sultans caused a 300-year period of decline. Final defeat came at the end of the First World War, when the victorious French and British carved up much of the empire between them. The Ottoman legacy can be seen in the patchwork of Muslim and Christian peoples in the Balkans, and in the contested borders of the Middle East.

THE OTTOMAN EMPIRE
1300 – 1922

IN THE 11TH CENTURY THE SELJUK TURKS, originally nomads from Central Asia, inflicted a crushing defeat on the Byzantine empire at the Battle of Manzikert (1071), driving them out of Anatolia. Seljuq power, however, fell victim to the Mongol invasions of the 13th century and by 1300 their state was crumbling.

Alongside them, in western Anatolia, a different race of Turks had established a small state of their own. Known as the Ottomans (from the name Uthman, the leader who originally wrested their independence from the Seljuqs), over the next 100 years they gradually extended their influence throughout Anatolia, and even into the Byzantine provinces of Macedonia and Bulgaria in Europe.

SUSTAINED ATTACKS ON THE BYZANTINE EMPIRE
During the 14th and 15th centuries there were conflicts with the Hungarians and the Venetians in Europe, but the sustained efforts of the Ottomans were directed against the Byzantines. Seizing Constantinople would not only give them undisputed control

LEFT *A portrait of Suleyman I the Magnificent by an unknown Venetian painter. Under Suleyman, the Ottoman empire conquered a swathe of European territory from Croatia to the Black Sea.*

of the profitable trade routes between east and west, but it would be a powerful symbol of their military and political power.

The Byzantines repeatedly either beat off or bought off Ottoman sieges of their city. Sultan Mehmed II (r. 1444–6; 1451–81), the ruler who finally broke their resistance, had first come to the throne as a boy of 12, when his father, Murad II (r. 1421–44; 1446–51), had abdicated in his favour. Murad returned, at his son's insistence, to rule for five years until his death, and then Mehmed, by then 19 years old, resumed power. Two years later, in 1453, the capture of Constantinople earned him the name of Mehmed the Conqueror. From then on, the city was known as Istanbul, and for nearly 500 years was the capital of the Ottoman empire.

EXPANSIONIST POLICIES

Over the next few decades, Mehmed pursued a policy of ruthless expansion in southeastern Europe, annexing Serbia and conquering the former Byzantine principality of Morea on the Greek Peloponnese. He took over the Genoese colonies on the coast of Asia Minor, seized Bosnia and fought against Venice to gain control of the Aegean ports of the Morea.

In the east, Mehmed pushed the boundaries of his expanding empire as far as the Euphrates, and defeated attacks by the Turkmen ruler Uzun Hassan (r. 1453–78) in western Persia. His conquests abroad, together with his military and administrative reforms at home, laid the foundations of empire. During the century that followed his death, the Ottomans enjoyed their greatest power.

In fact, Mehmed's reign ended with a period of near civil war, brought about by the high taxes necessary to fund his military conquests. His successor, Bayezid II (r. 1481–1512), was forced to call a halt to the rapid expansion of the empire. At home, Bayezid won the name of 'The Just' and for over 30 years struggled with managing the economy and taxation and replenishing the treasury.

But Bayezid's supporters in the army, who had originally put him on the throne, were dissatisfied with his lack of military ambition. In 1512 he was deposed in favour of his son, Selim I ('the Grim'; 1512–20), who showed his determination to survive by wiping out every other claimant to the throne except one: four of his sons, all his brothers and all seven of his nephews were eliminated. One favoured son survived.

Selim was determined to revive Mehmed's policy of aggressive expansion, and started a lightning and devastating campaign against the Mamluk armies of Syria, who were ruling what had once been the lands of the 'Abbasid caliphate. Cities all over Syria and Egypt welcomed the Ottomans as a new, disciplined and efficient government. Selim now controlled most of the old empire of the caliphate, together with its possessions in Europe, and revenues from the fertile lands and prosperous trading cities of these new provinces transformed his economy.

SULEYMAN, THE MAGNIFICENT LAWGIVER

Selim had virtually doubled the size of the empire, but it was under his son Suleyman (r. 1520–66)– the only son to survive the precautionary bloodbath at the start of his reign – that it would reach the zenith of its power and glory. Suleyman – known as 'the Magnificent' in Europe, and as *Kanuni* ('the Lawgiver') in Turkish – not only extended the frontiers of the empire but also fostered an artistic and cultural revival that spread the fame of his court around the world.

First, came the fall of the kingdom of Hungary. Belgrade was occupied by the Ottomans in 1521, and the king's finest troops and their European allies were put to flight at the battle of Mohács five years later. Then, when the Habsburgs – heirs to the old Holy Roman Empire – tried to absorb part of Hungary into their own Austrian lands, Suleyman forced them to retreat and laid siege to Vienna in 1529. Europe, already convulsed by the Reformation, seemed to be ripe for the plucking, but the supply lines were too long, and the battles would have had to be fought too far from home. The unsuccessful siege of Vienna, which was ended by the onset of winter, marked the western limit of his rule.

In the Mediterranean, the Ottomans defeated an allied European fleet at the Battle of Preveza off the coast of Albania in 1538, giving them unchallenged command of the eastern Mediterranean. Ottoman vessels were also active in the Red Sea and the Arabian Gulf, where Suleyman established bases at Suez and Basra and even mounted unsuccessful attacks on the Portuguese town of Diu, on the west coast of India.

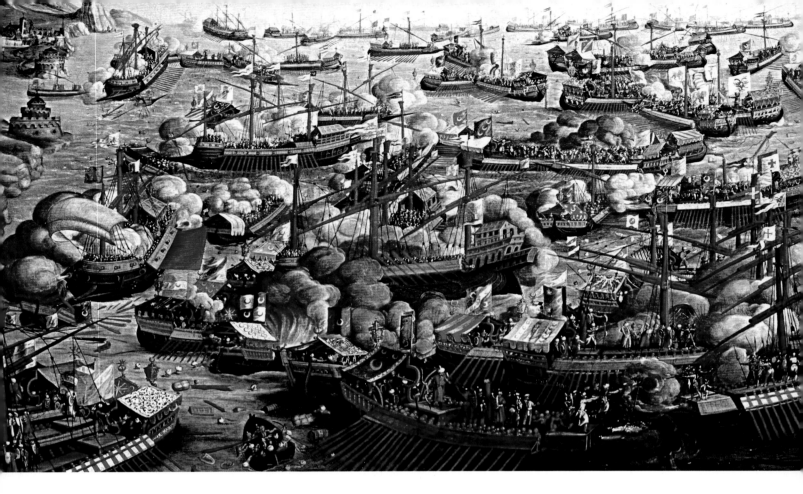

ABOVE *The Battle of Lepanto off Greece in 1571 saw the Holy League of Austria, Venice and the Papal States defeat the Ottoman fleet of Ali Pasha. This was the last major naval engagement to be fought by galleys.*

THE SULTAN'S RULE

Beneath the sultan, a small class of *osmanli* – all loyal Muslims – enjoyed authority over the mass of the population. They were divided into four groups: the first was responsible for the running of the palace and the sultan's personal and imperial institutions; the second for maintaining the efficiency of the army, keeping order within the empire and protecting its boundaries; the third for the civil administration, taxation and the treasury; and the fourth for the state religion of Islam and the observance of shari'a, or religious law. The sultan, for his part, gave legal rulings, or kanuns, which applied shari'a law to specific civil issues, and gradually built up into a body of civil law – Suleyman was particularly respected for the wisdom of his judgements.

When he died in 1566, while besieging the town of Szigetvár in Hungary, Suleyman left behind an empire which stretched from the Balkans in Europe to Central Asia, and a capital city which had become the new centre of Islamic civilization, complete with magnificent bridges, mosques and palaces. Ottoman culture was at its height.

During his reign, the office of grand vizier emerged as the sultan's deputy, answerable only to him, and with absolute power over *osmanli* and commoners alike. The *devsirme*, slaves recruited from the conquered Christian lands and employed by the sultan in much the same way as the 'Abbasids had earlier

employed the Mamluks, also grew in power, some of them rising through Ottoman society to become important landowners. As he grew older, Suleyman himself had begun to withdraw into his magnificent Topkapi Palace. Despite the theoretical strict punishments for offenders, the court and the administration had become notorious for corruption.

SELIM THE DRUNKARD

Ottoman culture flourished under Suleyman's successor, his son Selim II (r. 1566–74), but the new sultan himself played very little part in it. His two brothers had been executed for plotting to overthrow their father, and when Selim came to the throne at the age of 42, he was the first of a line of sultans to have been kept in virtual imprisonment in the harem as he awaited the succession. Thus had Suleyman chosen to protect himself from further intrigues.

Where the father had been known as the Lawgiver, the son earned himself the name of Selim the Drunkard, increasingly handing the affairs of state over to the management of his grand vizier while he devoted himself to his harem. There was peace in the empire, and even some additions to the Ottoman lands with the capture of Cyprus from the Venetians and Tunisia from the Spanish. There was also a humiliating defeat at the hands of the allied European powers at the Battle of Lepanto, off the western coast of Greece, in 1571. It was the first significant defeat at sea for nearly 100 years, and only dissension among the Europeans prevented them from pressing home their advantage with an attack on Istanbul itself.

The process of decline continued under Murad III (r. 1574–95), who succeeded Selim, although he adopted a more aggressive policy of attempted expansion, capturing Fez from the Portuguese, Tunis from the Spanish and Crete from the Venetians – conquests which helped to disguise the weakness of the empire. The navy was rebuilt after the disaster of Lepanto, and a 12-year war with the Persians led eventually to the seizure of more territories around the Caspian Sea.

Over the next few decades, the empire reached its peak in terms of the lands it ruled but the Ottoman economy could no longer sustain constant warfare. Another long war in Europe – fought against Austria – encouraged several central European rulers to try to break away from Ottoman rule and added to the economic problems at home, with heavy taxation and rampant inflation fanning the flames of discontent among the people.

TIMELINE

1529 Siege of Vienna; capture of Algiers

1534–54 Repeated campaigns in eastern Anatolia

1538 Ottomans defeat European fleet at naval battle of Preveza

1566 Death of Suleyman marks start of period of decline

1571 Destruction of Ottoman fleet at Battle of Lepanto

1574 Seizure of Tunis from Spanish

1578 Seizure of Fez from Portuguese

1593 War with Habsburgs; loss of territory in southeastern Europe

1606 Peace of Zsitvatorok

1618 Start of period of administrative reform under Osman II

1683 Siege of Vienna; start of Habsburg–Russian alliance against Ottomans

late 17th century Increasing European involvement in empire

1717–30 'Tulip Era' at court of Ahmed III and Ottoman artistic renaissance

1798–1801 French expedition to Egypt under Napoleon Bonaparte

1807 British invade Egypt

1826 Slaughter of Janissaries in 'Auspicious Incident'

1829 Greeks achieve independence

continued

CHALLENGES ABROAD

Murad III was known for the political influence which he allowed the women in his harem to wield – the degree of interest he took in them is reflected in his reputedly having fathered more than 100 children during the 21 years of his reign. His successor, Mehmed III (r. 1595–1603), made his reputation in a different way – by having 27 of his brothers and 20 of his sisters murdered to secure his place on the throne.

Although Mehmed lost no significant territories, he found it impossible to push further into Europe, where the emerging nation states offered stronger and more determined opposition than Suleyman had faced. At the end of the 16th century, open war broke out with the Austrians again, resulting in the loss of most of Hungary and parts of Romania, and although the Ottomans subsequently recouped much of the lost territory, the Peace of Zsitvatorok which ended the war in 1606 cost them the annual tribute that had been paid ever since the victory at Mohács 80 years before. Under the peace treaty, the Ottomans also formally recognized the Habsburg rulers as their equals in Europe, and agreed to stop raiding their territory.

In the east, a resurgent Persian monarchy caused even greater concern. Shah 'Abbas I (r. 1587–1629) reoccupied Iraq for some 15 years and, although once again the Ottomans managed to regain much of the lost territory, the new Persian strength meant that troops which could otherwise have been fighting in Europe were needed in Asia Minor. The Ottoman empire was suffering the strain of trying to fight constant campaigns on two fronts.

WARS IN EUROPE

During the 17th century, partly spurred on by the obvious vulnerability of the empire abroad, there were repeated attempts at administrative and organizational reforms at home, led frequently by the grand viziers rather than the sultans themselves. These were never radical enough to reverse the process of decline, but they helped successive sultans to rebuild their armies to such an extent that, by 1683, the grand vizier Kara Mustafa Pasha (c.1634–83) felt strong enough to renew the old efforts against the Habsburgs in Europe. He laid siege to Vienna again, as the prelude to another full-scale invasion of the Habsburg empire. However, his attack provoked the formation of an alliance between the Habsburgs and the Russians, which turned the tide in the Battle of Vienna and began to drive the Ottomans out of Hungary, Serbia and the Balkans.

The Ottoman empire, which had once been seen simply as a threat by the European powers, now became the subject of bitter rivalries and disagreements among them. Other European nations, concerned at the prospect of a resurgent Habsburg empire in Europe, tried to dissuade the Austrians and Russians from pressing on with their campaigns, to no avail. A series of wars in Europe saw the

empire suffering repeated defeats which left it bereft of all its former possessions north of the Black Sea. In addition, the sultan was forced to sign a humiliating agreement which gave the Russian tsar and the Habsburg emperor the right to intervene in the internal affairs of the empire if they felt that its Christian subjects were in danger.

By this time, the outlying provinces of Egypt and Algeria, added to the empire by Selim and Suleyman some two centuries before, were effectively ruling themselves. There were sporadic nationalist revolts in the Balkans. All over the empire, including the heartland of Anatolia, central government was weakening, and local leaders were becoming increasingly powerful.

In the midst of this political anarchy, the empire's rulers lived in splendour and luxury. In the early 18th century, for instance, under the rule of Sultan Ahmed

ABOVE *The joint Habsburg and Polish armies defending Vienna successfully withstood the onslaught of the Ottoman forces besieging the city in September 1683, inflicting heavy casualties on the Turks. The failure of this siege marked the Ottoman empire's last major challenge to Christian Europe.*

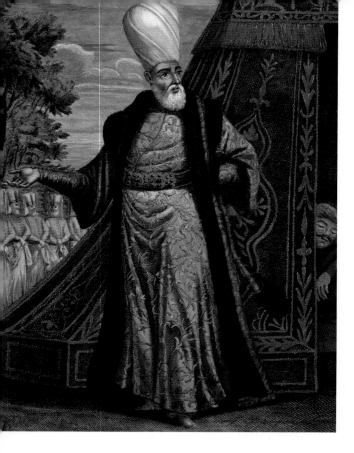

III (r. 1703–30) and his grand vizier Nevsehirli Damat Ibrahim Pasha (d.1730), came the 'Tulip Era', when a passion for growing tulips spread among the wealthy members of the Ottoman court, with the bulbs changing hands for huge amounts of money. This coincided with a revival in poetry, painting and ceramics. Ottoman clothes and fashions, which had been virtually untouched by European ideas for centuries, began to reflect those of the West.

REFORMS AND REVOLTS

At the end of the 18th century, Sultan Selim III (r. 1789–1807) began to form alliances with European powers such as Britain and Russia as a way of dealing with the threat of Napoleon Bonaparte, who invaded Egypt in 1798. These alliances were successful in the short term, and Napoleon was driven out of Egypt (although a later unsuccessful attempt to call on French aid to resist Russian incursions in the Balkans led to the loss of huge tracts of territory). For the European powers, the Ottoman empire was now clearly an opportunity rather than a threat – while the Russians seized the Balkan provinces of Moldavia and Wallachia, Britain mounted an invasion of Egypt. At home, meanwhile, the cumulative effect of the changes imposed on a society that was inherently conservative and backward-looking, was to encourage bitter internal opposition. In 1807 Selim III was overthrown, and his successor, Mustafa IV (r. 1807–8), reversed many of his reforms.

ABOVE *An 18th-century colour engraving of the chief of the Janissary corps. This élite force of the Ottoman empire originally comprised Christian youths taken from Balkan families.*

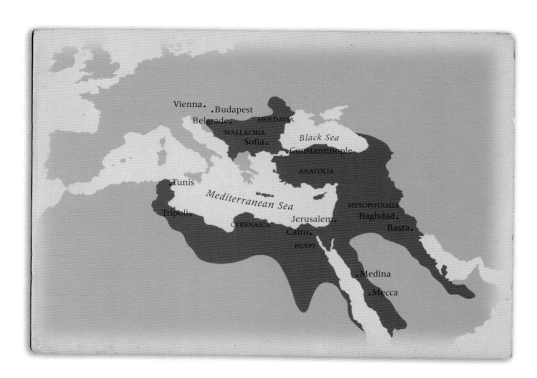

RIGHT *The extent of the Ottoman empire in the late 17th century. Thereafter, a long decline set in that would see the empire contract to its Anatolian heartland, the Levant and Mesopotamia by 1914.*

Within a few months, however, Mustafa was toppled in his turn, and the reform movement began once more. This time, the sultan, Mahmud II (r. 1808–39), was more ruthless. His élite force of Janissaries mutinied when they realized that their privileged position was under threat, and Mahmud turned his cannon on their barracks, killing hundreds of them and executing the survivors. This bloodbath later became known, in a masterpiece of political understatement, as the 'Auspicious Incident'.

The creation of a new and modernized army under the command of the sultan marked the start of a new attempt to enforce the authority of central government. This was relatively successful in Anatolia but, in the further reaches of the empire, nationalist uprisings continued to chip away at Ottoman power. In Greece, intervention by the European powers helped nationalists throw off Turkish domination in 1829, while in Egypt, a revolt led by the nationalist leader Muhammad 'Ali (c.1769–1849) gained independence in 1841.

In the territories that remained, however, the authority of the imperial government was stronger, and modernization and reform continued. Mahmud's two sons, Abdülmecid I (r. 1839–61) and Abdülaziz (r. 1861–76), who succeeded him as sultan in turn in 1839 and 1861, presided over a period known as the *Tanzimat*, or Reorganization, which included administrative changes in the tax system, in education and the law. Reforms were pushed through in central and local government, and there were rudimentary moves towards greater equality for the sultan's Christian subjects.

But the nationalist and separatist pressure in the wider empire continued, exacerbated by the suffering caused by droughts and flooding at home. The European powers intervened again, forcing the Ottomans to accept the independence of modern-day Romania, Serbia and Montenegro, and acknowledge Russian claims to territory in the eastern part of Asia Minor. The Ottomans' hold on their empire was loosening.

THE FIGHT FOR A CONSTITUTION

Alongside the administrative reforms, the personal power of the sultan had grown until Abdülaziz, supported by his grand vizier, Mahmud Nedim Pasha (c.1818–83), seemed to be governing like an old-fashioned autocrat. There was opposition both from those who thought reform betrayed traditional Ottoman customs and values and from those who thought it failed to go far enough towards establishing a modern state, and who therefore wanted to curb the power of the

OTTOMAN SULTANS

1281 – 1326 Uthman I
1326 – 59 Orhan I
1359 – 89 Murad I
1389 – 1402 Bayezid I
1402 – 13 Ottoman interregnum
1413 – 21 Mehmed I
1421 – 44 Murad II (first reign)
1444 – 6 Mehmed II (the Conqueror) (first reign)
1446 – 51 Murad II (second reign)
1451 – 81 Mehmed II (the Conqueror) (second reign)
1481 – 1512 Bayezid II
1512 – 20 Selim I (the Grim)
1520 – 66 Suleyman I (the Magnificent or the Lawgiver)
1566 – 74 Selim II (the Drunkard)
1574 – 95 Murad III
1595 – 1603 Mehmed III
1603 – 17 Ahmed I
1617 – 18 Mustafa I (first reign – deposed)
1618 – 22 Osman II
1622 – 3 Mustafa I (second reign)
1623 – 40 Murad IV
1640 – 8 Ibrahim I (the Mad)
1648 – 87 Mehmed IV
1687 – 91 Suleyman II
1691 – 5 Ahmed II
1695 – 1703 Mustafa II
1703 – 30 Ahmed III
1730 – 54 Mahmud I
1754 – 7 Osman III
1757 – 74 Mustafa III
1774 – 89 Abdülhamid I
1789 – 1807 Selim III
1807 – 8 Mustafa IV
1808 – 39 Mahmud II
1839 – 61 Abdülmecid I
1861 – 76 Abdülaziz
1876 Murad V
1876 – 1909 Abdülhamid II
1909 – 18 Mehmed V
1918 Mehmed VI

sultan. Riots in 1876 brought about the downfall of Abdülaziz and the removal of his grand vizier, clearing the way for the adoption of a constitution which would establish the Ottomans' first representative assembly.

It was certainly not a democracy – full executive power remained in the hands of the sultan, who could order the deportation of any individual he thought harmful to the state – but it was too great a step for the new sultan, Abdülhamid II (r. 1876–1909). The first parliament was summoned in 1877 but then dissolved within a few months. It was 20 years before another parliament was called and by that time most of the liberal agitators who had been responsible for the experiment in representative government had been either exiled or executed.

Abdülhamid maintained an elaborate spy network and brutally crushed dissent both at home and abroad, where he was responsible for the first of a series of massacres of thousands of Armenians in 1894. But opposition continued to smoulder, until in 1908 Abdülhamid was forced to call another parliament. It was too late: within a year a fresh revolution had forced him from power to be replaced by a new ruler, Mehmed V (r. 1909–18), who agreed to rule according to the constitution.

ABOVE *By the late 19th century, Ottoman power had declined so far that Turkey was known as the 'sick man of Europe'. Its lands were eyed greedily by both the Russian Tsarist Bear and John Bull of England, keen to expand their own empires. A popular music-hall song of the time ran:*
'We don't want to fight
But, by Jingo, if we do,
We've got the ships,
We've got the men,
We've got the money too.
We've fought the Bear before
And while we're Britons true,
The Russians shall not have
Constantinople!'

MILITARY RULE

With the fall of Abdülhamid, the Ottoman army emerged as the real political power in Istanbul. The empire staggered on, but its power was broken. In 1908 Bosnia and Herzegovina were annexed by the Austro-Hungarian empire, Bulgaria seceded from the empire and Italy seized territory in North Africa and on the Greek mainland. More fighting in 1912–13 resulted in the loss of most of the remaining Ottoman empire in Europe.

It seemed briefly as if joining the First World War on the German side might signal an Ottoman revival. Despite early defeats, the empire saw Allied forces repulsed at the Dardanelles, and then recovered territory on the Caspian Sea from Russia after the Russian Revolution. But the war also saw bloodshed on an almost unprecedented scale, with an estimated 600,000 Armenians either killed or deported from their homeland in eastern Asia Minor, as the military government sought to pre-empt any pro-Russian activity among the Christian population of Armenia.

Following the defeat of the Central Powers, the empire was partitioned by the Allies, drawing the boundaries of the modern Middle East. The League of Nations granted France a mandate to control Syria and Lebanon, while the

LAWRENCE OF ARABIA

T.E. Lawrence (1888–1935) – who gained worldwide fame as 'Lawrence of Arabia' – led an Arab uprising against the Ottoman empire on behalf of the British during the First World War. But the vision of the post-war Middle East that he presented to his allies – broadly supported by the British government in the McMahon Letter sent to Arab leaders in 1915 by Britain's high commissioner in Egypt – differed substantially from the eventual partition settlement.

Lawrence of Arabia, a fine military tactician, was a thorn in the side of the Ottoman empire.

Lawrence called for a separate state for the Kurds in what is today northern Iraq along with an Arab state, based on tribal loyalties, uniting the peoples of modern Syria, Jordan and parts of Saudi Arabia. He also envisioned a separate state of Palestine.

But in the Sykes–Picot Agreement of 1916, the British and French carved up the empire into their separate zones of control. Britain was responsibile for administering Palestine and Transjordan, on the east and west banks of the River Jordan. In 1917 the British foreign secretary Sir Arthur Balfour (1848–1930) guaranteed British support for *'the establishment in Palestine of a national home for the Jewish people'*. (the 'Balfour Declaration')

What were seen as conflicting promises by the British sowed the seeds of decades of conflict, but 30 years later, after the Second World War, the partition of Palestine into a Jewish state, an Arab state and an international zone around Jerusalem was agreed by the United Nations.

British were appointed to rule in Iraq, Transjordan and Palestine. The Ottoman empire in the Arabian Peninsula was incorporated into modern Saudi Arabia and Yemen.

In the heartland of the old empire, the nationalist leader Mustafa Kemal (1881–1938), later given the name Atatürk ('Father of the Turks') led a lengthy struggle against the official soldiers of the Ottoman government, Greek occupation forces and various local uprisings. On 1 November, 1922, the sultanate was formally abolished, and the 600-year-old Islamic Ottoman empire was replaced by the secular modern state of Turkey.

In the 15th and 16th centuries, the trading empire of the Songhai covered huge tracts of western Africa, stretching north almost as far as the borders of modern Algeria, west to the Atlantic Ocean and south down into what is now Nigeria. Most of its people lived in small farms, but there were also large cities serving as merchant centres for the trans-Sahara trade in gold, ivory, salt and slaves. The empire fell apart in the late 16th century after a military defeat by forces of the sultan of Morocco and was split into small, independent kingdoms. Today, about three million Songhai people are scattered along the River Niger in Mali, Niger and Nigeria.

THE SONGHAI EMPIRE
c.1460 – 1616

IN THE MID-15TH CENTURY THE SONGHAI KINGDOM was limited to the area immediately around its prosperous capital city of Gao. Since the decline of the trading empire of Mali a century or so before, it had been a region of almost constant tribal warfare, with attacks from desert raiders such as the Tuareg and the Fulani peoples. About 1464, a new ruler named Sonni 'Ali (r. 1464–93) succeeded to the throne and immediately began the process of conquering the neighbouring tribes.

He was a Muslim, although many of the people of Songhai followed traditional West African religions. There were victories over the Mossi people to the south of Songhai, and the Dogon in the north, which helped to develop Sonni 'Ali's reputation as a military leader. In 1468, Muslim residents of Timbuktu, to the northwest of Gao, asked for his help in driving away Tuareg tribesmen, who had occupied the town for some 30 years.

A REPUTATION FOR CRUELTY
He took the town and sacked it, allegedly with great slaughter, putting in place another aspect of his reputation, the name of a cruel and implacable enemy. From Timbuktu, he moved on to the wealthy town of Jenne (modern Djenné) to the southwest, which had always fiercely maintained its independence from the Mali

LEFT *The Great Mosque of Djenné in Mali, built in the 13th century, once lay within the bounds of the Songhai empire. Under Songhai rule, Djenné became a major centre of islamic scholarship.*

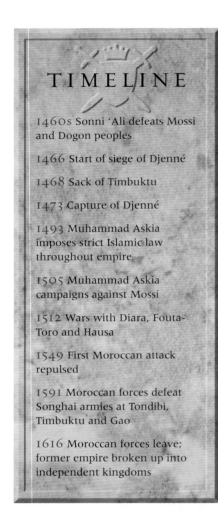
empire. Sonni 'Ali only managed to capture it after starving the inhabitants into surrender in a seven-year siege; but by the mid-1470s he had also brought much of the eastern half of the former Mali empire under his rule. By so doing, he established a power base along the River Niger, where his army imposed a strict discipline on the local tribes, forbidding the raids which had previously terrorized the small farmers.

On his death in 1493, his son Sonni Baru (r. 1493) was deposed in a swift and efficient coup led by a military leader – possibly a distant relative of Sonni 'Ali – who seized the throne as Muhammad I Askia (r. 1493–1528).

AN ISLAMIC EMPIRE

Where Sonni 'Ali had tried to maintain a balance between the Muslim faith of the townspeople and the animistic religion of the countryside, Muhammad Askia tried to impose strict Islamic law – although some of the peoples he conquered refused to accept it. It was under his rule that Gao, Djenné and Timbuktu gained prominence as centres of scholarship and the homes of impressive libraries. The Spanish–Moroccan writer Leo Africanus, visiting Gao in the early 16th century, commented on the number of learned men in the town, and said that books and manuscripts from North Africa reached high prices in the market there.

Muhammad Askia also mounted military campaigns to extend the boundaries of the empire, which reached its greatest extent under his rule, stretching as far as the Atlantic coast in the west. Huge caravans crossed the Sahara, carrying slaves, ivory from the interior, salt from the ancient mines in the desert north of Timbuktu, and gold, mined along the River Niger.

BELOW *The Songhai empire was one of the largest African empires in history, centered in eastern Mali.*

But perhaps his greatest achievement was the creation of a sophisticated administration, with separate ministries to oversee the different areas of government. Local chiefs were allowed to maintain control of their own areas, but had to acknowledge the primacy of Songhai rule.

Muhammad was deposed in 1528 by one of his sons, but the administrative system he had built up survived, with a large standing army keeping order and allowing peaceful trade across the empire. Askia Dawud (r. 1549–82), who succeeded to the throne in 1549, ruled for 33 years of relative peace behind fairly secure borders.

INVADERS WITH FIREARMS

Soon after his death, the forces of Sultan Ahmad Saadi (r. 1578–1603) of Morocco invaded the empire from the northwest, wanting to seize control of the valuable salt mines. They came at a time when the empire had been weakened

GLORIOUS GAO

The city that was to become capital of the Songhai empire under Sonni 'Ali was originally known as Kawkaw, and had established itself centuries before as a centre for the profitable trade across the Sahara, along with Jenne (modern Djenné) and Timbuktu. From Gao, goods from the north could be transported down the River Niger to the coast. Under Sonni 'Ali, the town grew until its population reached about 70,000, but it was virtually destroyed in the Moroccan invasion of the late 16th century which destroyed the Songhai empire.

Gao began to recover under the French colonial administration of the 20th century, as traffic began to flow through its port again. Today, surrounded by shimmering pink sand dunes, it is the capital of Mali's Gao region, a small trading centre, and a port of call for tourists and backpackers.

It still contains the tomb of Sonni 'Ali's successor as Songhai emperor, Muhammad I Askia, a 200-metre- (60-ft-) tall pyramid-shaped building of dark grey mud, studded with wooden spikes.

by a succession of natural disasters, when the valuable trade with the Atlantic coast had been disrupted by the activities of Portuguese slave traders and when arguments over the succession had led to an outbreak of civil war. But the main reason for the collapse of the empire was simple: gunpowder.

The primitively armed Songhai army of war canoes, horsemen and foot soldiers which had subdued the kingdoms of West Africa so effectively had no answer to the firearms of the invaders. In 1591, more than 40,000 Songhai men met a Moroccan army of less than a tenth that number, which had just completed an epic four-month trek across the Sahara. There was a brief and inconclusive cavalry skirmish between the two forces, and then the invaders opened fire with their muskets and cannon. The Songhai forces fled, and from then on there was no organized resistance. Gao, Djenné and Timbuktu were all plundered by the invading army.

For the Moroccans, it was a cheap victory but an expensive peace. Over the next 25 years they struggled to maintain control over the territory they had won, losing an estimated 25,000 men to disease and sporadic attacks by the Songhai and other tribes until the sultan finally recalled what was left of his forces. They left behind a ravaged country, which remained fractured into a kaleidoscope of separate, independent kingdoms.

SONGHAI EMPERORS

c.1464 – 93 Sonni 'Ali

1493 Sonni Baru

1493 – 1528 Muhammad I Askia

1528 – 31 Askia Musa

1531 – 7 Muhammad II Askia

1537 – 9 Askia Ismail

1539 – 49 Askia Issihak I

1549 – 82 Askia Dawud

1582 – 6 Internal fighting

1586 – 8 Muhammad Bani

1588 – 91 Askia Issihak II

Like other civilizations of the Andes, the Incas left no written records, so their history is known only through oral traditions and from written accounts made by their Spanish conquerors in the 16th century. As a result, the empire established by the Incas in the highlands of the Andes and along the Pacific coast of South America is now more generally known outside Peru for the suddenness of its destruction than for its culture or conquests.

THE INCA EMPIRE
c.1400 – 1535

THE EMPIRE THAT THE SPANISH ADVENTURERS CONQUERED stretched from modern Ecuador in the north to central Chile in the south and contained around 12 million people of different tribes and races, speaking more than 20 different languages. Modern estimates suggest that the Incas numbered about 12 million when the Spanish arrived in 1532; less than 100 years later, epidemics, disease and war had reduced their numbers to around 600,000.

The Incas traced their ancestry to a probably mythical figure named Manco Capac, who led them as nomads to the fertile Cuzco Valley, high in the Andes. From him, according to the legend, the leadership of the Inca nation was generally passed from father to son, with the ruling emperor nominating his own successor, and the chosen heir being approved by the priests. Some time in the 14th century, Mayta Capac, referred to as the 'fourth emperor', began to conquer other tribes in the region and seize their lands, an aggressive policy that was continued over the next 100 years by the three succeeding rulers.

A MYTHICAL PAST
Much of this early 'history' of the Incas is inseparable from myth. In the early 15th century it was Viracocha Inca (r. *c*.1410–*c*.1438) – the eighth ruler according to the traditional reckoning, and one of the first for whom there is any firm historical evidence – who began the sustained process of territorial expansion beyond the Cuzco Valley that would lead to the creation of the empire. At the beginning of his reign, the

LEFT *A gilded statue of the Inca king Atahualpa (r. 1532–3) in Cuzco, Peru.*

Incas seem to have lived more or less as mountain-dwelling raiders, launching attacks for plunder against surrounding tribes and ethnic groups, but not adopting any long-term strategy of dominance or conquest. Under Viracocha, all of that changed. First, they conquered the people of the Ayamarca kingdom, who lived further south in the Cuzco Valley, and then clashed with the Chanca, who had been making conquests of their own immediately to the west.

The clash with the Chanca was significant because it sparked a civil war within the Inca hierarchy, where there was already a dispute between two of Viracocha's sons over who would succeed him to the throne. Viracocha and his chosen successor, Inca Urcon, retreated to a fortified refuge, but Cusa Inca Yupanqi, his other son, won two major battles as he mounted a successful defence of the city of Cuzco. The victory gave him the power and prestige to announce himself not just as the rightful heir on his father's death, but as his immediate replacement as emperor. It also firmly established the Incas as the paramount power in the Cuzco Valley.

PACHACUTEC'S CONQUESTS

Cusa took the name Pachacutec Inca (r. 1438–71) and, when first his father and then his brother died, leaving him as undisputed ruler, he established a shaky truce with the Chanca. This developed into a suspicious and uneasy alliance, with the two nations uniting for a series of attacks on other neighbouring tribes, until Pachacutec secretly ordered the murder of the Chanca leaders, and had his forces chase their one-time allies deep into the rainforest.

There were still other powerful tribes to contend with, and Pachacutec also felt his position in Cuzco might not be secure. He dealt with the second problem by having the brother who had led his forces against the Chanca secretly murdered, and with the first by sending his two sons on a series of expeditions into the surrounding regions. By the time he had finished, the Incas controlled all the territory between Cuzco and the southern shores of Lake Titicaca in modern Bolivia, some 300 miles (500 km) to the south, and as far as the modern city of Quito in Ecuador to the north.

In the north, the Inca victories included the decisive defeat of the Chimú people of northern Peru, who had been one of the strongest nations in South America for some 200 years. The Incas sacked the Chimú capital of Chan Chan, whose ruins can still be seen on the northern coast of Peru, some 300 miles (500 km) north of Lima. Many of its inhabitants were slaughtered: it was the Incas, not the Chimú, who were now the rulers.

THE FOUR REGIONS

Back in Cuzco, Pachacutec started an ambitious programme of public works that included the rebuilding of much of the city and the construction of Sacsahuaman, the hill fortress that overlooked it. He supervised the building of Coricancha, a great shrine to the sun god, in front of which scores of boys and girls are said to have been buried alive in tribute to the god, and also set in train an ambitious series of agricultural terraces on the steep hillsides around the city. Cuzco was now the capital of an empire known as Tawantinsuyu, or The Four Regions, with four main highways leading from the centre of the city to the four *suyus* (quarters) of the empire. Separate provincial governments ruled over the conquered peoples under the personal leadership of the Inca himself.

To maintain control of this empire, Pachacutec also instigated a new policy of forced resettlement. Tribes were split up and some of their members sent off to distant parts of the empire so that they would be less able to foment revolution and would be more dependent on the power of the Inca state. Others were recruited as slave labour to work on Pachacutec's ambitious building programmes in Cuzco and elsewhere. Conquered peoples were largely left alone to follow their own religions, but they also had to acknowledge the Inca creator-god Viracocha, Illapa, the thunder god, and Inti, the sun god – who was specifically identified with the power of the Inca empire. The tribes were expected to provide tribute both for Viracocha and for the Inca government.

TUPAC INCA YUPANQUI BUILDS AN EMPIRE

It is Pachacutec's son, Tupac Inca Yupanqui (r. 1471–93), who is considered to be the greatest of the Inca leaders. Shortly after he succeeded on Pachacutec's abdication in 1471, he launched an invasion into the tropical rainforest around the Tono Valley. It had to be cut short when news reached him of a revolt in the Titicaca basin southeast of Cuzco. The conquered tribes

BELOW *The ruins of the Inca fortress and religious site of Sacsahuaman.*

there had risen up against the Incas, apparently after hearing rumours that Tupac Inca Yupanqui had been killed in battle. After destroying their fortresses in the mountains and restoring Inca control, he continued into what are now the highlands of Bolivia, and then on into northwest Argentina and as far as the River Maule in modern Chile.

In a lengthy campaign, he moved from valley to valley through the coastal lands, accepting the surrender of those tribes which submitted to him and conquering those which resisted, linking his father's conquests in the north with his own. Often, tribes would accept Inca authority peacefully on the promise – which was often fulfilled – of greatly increased prosperity within the empire. Once the conquests were complete by the end of the 1470s, he devoted himself to the administration of what was by now the biggest and most powerful empire in South America.

He continued his father's policy of allowing the conquered tribes largely to govern themselves under Inca supervision, although they could be called upon to supply labour for public works, and soldiers for the Inca armies. Some might be drafted in to work on the huge state-run farms which produced corn for distribution among the soldiers, while others would be sent to work either building or maintaining the network of over 15,000 miles (24,000 km) of roads that crisscrossed the empire. Tupac Inca Yupanqui also started a sophisticated system of dividing the male population of his empire into units of 100, 500, 1000, 5000 and 10,000, which he used in the administration of his vast labour forces.

The conquered tribes also had to provide young girls to serve as Aclla Cuna, or Virgins of the Sun, in temples to the sun god. There were several thousands of these temple maidens, from all over the empire, who were responsible for preparing food and holy garments for the emperor and also for maintaining the sacred flame in the temples. Some were chosen as sacrificial victims, while others, on puberty, were taken as brides or concubines either by the emperor or members of the Inca aristocracy.

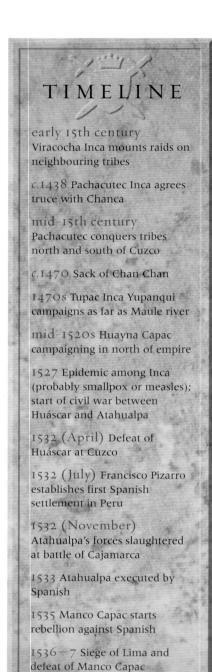

IMPENDING DESTRUCTION
Tupac Inca Yupanqui spent the last 15 years of his reign travelling in state from tribe to tribe and overseeing the distribution of lands among local leaders and members of the Inca aristocracy. His son,

RIGHT *Gold figurine from 1430–1532, representing a Virgin of the Sun.*

Huayna Capac (r. 1493–1527), inherited a strong and stable administration, and followed his father's policy of maintaining direct personal government, with constant visits to the four different provinces. But in addition, Huayna Capac set out to push the boundaries of the empire still further, assimilating new territories in the mountains of northeastern Peru and in the coastal regions of modern Ecuador.

While Huayna Capac was away campaigning in the north, he received word of a virulent epidemic that was sweeping through Cuzco and the heartland of his empire. Although he could have had no inkling of it at the time, this was the first sign of the approaching destruction of his empire: it seems likely that the disease that was killing Huayna Capac's people was either smallpox or measles, both of which had been brought to South America from Europe by the Spanish, and against which the tribes of the Andes had no defence. Hurrying back to Cuzco, Huayna Capac himself became one of the victims – he fell ill during the journey and died before reaching his capital.

ABOVE *A drawing from c.1615 depicting Manco Capac, the last Inca puppet ruler installed by the Spanish, who conducted a failed revolt against them in 1535–44.*

CIVIL WAR

Huayna Capac's death before he had had time to nominate a successor led to a bitter civil war among his three sons, Ninan Cuchi, Atahualpa and Huáscar. Ninan Cuchi died soon after his father, apparently from the same disease, leaving Atahualpa, who had been campaigning alongside Huayna Capac in the north, and Huáscar, who had remained in Cuzco. The empire was effectively split between the two of them, with Huáscar (r. 1527–32) controlling the south and Atahualpa (r. 1532–3) at large in the north with an extensive and battle-hardened army.

Huáscar brought an army north, but was defeated by Atahualpa's forces at a battle fought near the River Riobamba, in the central highlands of what is now Ecuador. However, he managed to escape with enough forces to challenge Atahualpa again at nearby Tumipampas – and this time the roles were reversed. Atahualpa's soldiers were defeated and he was captured, but then escaped to rejoin his scattered army. The stable administration which their father had inherited was in ruins as each brother slaughtered local tribesmen he believed to have supported his rival, turning the local tribes into ready allies for the Spanish when they arrived shortly afterwards.

Atahualpa sent his generals south with his army, where they won a series of victories which culminated in the defeat of Huáscar just outside Cuzco in 1532. Huáscar himself was kept alive to be sent north to pay homage to Atahualpa, but his entire family and scores of his supporters were slaughtered and their bodies fixed to poles as a warning to the people of the consequences of resistance.

THE SPANISH CONQUEST

Atahualpa was still celebrating the defeat of his brother when he heard the first news of the landing of Francisco Pizarro (c.1471–1541) and his tiny force of Spanish adventurers. Pizarro had made two previous exploratory landings in the north of the Inca empire, in modern Ecuador; but this time, urged on by stories of the immense wealth of the Inca rulers, he led his 106 foot soldiers and 62 horsemen on a march into the interior to seek out the Inca emperor.

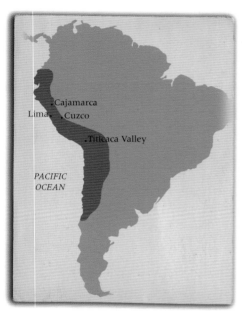

ABOVE *Stretching for some 2000 miles (3200 km), the Inca empire was comparable in size with the conquests of Alexander the Great (336–323 BC) in Central Asia.*

Atahualpa's envoys met him and invited him to the city of Cajamarca, where the emperor was waiting with several thousand men. Some accounts say the Inca bodyguard was unarmed, others that it included bowmen and men armed with clubs; in any case, the bulk of Atahualpa's army of some 30,000 men was camped outside the walls of the city. The emperor felt secure enough against such an insignificant number of foreigners to reject with contempt their audacious demand that he should accept Christianity and subjection to the king of Spain.

Pizarro and his men fired a sudden volley with their guns into the thronging Inca bodyguard and launched a concerted attack, with horsemen and foot soldiers fighting side by side. The Inca warriors, who had seen neither horses nor guns before and had no weapons to match the steel swords and armour of the Spanish, were cut down where they stood. In less than 30 minutes, Atahualpa had been seized and imprisoned, and all his senior commanders killed.

Leaderless, and shocked by the sudden slaughter, the rest of the Inca army offered no resistance. Atahualpa was imprisoned and, to the amazement of his captors, offered to give them a whole room filled with the gold they seemed to value so highly in return for his life. The room – 7 metres long by 5 metres wide (22 ft x 17 ft) was eventually filled with over 5800 kilograms (13,000 lb) of the finest masterpieces produced by the Inca craftsmen, all of which was reduced to ingots by Pizarro and his men. Two more rooms were filled with similar quantities of silver artefacts, which were also melted down – but even all this ransom did not save Atahualpa. The Spanish decided they could not risk the uprising that might result if they released the emperor, and he was garrotted after being found guilty on a trumped-up charge of plotting against them.

CUZCO FALLS

Resistance continued, although Pizarro tried to legitimize his position by installing Atahualpa's younger brother, Tupac Huallpa (d.1533), as a puppet ruler. While Atahualpa had been imprisoned by the Spanish, he had ordered Huáscar's execution and, as a result, the Spanish were seen as being allied in some way to the defeated faction in the recent civil war. Now, as they struggled towards Cuzco, they had to fight four battles against armies drawn from the north of the empire, under the leadership of Atahualpa's general, Quizquiz. They took Cuzco after a final desperate defence – the city was, Pizarro told King Charles (r. 1516–56) in a triumphant dispatch, *'the greatest and the finest ever seen in this country or anywhere in the Indies … It is so beautiful and has such fine buildings that it would be remarkable even in Spain'*.

'SAPA INCA' (EMPERORS) OF THE INCA EMPIRE

c.1410 – c.1438 Viracocha Inca

c.1438 – 71 Pachacutec Inca

1471 – 93 Tupac Inca Yupanqui

1493 – 1527 Huayna Capac

1527 – 32 Huáscar

1532 – 3 Atahualpa

1533 – 44 Manco Capac

BELOW *A 19th-century print shows Spanish soldiers capturing Atahualpa, the Inca king.*

INCA HISTORY

The Incas had no written history. Instead they had *quipus* – knotted cords which allowed them to keep an astonishingly accurate record of information such as crop yields, how many men from a particular village might be available for army service or what tribute was due or had been paid.

Each province of the empire had *quipucamayocs*, highly trained individuals who were responsible for collating this information. Exactly how they used the quipus is not known, but the records depended on the number of knots tied, the space between them and the length and colour of each individual piece of string.

The *quipucamayoc* of one province was able to demonstrate to a Spanish chronicler exactly

Peruvian print of an Inca man counting on a quipu. Quipu *is the word for 'knot' in the Inca language, Quechua.*

what had been given to the Spanish authorities in gold, silver, textiles, maize or other produce. The skilled users of the *quipu* were expected not only to be adept in manipulating the strings and reading the meaning of the cords, knots and colours, but also well versed in what was stored in past records.

Such information was vital for the efficient running of the empire and was also considered part of Inca history – but to the frustration of later European historians, the Inca only recorded information they thought important. They had little interest in precise chronology, and details such as the exact dates of the accession, abdication or death of individual emperors were simply not considered worth keeping.

Over the next few months, more conquistadores arrived to destroy any remaining opposition. Three years later, in 1535, the Spaniards' new puppet ruler, Manco Capac (r. 1533–44), escaped to lead a great rebellion, which included a lengthy siege of Cuzco. But the power of the Incas had been shattered. A last, desperate attack on Lima, the city the conquerors had built on the coast as their new capital, was repulsed by cavalry charges. The Incas had no answer to the awesome power of mounted cavalry, and retreated to a hilltop refuge at Vilcabamba, high in the Andes. Their empire had been destroyed by fewer than 200 men in less than half an hour's slaughter in the city of Cajamarca.

A LOST EMPIRE

In its short life, the Incas' empire extended over more than 2500 miles (4000 km) of territory. Almost all the towns and cities they built are lost, either destroyed by the Spanish settlers or swallowed by the jungle. But remains such as Machu Picchu, with intricate terracing up the steep hillsides, demonstrate how effectively they exploited the harsh mountain landscape. The accounts of the Spanish conquerors of whole buildings full of tribute, from cloaks, rare feathers and cloth to pure gold ornaments, show how completely they had dominated the tribes they conquered.

Already weakened by a bitter civil war, the Incas were completely overwhelmed by the Spanish, with their concept of total war, their steel weapons and armour and, above all, their horses. But if the Spanish had never come to South America – or if Atahualpa had acted more circumspectly and attacked Pizarro with the full force of his army, instead of treating him as a harmless guest – there is no reason to suppose that their empire might not have lasted for centuries.

BELOW *An engraving from 1596 depicts Incas gathering gold items to use as ransom for the Inca king Atahualpa, who was captured by Pizarro. Although the Spaniards were provided with large amounts of gold, the king was executed.*

The Aztecs were the first native people of America to face the full force of the Spanish conquistadores of the 16th century. By the time Hernán Cortés arrived in 1519, they ruled an empire that stretched across much of Central America. There was little attempt to impose direct day-to-day rule on the conquered tribes, but the Aztecs demanded payment of tribute and also the supply of human victims for the mass sacrifices they practised to their gods. Cortés conquered the Aztecs only after a long siege of their capital, Tenochtitlán, and after they had been seriously weakened by disease brought by the Spanish to the New World.

THE AZTEC EMPIRE
c.1400 — 1521

ALTHOUGH THE AZTECS DEVELOPED A REPUTATION AS FEARSOME WARRIORS – not least because of their practice of sacrificing their captured enemies to the sun god Huitzilopochtili in ceremonies of mass slaughter – their empire began with diplomacy rather than military conquest. In the early 15th century the city of Tenochtitlán, under its ruler Itzcóatl (r. 1427–40), formed a strategic alliance with the neighbouring cities of Texcoco and Tlacopán.

THE TRIPLE ALLIANCE

At that time the region was dominated by the Tepanec people, who controlled nearly all the Valley of Mexico, and the original aim of the so-called Triple Alliance was to establish the independence of the three cities. Over the next 100 years, however, Tenochtitlán gradually became the dominant member of an alliance that slowly extended its power over hundreds of other small city-states. At the height of their empire, the Aztecs ruled around six million people, spread over around 80,000 square miles (207,000 sq km).

Itzcóatl started his conquests with the capture of important agricultural areas in the southern part of the Valley of Mexico and then began to extend beyond the valley itself, leading an attack on the people of Cuauhnáhuac, modern-day Cuernavaca,

LEFT *A 15th-century gold pendant representing Mitlantecuhtli, the Aztec god of the dead.*

about 50 miles (80 km) to the south of his city. At the same time, he had started a massive building programme in Tenochtitlán itself, which was erecting temples, grandiose state buildings and a massive causeway to the mainland.

THE EMPIRE AT ITS PEAK

When Itzcóatl died in 1440 he was succeeded by his nephew Moctezuma I (r. 1440–69). He ruled with his brother Tlacaelel as his councillor and right-hand man for 29 years, leading expeditions as far as the Gulf coast. He oversaw the development of a successful trading economy based largely on goods from the coastal region such as cocoa, rubber and cotton. Meanwhile, tribute from conquered peoples was flooding into the Aztec capital. Spanish sources from the 16th century describe the offerings from the Mixtec people of Coixtlahuaca as including bowls of gold dust, bags of cochineal dye, exotic feathers and thousands of richly embroidered blankets.

This expansion of the empire continued under Moctezuma's successors, notably with the emperor Ahuitzotl (r. 1486–1502) who extended the area of Aztec dominance west to the Pacific coast and south into modern Guatemala. During this time, the Aztecs continued to exact tribute from the the cities they conquered, but otherwise left them generally in charge of their own affairs. Rather than being a centrally governed and united organization, the empire was always a loosely organized collection of semi-independent city-states that all accepted Aztec overlordship.

By the time Ahuitzotl was succeeded by his nephew Moctezuma II (r. *c.*1502–20), the empire stretched as far as modern Honduras and Nicaragua. Its prosperity was based largely on the high productivity of the Aztecs' intensive agriculture, which used sophisticated systems of irrigation and drainage in order to cultivate both dry areas and swampy marshland. But it had two crucial weaknesses: disaffection among the conquered peoples, and the Aztecs' own fatalistic religious beliefs.

The Aztecs' religious practice of human sacrifice often involved the deaths of hundreds or even thousands of captives, whose hearts were ripped out of their bodies while they were still alive – Ahuitzotl is reported to have sacrificed 20,000 people in a single ceremony. Constant warfare and demands for tribute and sacrificial victims had created bitter enemies to the Aztecs among the other peoples of Central America – most notably, the Tlaxcalans who lived just to the east of them and whom, crucially, they never managed to conquer. When the Spanish adventurer Hernán Cortés (1485–1547) and his soldiers landed on the Gulf coast in 1519, they found many potential allies against the Aztecs.

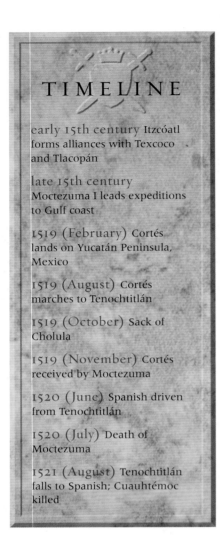

TIMELINE

early 15th century Itzcóatl forms alliances with Texcoco and Tlacopán

late 15th century Moctezuma I leads expeditions to Gulf coast

1519 (February) Cortés lands on Yucatán Peninsula, Mexico

1519 (August) Cortés marches to Tenochtitlán

1519 (October) Sack of Cholula

1519 (November) Cortés received by Moctezuma

1520 (June) Spanish driven from Tenochtitlán

1520 (July) Death of Moctezuma

1521 (August) Tenochtitlán falls to Spanish; Cuauhtémoc killed

THE COMING OF THE SPANISH

Among the Aztecs' religious myths was the story that a white, bearded god would eventually come to seize the empire. According to some accounts – although there are suggestions today that this may have been a story concocted after the conquest – the appearance of Cortés, a white, bearded stranger with his strange and terrifying guns, horses and steel weapons and armour seemed to fulfil this prophecy.

After initially fighting against the people of Tlaxcala, Cortés quickly formed an alliance with them. They saw him as a valuable ally against a powerful enemy, while he was desperate for knowledge about the Aztecs and their empire. With their backing, he marched first on the city of Cholula, where his troops killed several thousand of the inhabitants and burned the city to the ground. Some three months later, he reached Tenochtitlán.

TENOCHTITLÁN

The Aztec capital on Lake Texcoco was the biggest and most prosperous city in pre-Columbian America. When the Spanish arrived in 1519, more than 400,000 Aztecs lived either in the city or in the immediate vicinity.

It was originally constructed on a small island during the 13th century, where, according to Aztec history, the tribe had seen the sign they had been promised by their god Huitzilopochtili of an eagle devouring a serpent. The island would have been an easily defensible home for the newly arrived Aztecs, but the original settlement gradually spread as additional artificial islands were constructed, until by the 16th century it covered some 5 square miles (13 sq km) of the lake and the marshes beside it.

Three great causeways connected it to the mainland, and the city was divided into four administrative districts, or *calpulli*. Since the water of Lake Texcoco was salty, giant aqueducts brought supplies from freshwater springs on the mainland. These were cut by the Spanish during their siege of the city.

Within the busy metropolis, with its bustling agricultural market, were the 300-room palace of Moctezuma and hundreds of temples and other religious buildings. The main temple complex, where the mass sacrifices of human victims were carried out, included three large pyramids, the tallest more than 30 metres

Illustration showing Tenochtitlán, the capital of the Aztec empire on Lake Texcoco. Its ruins now lie buried beneath the teeming capital city of modern Mexico, Mexico-City.

(100 ft) high. Spanish chroniclers described a great wooden rack set up to hold the skulls of the sacrificial victims.

Bernal Diaz del Castillo (1496–1584), who served under Cortés, wrote in The Conquest of New Spain: *'It was all so wonderful that I do not know how to describe this first glimpse of things never heard of, seen, or dreamed of before.'* By the time he wrote those words, he and his fellow conquistadores had obliterated both the city and the Aztec empire of which it was the capital.

There were about 500 Spanish soldiers, accompanied by some 3000 native allies, and Moctezuma, unsure how to handle their arrival, welcomed them and ordered that they should be fed and looked after in one of the royal palaces. However, they turned on him, holding him hostage and demanding a huge ransom in gold. Reinforcements arrived from Spain, but the Aztecs, initially shocked by the fury of the Spanish assault, rose in rebellion. Hundreds of the Spanish were slaughtered as they were driven out of the city. Moctezuma was also killed, either by his Spanish captors or by the Aztecs themselves, who were angered by the submissive attitude he had taken to his captors.

Beating off several Aztec attacks as they retreated, Cortés and his men took refuge with the Tlaxcalans, who decided, along with several other smaller tribes, to join them in a fresh attack on Tenochtitlán. Cortés prepared the way by building warships to take control of Lake Texcoco, and mounted a siege of the city, cutting off its water supply and forcing many of its inhabitants to drink the salt water of the lake. They were also weakened by an epidemic of smallpox – a European disease to which they had no immunity – which struck them soon after the initial Spanish retreat and which killed about a third of the population.

After a siege of several weeks, the first Spanish soldiers forced their way into the city. Cuauhtémoc (r. 1520–1), the new emperor who had replaced Moctezuma, was captured, tortured and executed; those Aztecs who had survived the siege were driven from the city; and Cortés began to build his own capital over the ruins of Aztec Tenochtitlán. The capture of the city had taken three months, but it took the Spanish more than 150 years to conquer the rest of Central America, including the Yucatán Peninsula, where the Mayan people mounted a determined resistance.

SHATTERED REMAINS

But the Aztec empire fell with the destruction of Tenochtitlán. On the ruins of the old Aztec capital, the foundations of Mexico City were laid, with first a church and then a cathedral built over the temples where human hearts had once been ripped out for the Aztec gods. Destruction of the Aztecs' system of dams and canals led to constant problems with flooding, until Lake Texcoco was drained in the 17th century. Today, only a small lake surrounded by salt marshes survives. A modern version of the Aztec language, Nahuatl, is still spoken by 1.5 million people in central Mexico, but Tenochtitlán itself, and the Aztec empire, lie buried beneath Mexico City.

AZTEC RULERS

1428 – 40 Itzcóatl
1440 – 69 Moctezuma I
1469 – 81 Axayacatl
1481 – 6 Tizoc
1486 – 1502 Ahuitzotl
1502 – 20 Moctezuma II
1520 – 1 Cuauhtémoc

BELOW *The Aztec empire at its height after the expansion undertaken during the reign of Moctezuma II (1502–20), just prior to the Spanish conquest.*

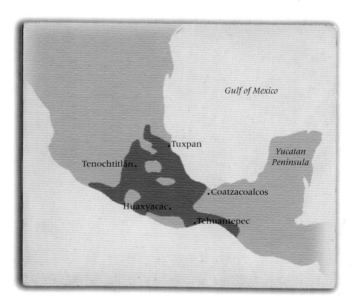

Gulf of Mexico

Tuxpan

Tenochtitlán

Yucatan Peninsula

Coatzacoalcos

Huaxyacac

Tehuantepec

QVARTI

GANGES FL

CAGAIREGIO

INTER

CIV

INDIAE

INDIA INTRA GA

ARDONS

GEM

SECVV

DVM

CABAIA

IN DVSF

CATABEDA

GARMA

REGNV

INDVSF

CAN

SINVS GANGETI CVS

RETIGO

INDICVM

Dabull
danda
os ylheos queymados
vilhas degoa
Gua de Rama
mergeo
anor
bacalor
montefremolo

INDIA

RI

BAZACATA ISVLA

PEALEGVS INDICVS

FEMALA

PEGVREGIO

M

ISVLE NICOBAR

FALS COMORLN

CEILAN ISVLA

Hic lapis gignitur herculeus obque hoc nauigia que claues ferreos habent retinentur harum incolae antropophagi sunt:

PORLANA

VS

EQVI

NO

C

CIAL

NE FORTVNAE

MANTOLE ISVLE

99

The short-lived union of Spain and Portugal in the early years of the 17th century created the first maritime empire to stretch right around the globe. The overseas empires were built on the great discoveries of 150 years before. Spain itself had only been united by the marriage of Ferdinand of Aragon and Isabella of Castile for 23 years when Columbus set off across the Atlantic in 1492, and the first Portuguese settlements in India followed the voyage of Vasco da Gama in 1498. It is hard to imagine the rapid expansion of knowledge about the world that followed those voyages – the size of the known world, as one explorer observed, doubled in size in a period of 80 years.

THE TRADING EMPIRES OF SPAIN AND PORTUGAL
1494 – 1898

IN THE TREATY OF TORDESILLAS OF 1494, Spain and Portugal divided the non-Christian world between them with the approval of the pope, drawing an imaginary north–south line around the world some 1300 miles (2000 km) west of the Cape Verde Islands. All the undiscovered lands to the west of the line were to be Spanish, and all those to the east Portuguese. The treaty laid the basis of the great trading empires of the Spanish and Portuguese that would dominate world trade. With its high-handed assumption of ownership, it also set the tone of European expansion for 450 years.

Although other nations such as France and England might protest at this unilateral take-over of the world, the treaty reflected the current reality. The Spanish-backed adventurer Christopher Columbus (1451–1506) had reached the Americas two years earlier, and four years before that the Portuguese explorer Bartolomeu Dias (c.1450–1500) had rounded the Cape of Good Hope to reach the Indian Ocean. None of the other nations in the Western world could match the shipping fleets of Spain and Portugal.

LEFT *India and Burma, as shown on an atlas of c.1519 by the Portuguese cartographer Pedro Reinel. Portugal's seaborne empire extended far into east Asia, where its cultural and linguistic heritage can still be found today.*

A SEA ROUTE TO THE EAST

The two nations adopted very different attitudes towards colonial expansion. While the Spanish concentrated on establishing colonies in Mexico and Peru to exploit the apparently limitless resources of the New World that Columbus had discovered, the Portuguese began establishing strategic fortifications and trading posts to guard the sea routes to the East Indies. The way forward was demonstrated in 1498 by the expedition of Vasco da Gama (*c*.1469–1524) to establish the first Portuguese outpost in India. From then on, Portugal concentrated on securing control of the valuable trade with the east.

As the first viceroy of Portuguese India, Francisco de Almeida (1450–1510) set out in 1505 to establish a chain of key staging posts along the eastern coast of Africa – including Mombasa in modern Kenya and the island of Zanzibar (now part of Tanzania) – and strengthened the fortifications of the port of Cochin, on the western coast of India. The Ottomans, Egyptians and Indians, who had previously controlled the region's trade routes, tried to drive them out of India, but were heavily defeated by the superior Portuguese ships at the Battle of Diu in 1509. The forces opposing the Portuguese were also supported by the Venetians, who could see the threat that a Cape route would pose to their own dominance of the overland eastern trade route into Europe, but the Portuguese victory established their dominance of the Indian Ocean for the next 100 years.

Almeida's successor as viceroy, Afonso de Albuquerque, extended Portuguese influence around the Indian Ocean. Between 1510 and 1515, he established Goa as the capital of Portuguese India, set up a trading post at Malacca on the southwest coast of the Malay Peninsula after massacring much of its Muslim population and captured Hormuz at the mouth of the Arabian Gulf, thus disrupting trade to Europe by the Red Sea route. The strategically placed fortifications which he established gave the Portuguese effective control over the sea routes and over the next few decades they pressed further east, establishing a settlement at Macau, which they later formally leased from the Chinese government.

Occasional foreign incursions such as the 1522 Spanish-backed expedition of Ferdinand Magellan (1480–1521) or the circumnavigation by Sir Francis Drake (*c*.1540–96) in 1577 caused angry diplomatic protests, but did not threaten Portugal's supremacy. With their network of supply stations, trading posts and military fortifications, the Portuguese dominated this prosperous eastern trade for 100 years without effective European competition.

AMERICAN POSSESSIONS

Despite sporadic revolts, the Spanish had, meanwhile, consolidated their empires in South and Central America. To ensure that they maximized the profit from their American possessions, they set up a trading organization, the Casa de Contracion. This body achieved its aim with notable success: the value of the gold and silver brought back to Europe in the first decade of the 16th century was around 195,000 ducats a year; by the 1550s it had reached some 2.4 million ducats a year; and by the 1590s it was running at nearly 8.5 million ducats. The treasure created a flood of wealth that helped to finance the constant European wars of the Holy Roman Emperor Charles V (r. 1519–56), but also, according to some historians, caused rampant inflation across the entire continent.

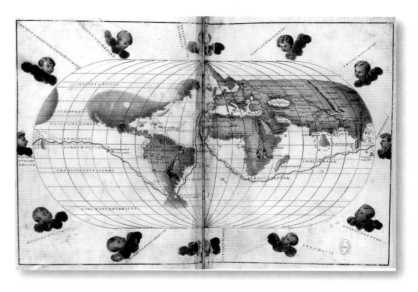

In 1524 Charles, realizing the importance of maintaining control over the explorers and adventurers who were opening up the New World, established the Council of the Indies as a legislative body. He followed it ten years later with the appointment of the first viceroy, who was sent to represent the royal power in Mexico; but the settlers continued to enjoy a great degree of *de facto* independence from Spain.

For Charles V, the Spanish possessions were just part of a personal empire that already stretched through much of Europe. Before he was six, he was duke of Burgundy and ruler of extensive territories in eastern France and the Low Countries. At 16, as king of Spain, he also ruled part of Italy as well as the American possessions. Three years later, still not 20 years old and after an expensive campaign of bribery

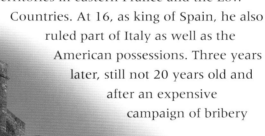

among the German electors, he inherited the Holy Roman Empire, with central European lands that encompassed Austria, Carinthia, Slovenia and the Tyrol. His realm was a vast and unwieldy patchwork of dynastic inheritances and was virtually impossible to govern, but it was the first empire on which, literally, 'the sun never set' – a phrase that is reputed to have originated with Charles himself.

THE PORTUGUESE REACH AMERICA

To follow the route east around the Cape, navigators would sail southwest into the Atlantic to pick up the trade winds. In 1500, Pedro Alvares Cabral (*c.*1467–1520) sailed so far into the Atlantic that he became the first European to sight the coast of Brazil. When the Treaty of Tordesillas had been signed, no one had dreamed that the Americas might extend so far east, but since it lay to the east of the agreed meridian, Brazil became part of the Portuguese empire.

There was no immediate sign that it would become a particularly profitable colony, but in response to landings by French settlers, King John III of Portugal (r. 1521–57) organized the administration of Brazil and the creation of the first towns, São Vicente and São Paulo. Sugar cane, largely produced by native or African-born slaves, became the country's most important export.

Brazil would remain a Portuguese colony until its independence in 1822. Initially, its importance was limited to the wood, sugar and coffee that could be exported from the coastal settlements. However, as settlers began to explore the hinterland to the west in search of more slaves for their plantations, deposits of gold and diamonds were found, especially in the state of Minas Gerais, and for a period during the 18th century Brazil became the main source for imports of gold into Europe.

An attempt to achieve independence in the late 18th century was defeated, and in 1815 Brazil was officially designated a kingdom on an equal footing with Portugal. For a while, the United Kingdom of Portugal, Brazil and Algarves was ruled from the Brazilian capital Rio de Janeiro by the Portuguese prince regent, who escaped from Napoleon's invasion of his own country, and was known as King John VI (r. 1816–26).

ABOVE RIGHT *The Portuguese and Spanish empires, the first truly global empires.*

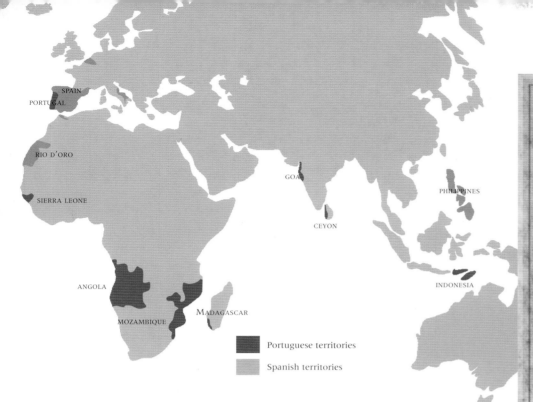

SPAIN
PORTUGAL
RIO D'ORO
SIERRA LEONE
GOA
CEYON
PHILIPPINES
ANGOLA
MOZAMBIQUE
MADAGASCAR
INDONESIA

◼ Portuguese territories

◼ Spanish territories

SPANISH POWER

Charles V's possessions in Europe were divided on his abdication in 1556. His son Philip II (r. 1556–98) became king of Spain, ruling the Low Countries, Naples and the American possessions, and his brother Ferdinand, who was invested as Holy Roman Emperor (r. 1558–64), inherited the Habsburg possessions in Austria.

Europe was convulsed by war through much of the 16th century, in the wake of the Reformation, and in the early years the Spanish armies were largely funded by the continuing flood of gold and silver from mines in Mexico and Peru. Elsewhere, Spanish explorers continued to push further into the Americas. In 1513 Vasco Núñez de Balboa (1475–1519) led the first European expedition to cross the isthmus of Panama. Fifty years later, in 1565, Admiral Pedro Menéndez de Avilés (1519–74) established a military base at St Augustine on the east coast of Florida, and in the same year Miguel López de Legazpi (1502–72) led a detachment of Spanish forces to create a settlement in the Philippines. This started a regular shipment of spices, silks and jewels back to the port of Acapulco on the west coast of central America, overland to the east coast, and thence back to Europe with the Spanish treasure fleets.

In Europe, meanwhile, Philip and his Venetian allies defeated the Ottoman fleet at the Battle of Lepanto off western Greece in 1571, restoring European dominance of the Mediterranean. But in the Low Countries he was engaged in a desperate struggle with Calvinist rebels as the Reformation flared across northern Europe. It was the start of 80 years of warfare that would end with the independence of the Netherlands, paving the way for the destruction of the Spanish empire in Europe.

TWO NATIONS UNITED

Philip was reeling with debt. The cost of the fighting in the Netherlands, the expense of the massive fleet that had been needed to defeat the Ottomans at Lepanto and the loss of income from his treasure ships – which were increasingly ransacked by pirates and privateers as they crossed the Atlantic – had brought him to the point of bankruptcy. But in 1580, on the death of Portugal's King Henry (r. 1578–80), a childless cardinal, he laid claim to the throne of Portugal, backing his demand with a massive invasion force. This gave Philip control, at least in theory, of the Portuguese trading empire to the east as well as his own possessions in the Americas. It also exposed him to another determined independence struggle, as the Portuguese people revolted against his seizure of power.

ABOVE *In 1513, the explorer Vasco Núñez de Balboa crossed the Isthmus of Panama and claimed the Pacific coastline of the Americas for Spain. The most famous account of this event, in John Keats's sonnet 'On First Looking into Chapman's Homer', describes the conquistador as having* 'star'd at the Pacific ... silent, upon a peak in Darien'. *Yet Keats wrongly attributed the feat to Hernán Cortés rather than Balboa.*

The religious wars in Europe continued: the Spanish were damaged first by the defeat of their armada at the hands of Drake and the English, and then – after Philip III (r. 1598–1621) died in 1621, to be succeeded by his son Philip IV (r. 1621–65) – by an even more crushing naval disaster at the hands of the Dutch in the Battle of the Downs off the southern coast of England in 1639. A force of 80 Spanish and Portuguese ships carrying more than 20,000 soldiers to reinforce their troops in Flanders was intercepted and destroyed by Dutch forces. Some two-thirds of the soldiers were killed, Spain's war effort in the Netherlands was crippled and the country's power at sea was effectively destroyed.

With Spain and Portugal unified under one crown, these conflicts also directly affected the Portuguese. The Dutch had concentrated on developing their navy and began mounting raids on Portuguese shipping and bases in the East Indies and Brazil. Attempts to establish a Dutch foothold in Brazil were repulsed but,

REMINDERS OF EMPIRE

The boundaries of Portuguese and Spanish influence in the New World and the Far East are reflected today in the languages of South America. Native Americans in Brazil speak over 180 different languages, but the vast majority of the country's 188 million population speak Portuguese. Spanish dominates the rest of the continent, including Central America.

In Asia, Spanish is widespread in the Philippines, while communities speaking at least some form of Portuguese survive in Malacca, Macau, Hong Kong and Indonesia; it is also used by a few thousand people in Goa, India. Portuguese colonies established in Africa in the 19th century included Angola and Mozambique, and the language remains widely spoken there as well.

during the second half of the 17th century, Dutch forces took control of Ceylon, the Cape of Good Hope and most of the East Indies' possessions from the Portuguese. By the end of the century all that remained of what had been a formidable chain of Portuguese fortifications and supply stations were Macau, East Timor and the remaining settlements in India.

DEFEATS AT SEA AND ON LAND

By that time, the forcible union of Spain and Portugal was over. In 1640 a Portuguese aristocrat named John of Braganza was encouraged by the demonstration of Spanish vulnerability at the Battle of the Downs to lead a successful rebellion in Portugal. He took the throne as King John IV (r. 1640–56) and ended 60 years of unpopular Spanish rule, although fighting with the Spanish lasted for another five years. King John was supported, at least diplomatically, by King Charles I of England (r. 1625–49); his daughter, Catherine of Braganza (1638–1705), was eventually married to Charles' son, Charles II (r. 1660–85). As a dowry, she brought with her the right to free trade

ABOVE *The defeat of the Spanish Armada by Drake's English fleet in 1588 (shown here in a contemporary English painting) ushered in a steady decline in Spanish sea power. This was completed 50 years later when Dutch forces inflicted a major defeat on Spain at the Battle of the Downs off the southeast coast of England in 1639.*

with Brazil and the East Indies, the Berber city of Tangier in Morocco and – crucially – the islands of Bombay (present day Mumbai) in India. The foundation of the modern city a few years later by the British East India Company provided an early foothold for the establishment of the British in India (see also The British Empire, pages 194–213).

Elsewhere on the continent, Spanish reverses continued. At the Battle of Rocroi in the French Ardennes in 1643, a joint army from Spain and the Holy Roman Empire was destroyed by French troops. More than half of its 27,000 men were either killed or captured – the first time Spanish forces had been defeated in a major land battle for more than a century. King Philip continued to struggle to hold together his European possessions, but the myth of Spanish military invincibility on land had been shattered as effectively as the Battle of the Downs had destroyed the reputation of Spanish sea power.

The Battle of Lens in Flanders finally brought about Dutch independence in 1648 with another Spanish military defeat at the hands of the French. Ten years later, the Battle of the Dunes in northern France led to a peace agreement that saw the loss of Spanish possessions in Lorraine and the Pyrenees region of southwest France. Spain was worn out by conflict and bankrupted by constant economic crises, and Philip's successor as king, Charles II (r. 1665–1700), was mentally and physically incapable. Nevertheless, the fighting which had torn the country apart for most of the 17th century continued.

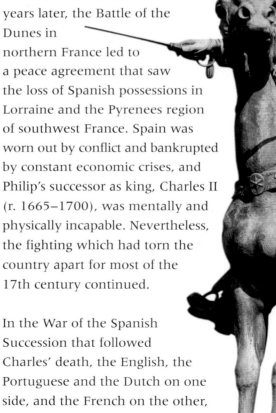

In the War of the Spanish Succession that followed Charles' death, the English, the Portuguese and the Dutch on one side, and the French on the other, fought over who should take the Spanish throne. The fighting took place not just in Europe but also in North America, where British and French colonists struggled for supremacy. Under the Treaty of Utrecht, which ended the war, the French candidate, the Bourbon Philip V (r. 1700–46), retained the crown and the American possessions but agreed to cede the Spanish Netherlands, Naples, Milan and Sardinia to Austria.

THE STRUGGLE FOR INDEPENDENCE

Although Spain had lost its European empire, the retention of the possessions in the Americas was crucial to its prosperity over the next 100 years. A compromise was eventually reached with Portugal over who should have control of the Amazon Basin, parts of which had already been occupied by colonists from Brazil. Spain had not recovered its status as a great power, but the decline experienced during the 17th century had been halted.

But the French Revolution and the Napoleonic Wars changed the face of Europe and the fortunes of Spain. First, defeat alongside the French at the Battle of Trafalgar (1805) left the Spanish navy virtually powerless to defend the crucial Atlantic sea lanes or to control her empire in the Americas. Then Napoleon's invasion in 1808 began the long guerrilla campaign of the Peninsular War. Portugal's prince regent (later to become King John VI) was forced to flee to Brazil, while Spain's King Ferdinand VII (r. 1813–33), who had turned to Napoleon for help in putting down the riots which had forced the abdication of his father, was imprisoned by the French for the next seven years.

The tumult in Europe was matched in America, where the example of the successful Revolutionary War against the British, coupled with the nationalist feelings fanned by reports of the French Revolution, encouraged a wave of independence movements. In 1811 Paraguay broke away, to be followed by Uruguay in 1815, Argentina in 1816, Chile in 1818 and Peru in 1821. Elsewhere, ten years of fighting resulted in the declaration of Mexican independence in 1821, rapidly followed by similar movements in the rest of Central America. Brazil, too, achieved its freedom when King John returned to Portugal at the end of the Napoleonic Wars, leaving his son Pedro behind as his regent. However, it became clear that Brazil would not accept the restoration of its colonial status, and within a few months Pedro declared the country an independent kingdom, with himself as its first constitutional ruler, Emperor Pedro I (r. 1822–31).

The defeat of Napoleon resulted in the release of Ferdinand VII and his return to power in 1814, but he was unable to stem the tide of independence. By the middle of the century only Cuba and Puerto Rico remained of what had been Spain's great American empire, and the Spanish–American War of 1898 resulted in their loss – along with Guam and the Philippines in the Pacific – to the United States.

ABOVE *A political cartoon from c.1899 showing a Spanish general fleeing from Cuba with a bag of money. After the Spanish–American War, large sums of capital held in Cuba were brought home, benefitting the Spanish economy and enabling major expansion of its industrial and financial sectors.*

OPPOSITE *The revolutionary campaigns of Simón Bolívar (1783–1830) won independence for vast territories, leading to the establishment of Venezuela, Colombia, Ecuador and Bolivia.*

At its high point in the second half of the 17th century the Mughal empire stretched across most of India and parts of modern Afghanistan and Pakistan. Like the Mongols from whom they claimed ancestry, the Mughals burst out of a small, remote kingdom and stormed into the surrounding region in an irresistible military fury. Like the Mongols, they employed shattering new military techniques to destroy their foes and harsh laws to maintain their rule – but the empire they eventually spread across most of the Indian subcontinent also brought a cultural, artistic and architectural flowering which lingers to this day.

INDIA AND THE MUGHAL EMPIRE
1526 – 1739

BABUR THE TIGER (r. 1526–30) succeeded to the throne of the Central Asian kingdom of Fergana, now in western Turkmenistan, when he was only 13 years old. He claimed descent both from Genghis Khan (r. 1206–27) and from Timur the Lame (r. 1369–1405), the 14th-century conqueror who ravaged much of Central Asia and left pyramids of skulls to establish his own fearsome reputation. By the time he inflicted a crushing defeat of the Afghan ruler of northern India, Sultan Ibrahim Lodi (r. 1517–26), at the first Battle of Panipat in 1526, Babur was in his forties. The victory came only after he had been driven out of his homeland by Uzbek tribesmen. First he conquered Kabul in Afghanistan and then made four unsuccessful crossings of the River Indus before succeeding at the fifth attempt to draw the sultan's troops into battle. The weapons he brought included mobile artillery – this was the first time the sultan's forces had seen the awesome power of gunpowder on the battlefield.

MILITARY CAMPAIGNS
Within a year of his success at Panipat, Babur's forces – again heavily outnumbered – had defeated the Rajput army of Rana Sanga (r. 1509–27) of Mewar at the Battle of Khanwa. Two years later at Ghaghra in present-day Uttar Pradesh, they overcame the armies of Mahmud Lodi, the brother of the defeated Sultan Ibrahim. Once more, it was the Mughals' use of gunpowder that was decisive.

LEFT *With the accession of Akbar in 1556, the Mughal empire underwent a period of rapid military expansion. This miniature (c.1590) by Tutsi the Elder shows the Battle of Bundi in Rajasthan in 1577.*

But Babur lived only four years after his triumph at Panipat. The Rajput and Afghan relatives of Sultan Lodi had not abandoned their hopes of recapturing their possessions, and Babur's son, Humayun (r. 1530–40; 1555–6), was plagued from the start of his reign by attacks from outside, and also from within by disputes with his brothers over the succession. In 1540, at the Battle of Kanauj, he was defeated by a former adherent of Babur, the Afghan leader Sher Shah Suri (r. 1540–5), who ruled in Bihar. Humayun was forced to flee north to take refuge in Persia.

Sher Shah Suri died five years later, but during his time in power he began to establish an imperial administrative framework for the empire he had seized. Humayun, meanwhile, married a Persian wife and immersed himself in the art and culture of the Safavid court. Both developments were to have a deep and lasting influence on the future of the Mughal empire.

RETURN OF THE MUGHALS

When Sher Shah Suri's son died eight years after succeeding to his father's throne, there was chaos across the former Mughal empire, with individual cities trying to claim their independence and three rival leaders marching on Delhi to try to seize control. Humayun's army marched back across the Punjab to find virtually no resistance, and on 23 July, 1555, 15 years after his flight north, Babur's son once more sat on the imperial throne.

Barely seven months later, though, Humayun died after falling on stone stairs in his palace. His 13-year-old son Akbar (r. 1556–1605) was crowned as his successor, with Bairam Khan (d.1561), the military leader who had commanded Humayun's forces on his return from exile, as his regent. Bairam Khan's strong leadership in the early years of his reign enabled the young Akbar to start a programme of renewed military expansion. The Rajput relatives of Sher Shah Suri continued with occasional campaigns against him, but after defeating them first at the second Battle of Panipat in 1556 and then at the Battle of Haldighat in 1576, Akbar embarked on a series of campaigns that eventually pushed the boundaries of the empire to Kabul in the northwest, Kashmir in the north, Bengal in the east and as far as the Narmada river in central India.

Militarily secure, he instigated a policy of reconciliation and assimilation of the Hindu majority in his lands – most significantly, abolishing the *jizya*, or poll tax, which had been levied on non-Muslims since Babur's day. He also began building on the administrative reforms that had originally been instituted by Sher Shah Suri, appointing zamindars to collect local taxes on his behalf, keeping a proportion as their payment. Aristocratic mansabdars, who paid direct allegiance to the emperor, were responsible for raising troops in return for the right to levy taxes on jagirs, or villages. In 1571, Akbar began the construction of the new city he intended to make his imperial capital, close to Agra, constructed from local red sandstone. It was given the Persian name Fathabad, or 'City of Victory'. The city was Akbar's principal residence for 14 years, but was then suddenly abandoned, possibly because of the lack of an adequate water supply, and the capital was moved first to Lahore and then back to Agra.

Akbar's reign lasted for 49 years, and it saw the Mughal court established as a cultural and intellectual centre that far outshone any of the great capitals of Europe of the same period. His library brought together books in Persian, Hindi, Arabic, Greek and English, and scholars from the great cities of India and Persia. Although Akbar remained firmly committed to his mystic and inclusive form of Islam, he encouraged religious and philosophical debate.

GRANDEUR AND DECLINE

Akbar's son, Salim (r. 1605–27), succeeded his father in 1605, with the title Jahangir, or 'Conqueror of the World'. Jahangir married a Persian princess, Mehrunissa, to whom he gave the name Nur Jahan, or 'Light of the World'. She was his 20th wife but, under her influence, the Persian culture of the court intensified and spread through the empire. Persian poets, scholars, artists and philosophers thronged the palace in what became a highpoint of Mughal culture. It is also possible, though, to see in the growth of corrupt, non-productive court officials the early signs of the weakening of the empire. The lean, efficient military strength that had characterized the early days of Mughal rule was slowly ebbing away.

This gradual decline continued under Jahangir's son, Shahjahan (r. 1627–58). Military operations to conquer the Deccan to the south and the northwestern lands beyond the Khyber Pass led to huge increases in taxation, while the economic problems of Shahjahan's treasury

ABOVE *18th-century painting depicting Timur, Babur and Humayun. Babur and his son Humayun, the first rulers of the Mughal empire, were said to descend from Timur.*

LEFT *By the time of Babur's death in 1530, the Mughals had established one of the largest empires in the world, extending from the Deccan plateau in the south to Turkestan in the north.*

THE TAJ MAHAL

The Taj Mahal was built by Shahjahan (r. 1628–58) on the southern bank of the Jumna river to house a mausoleum for his wife, Mumtaz Mahal, who died in 1631.

Skilled artists, masons and engineers from India, Persia, the Ottoman empire and Europe led a team of more than 20,000 workers who were employed in its construction, which took over 20 years and cost around five million rupees.

The white marble mausoleum itself stands on a 7-metre- (23-ft-) high plinth, its 73-metre (240-ft) central dome shimmering in the sun or moon, with four graceful minarets around it. Inside, in an octagonal marble chamber decorated with low relief carvings and mosaics, are memorials to Shahjahan and Mumtaz Mahal.

On either side of the mausoleum stand two identical buildings. One houses a mosque, while the other was designed as a *jawab*, or 'answer' – simply to provide balance and symmetry. Entrance to the complex is through a magnificent red sandstone gateway, embellished with intricate calligraphy spelling out verses from the Koran.

Shahjahan is supposed to have planned a similar mausoleum for himself on the opposite bank of the river, but he was imprisoned for the last eight years of his life in the nearby Agra Fort. From his prison window, he could see the great creation of his life – a monument today not just to Mumtaz Mahal, but to Shahjahan himself and to the flowering of the whole Mughal empire.

The Taj Mahal blends Indian, Persian and Islamic styles in one of the finest examples of Mughal architecture.

were intensified by his grandiose building schemes. The restrained, dignified red sandstone constructions of Akbar's reign were demolished and replaced with glittering marble: this was the age of the Taj Mahal, India's greatest monument to Mughal ostentation, and of the legendary Peacock Throne, encrusted with pearls, rubies and emeralds. Military adventures in the far reaches of the empire, and architectural adventures at home were draining the imperial coffers, and by the time Shahjahan's son Aurangzeb (r. 1658–1707) took over from his sickly father in 1658, the empire was massively in debt.

While Babur, 130 years before, had fought with the most modern and terrifying equipment, the weapons that the Mughals carried in the mid-17th century were outdated and inefficient. Like the armies of Sultan Ibrahim that Babur had conquered, the Mughals now relied on overwhelming numerical superiority – a policy that was unsuited to dealing with the rash of local uprisings and revolts during Aurangzeb's reign.

DISAFFECTION BEGINS TO GROW

His grandfather, Jahangir, had abandoned the traditional policy of religious tolerance in the empire, and in 1679 Aurangzeb reintroduced the hated *jizya* tax on non-Muslims that Akbar had abolished more than 100 years before. Islamic law, or shari'a, was imposed across his lands: representational art, such as the intricate Persian-style miniatures that had been such a feature of earlier Mughal courts, were forbidden, and Hindu shrines and temples were systematically desecrated. By now the empire had reached its greatest size – but many of its Hindu subjects were disaffected and angry, its treasury depleted and its enemies growing bolder.

In 1672, Pashtun tribesmen in the northwest surrounded and butchered a Mughal army that had been sent to reassert Aurangzeb's authority, while in Punjab Sikhs rose up in protest at attempts to force their conversion to Islam. Further south, the Marathas were not content to accept Mughal rule, and a series of bitter battles began in 1681 that later became known as the War of 27 Years. The ageing emperor was losing his grip. By the time the war ended in 1707, Aurangzeb had died at the age of 90, Hindu revolts were continuing across India and the Mughals were in retreat.

A CRUMBLING EMPIRE

Aurangzeb is remembered as the last of the great Mughals. The invasion of Delhi by Persian and Afghan armies in 1739, when the Peacock Throne and many of the other great treasures of the Mughal court were seized as the Persian soldiers slaughtered tens of thousands of the city's inhabitants, was one more step in the collapse. In the anarchy that followed, the British East India Company was finally able to extend its influence across the subcontinent.

ABOVE *Shahjahan's reign was considered to be the golden age of the Mughal empire. He is shown here on horseback, in an illustration from c.1628–58.*

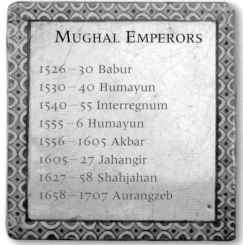

MUGHAL EMPERORS

1526–30 Babur
1530–40 Humayun
1540–55 Interregnum
1555–6 Humayun
1556–1605 Akbar
1605–27 Jahangir
1627–58 Shahjahan
1658–1707 Aurangzeb

The British empire started in the 16th century almost by chance, scrabbled together by trading companies and wealthy magnates seeking profit rather than imperial power, and by refugees looking for a new beginning. But by the end of the 19th century it covered about a quarter of the world's surface and ruled around a quarter of its population. Movements by former colonies for independence and self-rule led to the founding of the British Commonwealth of Nations in the early part of the 20th century. Today the Commonwealth – an association of 53 independent nation-states – remains like a ghost of empire which includes some two billion people, or around one-third of the world's population.

The BRITISH EMPIRE

1584–1997

ENGLAND'S FIRST MAJOR COLONIES WERE IN NORTH AMERICA, where the original settlers started from scratch, pushing the Native Americans westwards as they carved out farms and homesteads for themselves. Others joined them to escape religious persecution in Europe, and together they painstakingly built a new nation in the New World. The so-called second empire was based in India where, by contrast, British arrivals found an established and prosperous civilization with which to trade. Gradually, by means of diplomacy and military force, they became the dominant power on the subcontinent. These two very different types of colonies, one establishing itself in a largely unsettled land, the other developing a trading relationship with a flourishing and powerful nation, provided two contrasting models on which the British empire was eventually built.

THE BEGINNINGS OF EMPIRE IN AMERICA

The England of Elizabeth I (r. 1558–1603) lacked both the money and power to match the Spanish and Portuguese in the Americas and the east, but had the seamen and the ambition to mount raids on their overseas settlements and attack their shipping.

LEFT An Allegory of the British Empire, *painted in 1901 by Arthur Drummond (1871–1951), shows all nations under British sovereignty paying homage to Queen Victoria.*

They were mostly pirates, not pioneers – the famous circumnavigation of the globe by Francis Drake (*c*.1540–96) was more an extended series of ruthless attacks on settlements and ships than a voyage of exploration. What mattered was that it paid its investors, including Queen Elizabeth, dividends of some 4700 percent. An early attempt by Walter Raleigh (*c*.1552–1618) to establish a settlement at Roanoke Island, off the coast of what is now North Carolina, ended in disaster when the settlers either starved or were killed by Native American tribesmen. When a supply ship arrived at the settlement in 1590, the 117 original pioneers of the first settlement of the future British empire had vanished.

A few people talked about empire at Elizabeth's court – the astronomer, occultist and geographer John Dee (1527–1608) is said to have been the first person to coin the term 'British empire' – but the queen herself was more interested in quick profits than in long-term settlements. It was not until the reign of James I (r. Scotland 1567–1625; England and Ireland 1603–25) that any concerted efforts at establishing overseas possessions were made. In 1607, James granted a Royal Charter to the Virginia Company to launch a colony at Jamestown on Chesapeake Bay in present-day Virginia, in the hope that they would find gold in the same way that the Spanish explorers had done in the south. They were disappointed, but in starting the cultivation and export of tobacco, they were establishing a pattern of colonial trade that would remain throughout the empire for 350 years. The colonists grew and harvested the crop, English vessels shipped it home, English merchants sold it and the English government took its share through import duties.

THE PILGRIM FATHERS

Elsewhere along the Atlantic seaboard of North America, other groups of settlers were putting down roots too, driven not so much by the urge to profit by trade as by the desire to escape religious persecution at home. Puritans in England felt that King James was leaning towards Catholic Spain, and left first for Protestant Holland and then for the New World.

In 1621, the Pilgrim Fathers arrived in Massachusetts Bay on board the *Mayflower*, to form a new community that had no direct link with their old country. Within 30 years, new settlements had grown up along a 500-mile (800-km) stretch of the coast. Each one would have had little or no contact with the others, and the settlers would certainly not have thought of themselves as Americans, but from the moment they arrived there was a sense of separateness from England, a feeling that the New World would be somehow different from the old.

THE BRITISH IN INDIA

From the start, the growth in English overseas possessions was driven by trade.
In 1600, Queen Elizabeth had granted a charter to the newly formed East India
Company, giving it the monopoly of trade between England and the Spice
Islands of the East Indies. That trade was disappointing. The Dutch, who had
taken over control of the former Portuguese colonies, had established a trading
empire of their own and were highly efficient in keeping the English merchants
out, and the company was forced to concentrate on importing pepper from its
base at Surat in northwest India. There, the diplomat Thomas Roe (1581–1644)
established good relations with the court of the Mughal emperor Jahangir
(r. 1605–27) and built trading posts along the Indian coastline. These outposts
were protected by heavily armed English ships, and in turn provided a chain of
supply bases. As the foundations were being laid for an English empire in
America, so the East India Company, locked out of the Spice Island trade, was
making the first moves towards establishing English influence in India.

For decades it was exclusively a mercantile operation – the East India Company
was interested in trade, not territory – and although the Mughal empire was not
as powerful as it had once been, it remained too strong to challenge. The
English, like the Portuguese, the Dutch and the French, concentrated on
maintaining the small, self-contained coastal bases they had already established.

ABOVE *The British East India
Company set up trading stations
throughout India. The station
depicted here includes a church
residency and a warehouse.*

Then, in 1757, an attack on the trading post at Calcutta by the ruler of Bengal, Siraj ud-Dawla (r. 1756–7) caused the deaths of dozens of English prisoners, who suffocated in a tiny cell that became known as the Black Hole of Calcutta. An employee of the East India Company, Robert Clive (1725–74), led an army north to reassert the company's position. Victory over the Bengalis at the Battle of Plassey (1757) established the British as the authority behind the throne in Bengal as well as in their original power base of Madras, and led them inland from their coastal strongholds for the first time. While the settlers in America were driving out the original inhabitants of the lands they were taking over and establishing new communities of their own, the traders in India were taking over control of existing towns and villages, and imposing themselves as rulers. When, during the 1760s, the company decided to seize formal power in Bengal from its Indian nawab, it ruled over more people than the king of England himself.

SLAVES IN THE SERVICE OF SUGAR

Britain was pushing out its boundaries in other directions as well. In 1660, Charles I (r. 1625–49) granted a charter to the Royal Adventurers into Africa to import ivory and gold from Guinea in West Africa. But this trade was gradually superseded by the more profitable and morally questionable business of transporting slaves to the new sugar plantations in the West Indies. Other English companies had been doing this for at least 30 years, but the new society ran the slave trade on a different scale: within five years, it was making an estimated £100,000 a year from selling slaves bought from African rulers on the coasts of modern Guinea and Ghana. By the time it ceased trading in the early 1670s, transatlantic trade was one of the most profitable that British ships could engage in, and the writing began of one of the most shameful chapters in the story of the British empire. It was not until the early 19th century that Britain took a lead in abolishing the trade in slaves.

EUROPEAN WARS

England and Scotland had shared a monarch since James VI of Scotland had succeeded Elizabeth I in 1603 as James I of England; but it was only in 1707, following a disastrous attempt to establish a Scottish colony on the Isthmus of Panama (which virtually bankrupted the Scottish state), that the two governments were formally united by an Act of Union. The growing number of foreign settlements continued to be ruled under English rather than Scots law, but from that time on it is possible to think of a growing British, rather than a purely English, empire.

Wars in Europe, like politics, always had a strong effect on the settlements abroad. The start of the English Civil War (1642–51) between Charles I and his parliament had seen the level of control that England tried to assert over the American settlements diminish, and fighting between the English and the Dutch in the 1660s led to the capture of New Amsterdam, later renamed New York. Then, throughout the 18th century, England was at war in Europe.

In 1701, the War of the Spanish Succession started, in which England and its allies in Holland and the Holy Roman Empire tried to check French expansion by preventing a Frenchman from succeeding to the throne of Spain. The Treaty of Utrecht, which ended the war in 1713, left the Bourbon Philip, duke of Anjou as King Philip V of Spain (r. 1700–46), but brought the British big territorial gains in Canada, along with the possession of Gibraltar and the Mediterranean island of Minorca, and trading rights in Spain's South American colonies.

ABOVE *This undated illustration shows Britannia, a symbol of Great Britain for over 2000 years. She was often depicted as ruler of the seas of the British empire.*

DISPUTES OVER SETTLEMENTS

In theory at least, the treaty left France and England at peace – but in northern America, constant skirmishes continued over the borders between their respective settlements. There were also tensions with the Spanish over English trade with their colonies, and in 1739 war broke out again, spilling over into a wider European conflict concerning the succession to the Habsburg Emperor Charles VI (r. 1711–40). This was the time at which, responding to the nation's jingoistic fervour and hoping to curry favour with the new king, George I (r. 1714–27), the Scottish poet James Thomson (1700–48) wrote 'Rule Britannia'. In a way, it was the start of the first 'world war': for the first time, conflict in Europe extended to three continents, with French and British forces fighting for the next ten years both in America and India, where the French seized the East India Company's base at Madras.

The war in Europe paused in 1748, but within six years the French and British were fighting again in North America over who should control the vast hinterland of the continent between the Great Lakes and the Gulf of Mexico. In 1756, the Seven Years' War started in Europe, involving all the major European

powers in a continuing battle for supremacy in the Old World. Three years later, the French suffered catastrophic setbacks both in Europe and the Americas. First their forces were defeated at Minden, in Germany, and then, less than two months later, news came that troops led by General James Wolfe (1727–59) had scaled the Heights of Abraham to drive the French out of their Canadian stronghold at Quebec.

The Treaty of Paris, which ended the war in 1763, formalized British possession of what had been called New France, stretching across Eastern Canada, and also added the former Spanish territory of Florida to its colonies further south. In India the treaty returned the city of Pondicherry, which had been captured by British forces in 1761, to the French – but the war had already underlined Britain's dominant position in the subcontinent. Britain's empire, both in North America and in India, seemed to be at the peak of its power.

EMERGENCE OF A NEW NATION

The war that appeared to have entrenched British power had in fact created the conditions for Britain's first great imperial setback. Victory in 1763 would set the scene for defeat in 1781, the end of British rule in America and the establishment of the United States of America.

The Seven Years' War had to be paid for, and the government in London saw no reason why the American settlers should not pay a share. New taxes and restrictions on trade were imposed. Faced with a common threat, the colonists began to protest vigorously against the idea of direct or indirect taxation from Westminster. The dispute was damaging Britain's other imperial possessions – tea sales by the East India Company in America collapsed from over 136,000 kilograms (300,000 lb) a year to around 227 kilograms (500 lb).

THE BOSTON TEA PARTY

The company was unable to pay its taxes, and the government agreed to allow it to sell tea direct to the colonists without paying the tariff, so that it could undercut domestic merchants and smugglers alike. The fury in the port of Boston, where the East India Company ships were stormed and the tea hurled overboard, was originally criticized strongly among American settlers as well as in London – but the response from Britain, with its heavy-handed assertion of power, brought the demonstrators widespread support.

So the famous Boston Tea Party was, ironically, not so much about taxation imposed from London as about the high-handed sudden relaxation of tariffs by the imperial government. But there were other

1776 — WHO WAS FIGHTING?

British writers generally refer to the war that started in 1776 as the American War of Independence, while in the United States it is usually called the American Revolution. One other possibility, suggested by the numbers involved on each side, would be to think of it as the First American Civil War.

Most modern historians now believe that around 40 percent of the population of the 13 colonies involved in the conflict actively supported military action to end British rule, while some 15 percent remained loyal to King George.

Some 50,000 loyalists fought on the British side, including many black slaves who escaped from Southern plantations in response to a promise of freedom by the earl of Dunmore, the royal governor of Virginia. After the war, an estimated 70,000 loyalists – black and white – left the United States, mainly for Nova Scotia, the West Indies or Britain.

The Spirit of '76 *by Archibald M. Willard; a painting that instantly evokes the patriotism of the American War of Independence.*

issues too. After the peace with France in 1763, many of the settlers wanted to push further west. Until then, they had been deterred by the opposition of the French, who were unwilling to see British influence extended deeper into the continent, and now the army of King George also stepped in to prevent them. Worried that they could be drawn into a war against Native American peoples that might involve huge costs and very few possible gains, the British government stationed troops in the area west of the coastal settlements to prevent further expansion.

Rumours circulated that the British were aiming to establish a Catholic army from the French settlers under their rule in Canada, which might dominate the

American Protestants. Where once the fear of the French to the north had checked anti-British feelings, now it served to stoke the fires of revolt. On 4 July, 1776, the American colonies announced their independence from Britain. This Declaration of Independence changed everything: now the colonists, or many of them, certainly felt 'American'.

THE WAR OF INDEPENDENCE

An early British defeat, in which troops heading south from Montreal were forced to surrender at Saratoga in 1778, encouraged Britain's European rivals to offer what help they could to the Americans – French naval power was an important counter to the British warships, which would otherwise have enjoyed unchallenged control of the coastal cities. When General Charles Cornwallis (1738–1805) led his redcoats north through Georgia and the Carolinas, a French naval victory in the Battle of Chesapeake Bay (1781) cut them off from their naval support, and set the scene for victory by George Washington (1732–99) and the final British surrender at Yorktown – less than 30 miles (50 km) from Jamestown, where the original Virginia Company settlers had landed just 174 years earlier. A new nation was born, and the first stage of the British empire was over.

FORTRESS INDIA

BELOW Cartoon from c.1809 showing William Pitt and Napoleon Bonaparte dividing the globe between their two nations, after the signing of the Treaty of Amiens temporarily ended hostilities between the United Kingdom and France.

Within five years of his defeat at Yorktown, the British commander General Cornwallis was arriving in India as governor general, the first to be appointed by the government rather than the East India Company. The British were relieved that the loss of the American colonies had not jeopardized their position in what seemed at the time to be the infinitely more valuable empire in the east. There had been several French attempts to take advantage of Britain's preoccupations in America to increase their influence in the Indian Ocean, but the East India Company had strengthened its position by building alliances with local Indian rulers, partly through diplomacy and partly through military force.

Westminster, however, was no longer prepared to allow the company to operate with its old independence, and an act of parliament in 1784 gave the government explicit control over politics and foreign policy in India, with a governor general to represent its interests. Cornwallis' brief was to avoid military conflict and to see that the commercial empire in India ran efficiently. His time in India helped to restore his reputation after his defeat at Yorktown, and he was given the title of marquis in 1792 before returning to England the following year.

Europe, however, was convulsed by the French Revolution of 1789 and the start of another period of conflict. The government of William Pitt (1759–1806) declared war on France in 1793, and by the end of the decade, Napoleon Bonaparte (1769–1821) had emerged as the new French strongman, building a European empire of his own. Britain, at the heart of a series of European coalitions, remained at war (with two brief pauses) for the next 12 years.

After humiliation in America in 1781, Britain was only one of several European nations extending its power across the world; the remnants of its foreign possessions were matched by the trading empires of France, Portugal, Spain and Holland. Over the next three decades of conflict in Europe, however, all the other empires were lost, leaving the British supreme. The naval defeat of the French and Spanish at Trafalgar in 1805 not only gave Britain mastery over the French at sea, it also provided the basis for the growth of a new and powerful empire stretching around the world.

ABOVE *An 1875 depiction by maritime painter John Callow (1822–78) of the Battle of Trafalgar (1805). During this engagement, superior seamanship and fighting tactics saw the Royal Navy inflict a crushing defeat on a combined French and Spanish fleet.*

ADVANCING EASTWARD

Outside Europe, Pitt's main war aim was to seize the former Dutch East Indies possessions, which had come under French control with Napoleon's conquest of the Netherlands. British naval forces – now unchallenged around the world – had already given Britain control of Ceylon and the Cape of Good Hope, which effectively cut off communication between the East Indies and Europe.

In India, the threat of invasion by Napoleon's forces from their bridgehead in Egypt had galvanized the British government into action. A treaty signed in 1800 by the new governor general, Lord Wellesley (1760–1842), with the nizam of Hyderabad allowed the company to control the nizam's foreign policy. In return for British protection, the nizam agreed not to make alliances with any other rulers. It was a model for a series of political deals which secured the East India Company's position across nearly half of India.

Meanwhile, Wellesley's brother Arthur (1769–1852), the future victor at Waterloo and 1st duke of Wellington, had stormed the capital of Sultan Tipu of Mysore (r. 1782–99) at Seringapatam, after the sultan had incautiously expressed his support for the French. This British victory, in 1799, established another precedent: where diplomatic alliances could not be made, Arthur Wellesley was prepared to use the iron fist instead. Further military victories over the moribund Mughal empire extended his power towards Delhi, where the Great Mogul remained on his throne as little more than a puppet of the British.

By 1805, Britain was the unchallenged dominant force in India, and over the following years pressure increased on the East India Company to expand further. In 1819 the company signed a lease for the possession of Singapore, which secured the sea route between India and China. Then in the early 1820s, after border skirmishes in Bengal (modern Bangladesh) with the expanding Burmese kingdom, it started to acquire coastal land around the Irrawaddy Delta on the east side of the Bay of Bengal. The infamous Opium Wars (1839–42 and 1856–60), in which the company enforced its right to sell opium in China despite the opposition of the Chinese government, led to the Treaty of Nanking in 1842. This gave the company access to the markets in China, and also leased them a base at Hong Kong. Britain was establishing a network of naval bases from which its navy could, in Thomson's words of a century before, 'rule the waves'.

ON THE OTHER SIDE OF THE WORLD

Defeat in America had another effect on the British empire. The 13 colonies that had declared independence had been a useful place for the British government to send convicted criminals – a policy that had aroused considerable opposition in America during the 1770s – and the loss of the American possessions meant finding somewhere else for them to go.

In 1788, the First Fleet reached the eastern coast of Australia, the land that Captain James Cook (1728–79) had first charted more than 20 years before. It was a continent sparsely populated by 'aborigines', whose eventual fate would be similar to that of the Native Americans. The fleet carried around 780 convicts – pathfinders for some 160,000 involuntary immigrants, both men and women, over the next 80 years. Their average age was 26, and it is estimated that by 1831 almost three-quarters of the population of Australia and Van Diemen's Land, or Tasmania, were either serving convicts or the children of convicts. Even when they had completed their sentences, they were not allowed to return home: the British had found a new way of populating an empire.

FREE AUSTRALIAN SETTLEMENTS
In Australia, new settlements grew up around Melbourne and in South Australia, based on freed ex-convicts and people who had chosen to travel to Australia, rather than prisoners on transport ships. Other settlers moved on again, to the fertile and attractive islands of New Zealand to the east. In 1840, worried about the possibility of other European nations taking control, the British government signed the Treaty of Waitangi with a group of Maori leaders on North Island. In theory, at least, it gave the native New Zealanders the rights of British citizens in return for accepting British sovereignty and agreeing to sell land only to the British government. How well it worked and to what extent the Maori were cheated of their land by unscrupulous speculators remain controversial, but it provided a blueprint for New Zealand as another colony in the growing British empire.

BELOW *Britain discovered a different way of colonizing its empire by deporting convicts to their new – and permanent – home in Australia.*

DIVIDE-AND-RULE TACTICS

By 1850, Britain had the biggest and most varied empire the world had ever seen, based largely on its unchallenged control of the seas. In India, still the heart of the empire, a new generation of imperial administrators began drawing the different states into a single unified nation, aided by the development of a national railway network and the setting up of an all-India postal service on the model of the Penny Post which had just been established in Britain. But local, regional and linguistic loyalties remained strong, and when what the British called the 'Indian Mutiny' broke out in 1857 – sparked by rumours that the cartridges supplied to Indian soldiers were greased with a mixture of pork and beef fat, thus offending both Muslims and Hindus – the British were able to recruit soldiers from Bengal and Punjab to help them put it down. This tactic of 'divide and rule' was used throughout the history of Britain's relations with the native populations of its empire all over the world, along with the acceptance of local dignitaries like the Indian nawabs into the imperial power structure. These methods of asserting control were often coupled with the use of vastly superior military technology and ruthless slaughter.

The Indian Rebellion – which involved much more of the population than the word 'mutiny' suggests – shocked the British into establishing a more efficient administration, with a viceroy to represent the queen and report directly to a secretary of state in London. Earlier attempts to increase direct control over the semi-independent rulers of the various Indian kingdoms were quietly

BELOW At its peak, just after the First World War, it was literally true that the 'sun never set' on the British empire, as at any moment it was daylight somewhere in its far-reaching dominions.

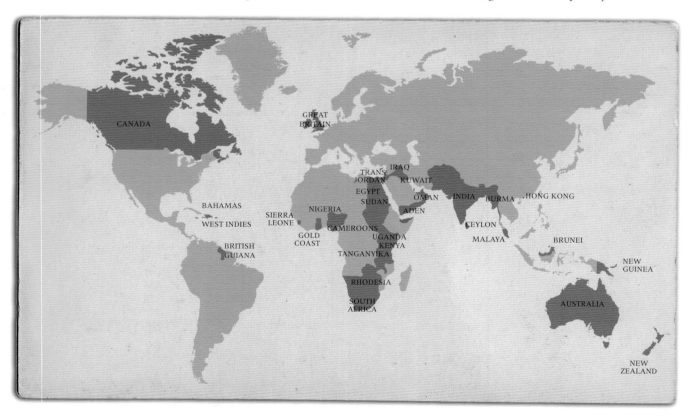

abandoned. In India and elsewhere, the next 20 years saw growing peace and prosperity. Parliaments were established in most of the new colonies – although the process was held up in Australia by the fear of a 'convict government' – and the expansion of this new British empire seemed to have come to a halt.

'A FIT OF ABSENCE OF MIND'

The historian Sir John Seeley (1834– 95) famously suggested in a lecture in 1883 that the British *'seem, as it were, to have conquered and peopled half the world in a fit of absence of mind'*. Events in Africa in the years immediately after his observation showed that they were still capable of doing exactly that.

There had been growing anxiety about the expense of supporting the existing colonies and the danger that they might drag Britain into conflict with other European powers – but in the late 1880s, separate trading companies in East, West and South Africa were receiving charters and starting to do the job of empire-building on their own account.

The government could not keep the various companies at arm's length. First, the Imperial British East Africa Company, facing bankruptcy, threatened to pull out from its area of influence deep within Uganda, and the government was forced to declare a protectorate in order to avoid the humiliation of withdrawal. Then in the south, the discovery of gold in the Boer territory of Transvaal encouraged the businessman, politician and adventurer Cecil Rhodes (1853–1902) to look for new deposits in the British South Africa Company's area further north. This venture, along with an abortive attempt to topple the Transvaal government in 1895 – the Jameson Raid – threatened to involve the British government in South Africa as well. And, in West Africa, the threat of clashes between the agents of the Royal Niger Company and their French rivals in the region led the government to take over the administration of what became Nigeria. As the century drew to a close, Britain found itself with the beginnings of an African empire which it had acquired almost while its back was turned.

WAR ON THE VELDT

There was a price to pay. The Transvaal had been established as a homeland by the Boers, Afrikaner farmers of Dutch origin, who left the Cape earlier in the century rather than accept British rule, and in particular the emancipation of

ABOVE *Attack by the Indian mutineers on the Redan Battery at Lucknow on 30 July, 1857. One of their leaders, waving his sword, shouted 'Come on, my braves'.*

slaves. The Great Trek of the 1830s and 1840s had taken thousands of them north of the Vaal river to carve out their own land against the bitter opposition of the Zulu tribes of the area.

In 1877, when the settlers had run into financial difficulties, an uneasy union had been declared with the British at Cape Colony. Shortly after that, they had seen Zulu tribesmen inflict damaging defeats on the British forces, and then watched as the British finally defeated the Zulus, effectively disarming the biggest threat faced by the Dutch settlers. After a brief war in which the lightly armed Boer guerrillas forced the British to restore their self-government under the sketchy and ill-defined authority of the crown, the two republics of Transvaal and Orange Free State had been given authority to run their own affairs again. To add to the Boers' new-found self-confidence, the discovery of gold had invigorated the local economy after its initial difficulties so that it promised to overtake that of Cape Colony.

PORTENTS OF WAR

To what extent the British government was involved in the Jameson Raid is still a matter for argument, but it had left the Boers deeply distrustful of British intentions. By the end of 1899, the British and the Boer settlers were at war in what proved to be the sternest test the empire had faced since the American War of Independence more than a century earlier.

The arrival of reinforcements from London enabled British guns and discipline to defeat the main Afrikaner army, but instead of meekly surrendering, the Boers then mounted a long and highly effective guerrilla war. It was the first time British soldiers had faced such a campaign, and they sustained heavy losses over

BELOW *A Boer guerilla commando near Ladysmith, c.1900. The Boers lost two independent republics to the British empire during a protracted guerrilla war.*

the next two years, before the war ended with the Treaty of Vereeniging. The Transvaal and Orange Free State republics became self-governing colonies within the British empire, and in 1910 the Union of South Africa was declared, bringing them together with the existing British colonies of the Cape and Natal.

THE LONG GOODBYE

In some respects, the empire was stronger in the aftermath of the Boer War than it had ever been. Troops to support the British effort had come from the self-governing colonies of Australia, New Zealand and Canada, where many people still thought of themselves as British; after the conflict, pro-British Boers rapidly gained influence in the new Union of South Africa; and in India there was widespread personal loyalty towards Queen Victoria (r. 1837–1901) as empress – a title she had taken in 1877. The scramble for Africa was complete, with virtually the entire continent now divided between half a dozen European powers. In the first 12 years of the new century, emigration from Britain to the colonies trebled, far outstripping that to the United States – but it is possible to see the beginnings of the long process of Britain's disengagement from empire in the Treaty of Vereeniging.

The cracks were beginning to show. The self-governing colonies – renamed dominions in 1907 – wanted to see the introduction of tariffs to protect their farmers, a policy that would have led to higher food prices for British electors, and which was roundly rejected at the polls in a Liberal landslide in the election of 1906. The racist attitudes inherent in the British vision of the future – the dominions were inhabited by whites, the colonies by a large black or Asian majority – were largely unacknowledged in Britain, although they caused angry protests in India and

ABOVE *As commemorated in this postcard, British colonies presented a united front during the First World War, with the dominions providing troops to fight for Great Britain.*

elsewhere. For all the personal loyalty to Queen Victoria in India, there was new growth of national feeling, with the development of separate Hindu and Muslim campaigns in the Congress and the Muslim League. It was becoming clear that India would at least have to move towards dominion status: the traditional certainties of the empire – that the British idea of civilization could be exported around the world, supported by unchallengeable military power – were being called into question.

A WORLD WAR AND THE LEAGUE OF NATIONS

With the outbreak of the First World War (1914–18), the old loyalties were on parade again, with the dominions sending troops around the world to fight for the mother-country. But relationships were subtly changing: at the Versailles peace conference at the end of the war, representatives of the dominions and India sat as a British empire delegation but, significantly, they each added their own signatures to the treaty, and they each became separate members of the new League of Nations that was established. It was a tacit acceptance that they had voices of their own. During the 1920s, the term Commonwealth of Nations, rather than British empire, began increasingly to be used in recognition of their role, as the government in Westminster put it, as 'autonomous communities within the British empire'.

The aftermath of the war saw the last big expansion of the empire. The former Ottoman empire possessions of Palestine and Iraq came under British rule through League of Nations mandates, along with the former German colonies of Tanganyika (now united with Zanzibar as Tanzania), Southwest Africa (now Namibia) and New Guinea. But the weakness of the whole structure of empire was rapidly becoming apparent.

Nationalist feelings in India were gathering momentum, helped by blunders such as the Amritsar Massacre of 1919, in which a British general gave the order to fire on an unarmed crowd, killing nearly 400 people, and by the non-violent tactics of M.K. Gandhi (1869–1948) (see Gandhi and Civil Disobedience, opposite). By 1929, Gandhi and his followers were no longer satisfied with vague promises about dominion status that carried no firm timetable.

In Africa, there seemed to be little, if any, movement towards independence, and still less towards any form of democracy. The government in London kept its involvement and its financial support to a minimum – a policy which often led to grinding poverty among the native populations. There certainly seemed to be no reason during the 1930s to expect any sudden change – but the start of the Second World War at the end of the decade provided a much quicker death blow to the British empire than anyone had expected.

THE FINAL YEARS

To the Britons who lived through it, it was the war in Europe that seemed to threaten Britain's existence. If Germany's annexation of the Sudetenland in 1938 had been to Prime Minister Neville Chamberlain (1869–1940) *'a quarrel in a faraway country between people of whom we know nothing'*, then the fighting in Southeast Asia took place in a place even further away, and involved people about whom the British knew even less. But that was the war that would be largely responsible for the end of Britain's empire.

The empire and Commonwealth seemed to be united again. Once again, in 1939, soldiers from the colonies and dominions fought in every theatre of the war. However, British possessions in Hong Kong, Malaya, Singapore, Burma and Borneo rapidly fell to the Japanese. The loss of Singapore, in particular, damaged British credibility in Australia, where it seemed to show that the empire was no longer capable of providing protection against military threats, and also in India, where it was taken as an indication of the imperial power's new weakness.

ABOVE *Led by General Edmund Allenby, British forces captured Jerusalem from Turkey in 1917, during the final expansion of the empire.*

GANDHI AND CIVIL DISOBEDIENCE

Mohandas Karamchand Gandhi (1869–1948) – known as Mahatma Gandhi, or Gandhi the Great Soul – was the inspiration behind *satyagraha*, the principle of non-violent resistance. As leader of the National Congress, he led nationwide campaigns for the liberation of women, the alleviation of poverty and an end to the caste system, and for independence from British rule.

A devout Hindu and vegetarian, Gandhi trained in England as a lawyer, and in 1891 went to work in South Africa, where he started a campaign against a new bill that would deprive Indians of the vote. He remained in South Africa for 20 years, campaigning against discriminatory legislation and helping the British in the Boer War by raising an Indian ambulance corps. On his return to India in 1914, he became increasingly influential in the Congress movement, and was jailed for two years because of his campaign of non-violent non-cooperation. On his release, he started a fast to force the warring Muslim and Hindu communities to cease violence, and led a 200-mile (320-km) march to the sea to collect salt in defiance of British laws and taxes. He was imprisoned several times but maintained his commitment to non-violence, and in 1946 was involved in the talks which finally led to Indian independence. Gandhi, who was bitterly disappointed that independence was accompanied by the partition of India and Pakistan, was assassinated in Delhi by a Hindu fanatic two years later.

Mahatma Gandhi addressing some of his thousands of supporters. The implicit faith of his followers is reflected in the faces of those who listen to his every word.

'QUIT INDIA!'

An attempt to buy off renewed demands from India for a commitment to independence after the war with the firm offer of dominion status were no longer enough, and the British authorities responded to a growing 'Quit India' campaign with a round of arrests and imprisonments. Similar tactics were employed in Egypt and in Iraq, where a pro-German rebellion had to be put down. Britain managed to hold its imperial possessions together through the war, but there was little prospect of being able to do so once peace came.

Victory in 1945 brought the colonies in Asia and the Pacific back to their pre-war European rulers, but not for long. The British found their hold on Malaya, Singapore, Burma and Borneo irrevocably weakened.

Britain had been virtually bankrupted by the war, and the next 25 years saw an undignified scramble out of the imperial connections in Southeast Asia, the Indian subcontinent and Africa. The whole process was faster than British administrators had expected, and a lot less peaceful and orderly than they had hoped. The biggest retreat, from India, came with tragic haste: with law and order rapidly breaking down, the viceroy warned the government that the British community should be prepared to leave. He was replaced by Lord Mountbatten (1900–79) in February 1947, with a brief to arrange for full British disengagement within 15 months. In the face of rising violence, he brought even that tight deadline forward, declaring Indian independence on 15 August, 1947. Hundreds of thousands of people died in ethnic and sectarian violence as they struggled to cross the demarcation lines that had been decreed between Muslim Pakistan and Hindu India.

STRENGTHENING OF COMMONWEALTH TIES

But if the withdrawal was a human disaster on the ground, it was counted a diplomatic success in London. Both India and Pakistan opted to join the Commonwealth, setting a precedent for the other former colonies. Burma chose to become a republic with no ties to Britain or the other former colonies, but most of the other states that achieved independence over the next 20 years maintained their links through the Commonwealth. There were conflicts in several places – notably Malaya and Kenya – and the racial policies of South Africa and Rhodesia (modern Zimbabwe) brought severe complications to the process of withdrawal, but the trend of British policy was clear.

By the time Prime Minister Harold Macmillan (1894–1986) made his famous speech about a 'wind of change' sweeping through Africa in 1960, that wind had already blown away many of the old trappings of colonialism. Most of the West Indies possessions became independent nations in their own right, after the failure of the West Indies Federation in 1962. Egypt – occupied by Britain in 1882, but formally independent since 1922 – nationalized the Suez Canal in

BELOW *The Egyptian president Gamal Nasser is cheered by a huge crowd on his arrival back in Cairo from Alexandria, where he announced he had taken over the Suez Canal Company.*

1956. The crisis that followed, when Britain was forced by American political and economic pressure to abandon a clumsy attempt to seize back control, was a brutal reminder of the new realities of post-war power. In 1971, British bases in Malaysia, Singapore and Aden were closed as the troops came home. By the time Hong Kong was handed back to China at the expiry of its lease in 1997, the British empire was little more than a memory.

Today, 14 tiny islands and other isolated communities scattered around the world are all that remain – places such as the Falkland Islands in the South Atlantic, the Pitcairn Islands in the Pacific and Gibraltar in the Mediterranean, where for various reasons the local people do not want independence. They are known as British Overseas Territories. There is also the Commonwealth of Nations, in which the United Kingdom, 52 former British colonies and Mozambique, formerly ruled by Portugal, are linked as a voluntary association of independent states. The greatest legacy of the 300 years of imperial rule is undoubtedly the English language, spread around the world by the expansion of the empire, and now widely accepted as an international means of communication.

BRITISH RULERS

Tudors (English ruler)
1558 – 1603 Elizabeth I

Stuarts
1603 – 25 James I
1625 – 49 Charles I

Commonwealth
1649 – 58 Oliver Cromwell
1658 – 9 Richard Cromwell

Stuarts (restored)
1660 – 85 Charles II
1685 – 8 James II
1689 – 1702 William III (of Orange) and Mary II (d.1694)
1702 – 14 Anne

Hanover
1714 – 27 George I
1727 – 60 George II
1760 – 1820 George III
1820 – 30 George IV
1830 – 7 William IV
1837 – 1901 Victoria (declared empress of India 1877)

Saxe-Coburg-Gotha
1901 – 10 Edward VII (also emperor of India)

Windsor
1910 – 36 George V (also emperor of India)
1936 Edward VIII (also emperor of India)
1936 – 52 George VI (emperor of India to 1947)
1952 – present Elizabeth II (also head of the Commonwealth)

The empire of Napoleon Bonaparte was created by war, grew through war and was destroyed by war. During 11 years of existence, it experienced only a few months of uneasy peace, but at its peak it controlled much of Germany, Italy, Spain and the Duchy of Warsaw – all of which were sacrificed at Napoleon's final defeat at Waterloo in 1815. However, his domestic reforms proved longer-lasting, and some 20 years after his death, the defeated, deserted emperor became the greatest national hero of the French state, interred in a magnificent tomb at Les Invalides, Paris.

THE NAPOLEONIC EMPIRE
1804–1815

NAPOLEON BONAPARTE (1769–1821), the creator of France's first empire, was the son of a Corsican lawyer. He was educated at France's military academy in Paris and joined the army shortly before the upheaval of the French Revolution in 1789. Napoleon's brilliant early military career in defence of the revolution – rising to brigadier general and Commandant of French Artillery in Italy at the age of 24 – quickly attracted the attention of the leading revolutionary figure Maximilien de Robespierre (1758–94) in Paris. But with the fall and execution of Robespierre, Napoleon himself was arrested and charged with conspiracy and treason in 1794. He was freed after a few weeks, but not restored to his command, and was considering offering his military services to the Ottoman sultan in Turkey when he was summoned back to Paris by the ruling National Convention to put down a royalist rebellion a few months later.

In the aftermath of this attempted rebellion, the Convention was replaced by a Directory, in which a five-strong executive ruled the country, with a two-chamber parliament. Success against the rebels brought Napoleon promotion first to the command of France's Army of the Interior, and then to the command of the army in Italy, where his energetic campaigning brought about the annexation of Nice and Savoy and the humiliating defeat of Austria. By now, Napoleon was a military hero – but he was also taking a close interest in domestic politics, and involved himself in a

LEFT *While Napoleon I will forever be remembered for his defeat at Waterloo as much as for his empire, the civil code that he constructed remains the basis of legal systems throughout the world today.*

TIMELINE

1789 Start of the French Revolution

1793 At the age of 24, Napoleon is promoted to brigadier general; the First Coalition of European nations is established, in an attempt to contain Revolutionary France

1794 Napoleon is charged with treason, but freed within a few weeks

1795 Leaders in the ruling National Convention instruct Napoleon to put down a royalist revolt in Paris

1796 Napoleon is appointed commander-in-chief of the French army in Italy; the same year he achieves the annexation of Nice and Savoy and continues the war on Austria

1797 A *coup d'état* eliminates royalist supporters from the Directory

1798 French attempts to block Britain's trade route to India defeated at the Battle of the Nile

1799 Coup du 18 Brumaire forces resignation of the Directory leaders and the creation of a Consulate

1800 Napoleon's position as First Consul formally approved; Battle of Marengo results in defeat of Austrian forces and French control of northern Italy

1802 Peace of Amiens sees French as the dominant nation in continental Europe; Napoleon is granted the title First Consul for life

continued

coup d'état in 1797, which finally destroyed royalist influence in the Directory and made him the dominant force in government.

With virtually the whole of Europe dedicated to toppling the revolutionary government, Napoleon masterminded a campaign to seize Turkey in an attempt to strike at Britain's all-important trade route to India. This bold stroke was initially successful, until Admiral Horatio Nelson (1758–1805) defeated the French fleet at the Battle of the Nile in 1798, effectively confining French forces to the eastern Mediterranean. Britain, Austria and Russia now formed a new coalition against France, and the initial defeat of French armies in Italy brought chaos to the government. Napoleon returned home, slipping past British patrols in a French frigate, and took part in the Coup du 18 Brumaire (the equivalent in the French revolutionary calendar of 9 November). The Directory was forced to resign, and three consuls – one of them the 30-year-old Napoleon – took power.

REFORMS AND A NEW CONSTITUTION

Napoleon – the one of the three who had the military backing and the hero's record – was duly appointed First Consul. The new constitution, which gave him virtually unchallengeable power, was confirmed by an overwhelming majority in 1800. Despite all the legalistic trappings of the Consulate, the 'liberty, equality and fraternity' of the French Revolution of 1789 had finally been superseded by the personal rule of one man.

This was the period when Napoleon set about the administrative reforms which would prove to be among the most lasting legacies of his rule. The Napoleonic Code, which sought to enshrine in law the revolution's achievements of individual liberty, a secular state and equality before the law, was the culmination of some 14 years' work, but the reorganization of the police, the educational system, the judiciary and above all the army, was driven by Napoleon's own enthusiasm. He also repaired relations between the French Republic and the papacy.

All these reforms were pushed ahead while war continued to rage in Europe. The revolution had been under attack from outside from almost its earliest days – the First Coalition of European nations dedicating to destroying it was set up in 1793, and was followed by six more similar alliances over the next 23 years. It is against that background that Napoleon's eventual ambition to create an impregnable French empire surrounded by a buffer zone of client states should be seen. But if, in its early days, the determined pushing outwards of the boundaries of French power could be interpreted as a defensive strategy by a nation under threat of destruction, it rapidly turned into a war of conquest that brought the old political structures of Europe crashing down.

AMBITIONS TO BECOME EMPEROR

By 1800, the Russians had withdrawn from the latest anti-French coalition, and Napoleon concentrated his forces on Austria, defeating the Austrian forces in the Battle of Marengo of 1800, and reaffirming French domination of northern Italy. With the British – now the only nation still at war with France – rapidly tiring of the struggle, the Peace of Amiens was signed in 1802, leaving France in an overwhelmingly dominant position in continental Europe. That was the moment at which Napoleon suggested, through friends in parliament, that he should be appointed First Consul for life in recognition of his success.

ABOVE *The Concordat of 1801, signed between Napoleon I and Pope Pius VII, assured the Roman Catholic Church's position as the majority church of France and restored some of its civil status, which was lost during the revolution.*

The peace was short-lived – and so was Napoleon's new position. After a few months, with war breaking out again between Britain and France over the provisions of Amiens, a British-backed assassination plot against Napoleon was discovered. This led the First Consul's allies to suggest – almost certainly at his instigation – that declaring the regime to be a hereditary empire with Napoleon and his heirs at its head would remove any hope that it might be ended by assassination. On 2 December 1804, Napoleon seized the crown from Pope Pius VII (r. 1800–23) and defiantly placed it on his own head. With that contemptuous act, France's first empire was formally declared.

Just 15 years after the revolution had driven the French aristocracy out of the country, and the heads of those who were foolish enough to stay had been cut off, one of Napoleon's first acts as emperor was to declare that princely titles were to be reinstated for members of his own family. The revolution had turned full circle and was creating a new aristocracy. Although the revolutionaries had guillotined their own king, the new emperor declared himself king of French-controlled Italy a year later; three years after that, he announced the creation of a new imperial French nobility.

TRIUMPH IN EUROPE

ABOVE *The Arc de Triomphe du Carrousel in Paris was commissioned by Napoleon I to commemorate France's military victories in 1805. These are depicted in friezes around the building's arches.*

Now, instead of a coalition of European powers, Napoleon had only the British to fight, and in an effort to gain control of the English Channel, he forced Spain to declare war on Britain, in the hope that their joint navies would be able to challenge the formidable British sea power. Britain, however, managed to organize a new anti-French coalition involving Austria, Russia, Sweden and Naples. French military victories at Ulm and Austerlitz in 1805 forced Austria out of the war, leaving Napoleon supreme in Europe – but defeat at sea in the Battle of Trafalgar the same year meant that his dreams of dominating the English Channel in order to mount an invasion of Britain were dashed.

In the Treaty of Pressburg (modern Bratislava), signed with Austria after the victory at Austerlitz, Napoleon put into practice his strategy of creating a defensive ring of client states beyond the Rhine, the Alps and the Pyrenees. The treaty effectively destroyed the moribund Holy Roman Empire, binding together the German states of Bavaria, Baden, Württemberg, Hesse-Darmstadt and Saxony into a new Confederation of the Rhine, which was entirely under

French domination. The takeover of Austrian possessions in Piedmont, Parma, Piacenza and Venice, meanwhile, left France in unchallenged domination of Italy. The Spanish Bourbon monarchs who had ruled the kingdom of Naples were ousted in favour of Napoleon's older brother, Joseph (1768–1844), who was crowned king.

Now Prussia joined the tottering European coalition against the French, only to see their outdated armed forces routed at the Battle of Jena (1806). Napoleon moved his troops quickly, and he moved at strength – the usual size of European armies during the 18th century had been around 70,000, but the French system by which every able-bodied man was at the disposal of the army meant that he often had more than 200,000 men under arms. After Jena came defeat for the Russians at Friedland (1807), and at the town of Tilsit, near the Russian border, Napoleon signed treaties with both Prussia and Russia, effectively dividing Europe between Napoleon and Alexander I (r. 1801–25) of Russia. Prussia was virtually halved in size, with territory going to create a new Grand Duchy of Warsaw and a new kingdom of Westphalia, with Napoleon's brother Jerome (1784–1860) ruling it. For the beleaguered British, the Treaty of Tilsit also saw the defeated Prussia dragged into an alliance with France and Russia with the creation of the so-called Continental System, a rigidly enforced blockade of British trade. French domination of western Europe was confirmed.

THE PENINSULAR CAMPAIGN

Under the Continental System, not only British ships but also any neutral vessels that had visited Britain or any of its foreign colonies were seized. The weak link in the system was Portugal, which relied on trade with Britain and refused to co-operate with the French. When the Spanish king, Charles IV (r. 1788–1808), agreed to allow Napoleon to march his troops across Spain, there was such an explosion of grievances against the monarchy and the presence of the French that Charles was forced to abdicate in favour of his son, Ferdinand VII (r. 1808). Napoleon sought to solve the problem by sweeping the Spanish monarchy away and replacing it with his brother Joseph, who was replaced as king of Naples by Napoleon's brother-in-law and military ally, Joachim Murat (r. 1808–15).

It was one of Napoleon's few strategic errors: the Spanish would not accept Joseph as king, and civil unrest turned into outright insurrection. For the British, the revolt provided an opportunity to get troops back onto mainland Europe, and under the command of Arthur Wellesley (1769–1852) – later the duke of Wellington – they poured

1804 Discovery of a British-financed assassination plot provokes Napoleon to declare France a hereditary empire with himself as emperor; promulgation of the Napoleonic Code; in an attempt to challenge British sea power, Napoleon induces Spain to declare war on Britain

1805 French victories at battles of Ulm and Austerlitz force Austria out of the war; Napoleon is defeated by the British at the Battle of Trafalgar; the French dethrone the Bourbons in Naples, and Napoleon replaces them with his brother Joseph

1806 Prussians defeated at the Battle of Jena

1807 Battle of Friedland sees the defeat of the Russians; Treaty of Tilsit divides Europe between France and Russia and creates the Grand Duchy of Warsaw and a new kingdom of Westphalia, ruled by Napoleon's brother Jerome

1808 The abdication of the Spanish monarch and Napoleon's attempt to install his brother Joseph as king of Spain leads to civil revolt; British troops land on the Iberian Peninsula

1812 Napoleon embarks on invasion of Russia; victory at the Battle of Borodino encourages him to push on to Moscow but once there he is forced to retreat

1813 French defeat at Leipzig at the hands of allied European forces

1814 In Napoleon's absence, Parisian authorities surrender to the allies and begin negotiations to reinstate the deposed royal family; Napoleon abdicates and is exiled to Elba

continued

THE LEGEND OF NAPOLEON

In his lifetime, Napoleon I inspired extraordinary passion and loyalty among intellectuals across Europe. Byron (1788–1824), shattered by the news of his defeat, wrote five poems about the man he referred to as a 'modern Mars'; the German writer Goethe (1749–1832) was another admirer; the French novelist Stendhal (1783–1842) was one of his biographers, and Sir Walter Scott (1771–1832) another.

The Eroica Symphony by Beethoven (1770–1827) was originally entitled the Bonaparte Symphony – a contemporary account describes how the composer ripped the title page in disgust when he heard that his hero has crowned himself emperor, and renamed the work the Eroica. The published version, though, still carried the dedication 'to the memory of a great man'.

Although Napoleon's star had come crashing down with military defeats in the wake of the Battle of Borodino in 1812 (which inspired Tchaikovsky's powerful study of disaster and destruction, the 1812 Overture) his legend grew among the general public after his death in 1821.

Following the return of his body from its simple grave on St Helena, Napoleon was given a magnificent state funeral in Paris in 1840. The emperor was carried solemnly beneath the Arc de Triomphe and was interred in a lavish tomb beneath the dome of Les Invalides – on the banks of the Seine, as he had requested in his will.

It is generally agreed that it was Louis-Napoleon's family connection that was largely responsible for the overwhelming support that took him to power in 1848 and enabled him to establish the second empire. He cultivated the Bonaparte legend assiduously during his years in power.

One of the most famous depictions of the emperor was painted in 1801 by Jacques-Louis David (1748–1825), showing him leading his troops into Italy to attack the Ausrian army besieging Genoa.

men and material into the Iberian Peninsula to support the Spanish and Portuguese. Over the next two years, they had significant successes against Napoleon's previously unbeatable troops, especially when Austria launched a fresh attack on Bavaria in 1809. But Spain at that time seemed little more than a distraction. When the Austrians were once again defeated, France added still more territory to its empire, seizing a further stretch of land along the Dalmatian coast, which Napoleon named the Illyrian Provinces.

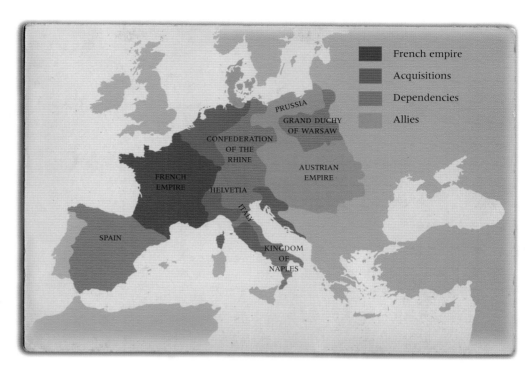

ABOVE *The extent of the Napoleonic empire at its height in 1812.*

The empire now stretched from the German states on the North Sea to northern Italy; and around it were semi-independent states ruled by Napoleon's own family in Westphalia, Naples and Spain. Helvetia (the Swiss Confederation), the Confederation of the Rhine and the Grand Duchy of Warsaw remained nominally independent, but were firmly bound to France by treaty – and even if Napoleon was unable to pacify the Iberian Peninsula and drive the British out, he still commanded by far the most powerful army in France. At the start of 1812, his empire was at its zenith and his power apparently unchallengeable.

DISASTER IN RUSSIA

But then came the strategic disaster which shattered the myth of French invincibility. Napoleon had been trying to persuade Alexander I of Russia to offer him more active support against the British, and was dissatisfied and suspicious at his lack of success. Perhaps, also, repeated military triumphs had led him to overestimate the power of his land forces. Whatever his motivation, he embarked on one of the most disastrous military campaigns in history. He gathered some 600,000 forces in Poland – pulling about 30,000 out of the Peninsular campaign, thus allowing Wellesley's British forces to start to make fresh headway – and in late June 1812, led them eastwards across the Niemen river at the start of the long journey to Moscow.

It was a fatal mistake. Now there were no armies for him to defeat, because the Russians simply retreated, burning the countryside behind them to deny the French food as their supply lines lengthened. It was not until Napoleon was within 70 miles (110 km) of Moscow, three months after he had set out, that the

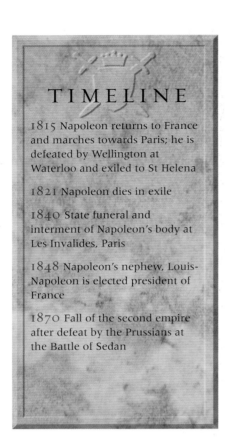

Russian general Kutuzov (1745–1813) first opposed him at the Battle of Borodino on 7 September, 1812. The French won the battle and entered Moscow about a week later – but, crucially, they had failed to destroy the Russian army. With Moscow on fire like much of the Russian countryside, Alexander refusing to negotiate with him and his supply lines impossibly stretched, Napoleon had no choice but to start an immediate withdrawal, as the Russian winter closed in. Kutuzov's forces harassed the French troops as they struggled back through almost impossible conditions. By the time they reached the Berezina river in present-day Belarus, where they faced another fierce battle, barely 10,000 of Napoleon's massive army were fit for combat. The emperor's army and his reputation were in tatters: for the first time, it looked as though the empire he had created might not survive.

A CATASTROPHIC DEFEAT

Wellesley was advancing towards French soil through the Iberian Peninsula; there were anti-French demonstrations in Germany and in Italy, and the Prussian forces that had joined the Grand Army deserted *en masse*. At home, meanwhile, Napoleon had to deal with an attempted *coup d'état* led by a dissatisfied general. Relentless news of military defeats and disasters had sapped his support, leaving much of the nation war-weary and disillusioned. Napoleon, however – still believing that he could achieve ultimate military victory – failed to seize the offer of an armistice which might have left his empire virtually intact.

Finally, in 1813, a combined force of some 320,000 Austrian, Prussian, Russian and Swedish forces faced the demoralized and depleted French army. Napoleon had responded to the disaster of his Russian campaign and the offer of peace which followed it with another defiant attack on Germany, but was forced to withdraw after failing to capture Berlin. The allied forces caught up with the French at Leipzig, outnumbering them by nearly two to one and surrounding them near the city. Even so, Napoleon beat off separate attacks by the Swedes and Prussians, and was defeated only when one of his officers panicked and blew up the only bridge over the River Elster while French troops were still crossing it. As a result, more than 30,000 men were left stranded in the city of Leipzig, unable to join the battle, and Napoleon's army crashed to the most catastrophic defeat it had ever suffered in a pitched battle.

Demonstrations against the French emperor intensified all over Europe. In Italy, the Austrians were gradually taking back the land Napoleon had seized, and his own brother-in-law, the man he had created King Joachim-Napoleon of Naples, was in negotiations with them about deserting him. At home, the legislative assembly and the senate, which he had dominated so successfully for so long, were calling for peace and for an easing of his personal rule. Repeated

announcements from the armies ranged against him that their fight was with Napoleon himself rather than with the French people intensified the feeling in France that it was time to make peace.

In a last, desperate effort in 1814, Napoleon led his troops away from Paris so that he could attack the enemy forces from the rear. As soon as he was out of the city, leading citizens began talks with the allies, and before he had gone 40 miles (60 km) from the capital, the city had surrendered. With nothing left to fight for, he abdicated and accepted the allies' offer of exile on the Mediterranean island of Elba. The terms were relatively generous – he would keep the title of emperor, command a guard of 400 men and receive an annual income of two million

ABOVE *The first sign of weakness of Napoleon's* Grande Armée *was at the Battle of Eylau in 1807, which resulted in a bloody stalemate against Russian troops. It is depicted here in a painting by Antoine-Jean Gros (1771–1835).*

THE EMPIRE STYLE

France's first empire was known not only for its military victories, but for its style. As Napoleon's armies were sweeping through Europe, so in the years that followed the Battle of Austerlitz (1805), French tailors and seamstresses, painters, sculptors and designers were spreading the glory of France in their own way.

The Empire Style looked back to the art of imperial Rome in art and architecture. It was marked by great buildings and monuments such as the Arc de Triomphe, commissioned by Napoleon himself following his victory at Austerlitz, but not completed until 1836, 15 years after his death. Painters and sculptors such as Jacques-Louis David (1748–1825) and Antonio Canova (1757–1822) strove to achieve a similar grandeur, and in the ballrooms of Paris, where the ornate furniture echoed Greek, Roman and ancient Egyptian design, the fashions recalled the most luxurious days before the revolution.

The men wore tailcoats, waistcoats and cravats, while the women had plunging necklines and high waists. Self-conscious elegance was the key note and, from city to city, it was copied by designers and the wealthy beau monde. Against this invasion, even the English Channel was no defence. The ships of the British navy had been successful in keeping Napoleon's soldiers away from Britain, but they could do nothing about the French fashions which swept even more irresistibly across Europe.

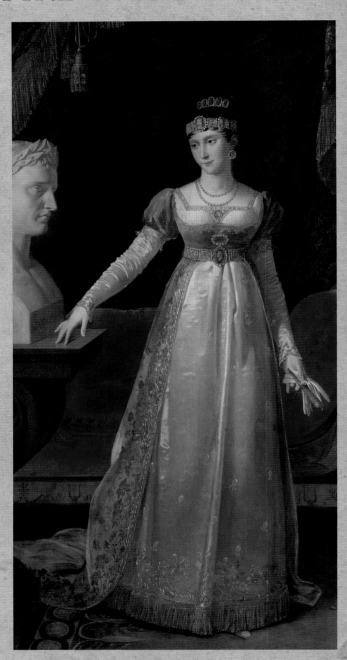

French couture spread from Napoleon's own family – Pauline Bonaparte, Napoleon I's younger sister, is shown here – to embrace France and the rest of Europe, prompting a style revolution.

francs. However, his territory would extend no further than the tiny, mountainous island, which was declared an independent principality under his rule. The dream of a French empire seemed to be over.

DEFIANCE AND DOWNFALL

Napoleon's view of the arrangements made for him was unambiguous: he tried to poison himself rather than accept the offer of exile. The view of many Frenchmen of the man they had cheered only a few years before also seemed clear: he narrowly escaped assassination on his journey through France to take ship for Elba. But there was an astonishing coda to be written to the story of the first French empire.

ABOVE *The Fox and the Goose; or Boney Broke Loose!.* The cartoon depicts the Congress of Vienna; a meeting between the major powers of Europe to divide up the Napoleonic empire following its defeat. The outcome was so unpopular within France that it allowed Bonaparte to escape Elba and regain power for a few brief months, before his final defeat at the Battle of Waterloo.

There was little support for the return of the Bourbon royal family in France, where the new Louis XVIII (r. 1814–24), brother of Louis XVI (r. 1774–93) who had died on the guillotine, was seen accurately enough as a king imposed by foreign power and with foreign loyalties. In Vienna, the victorious allies seemed to be close to war among themselves as they argued over the aftermath of the fighting. There seemed therefore to be the opportunity for one final effort, and on 1 March, 1815, less than a year after he had gone into exile, Napoleon landed at Fréjus, near Cannes in the south of France.

Volunteers flocked to him as he marched north towards Paris, as did the soldiers who were sent to arrest him. Louis XVIII fled in fear for his life as the emperor took power again in the French capital, astutely announcing the liberalization of the old imperial constitution. But whatever concessions he made, he could not offer the peace that the people wanted: allied troops were already massing on the French borders, and Napoleon knew that he would have to defeat them if he was to survive. On 16 June, leading a hastily assembled army to meet them, he defeated a Prussian army at Ligny, but two days later he faced the duke of Wellington, the victor of the Peninsular War, at Waterloo, in modern Belgium.

It was, as Wellington declared later, '*a damned nice thing – the nearest run thing you ever saw in your life*'. Just as the British troops seemed to be about to crack, the Prussian field marshal von Blücher arrived at the battlefield with 45,000 Prussian reinforcements, and Napoleon's final defiance was over. Forced by the parliament in Paris to abdicate for a second time, he made a dash for the Atlantic coast at Rochefort in the hope of boarding a ship for the United States, but was prevented from leaving port by a British naval patrol. Eventually, faced with the likelihood of capture and summary execution, he appealed to the British government for protection.

A DISTANT EXILE

There had been talk among the allies even before Napoleon's return from Elba of the possibility of confining him on a more secure, remote island, and now the decision was taken to send him to St Helena in the South Atlantic, more than 1200 miles (1900 km) off the southwest coast of Africa. There he lived quietly, reading, writing and walking, until after about two years he showed the first signs of illness. On 5 May, 1821, after six years in this second, final exile, he died. There have been suggestions since that he may have been slowly poisoned by the British – Napoleon himself, in his will, declared *'I die before my time, killed by the English oligarchy and its hired assassins'* – but the more common view is that he suffered from a progressive cancer of the stomach.

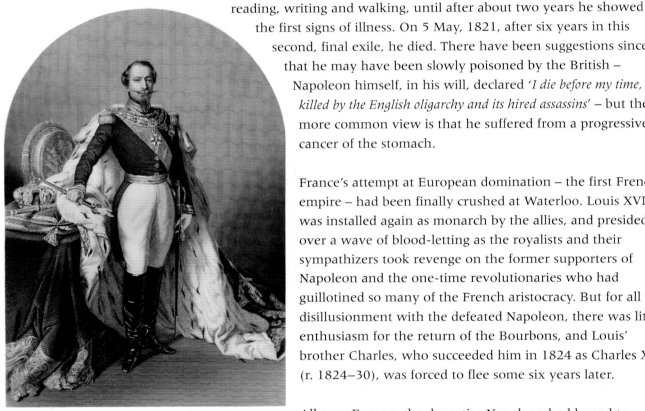

ABOVE *Napoleon III was both the first president and last monarch of France, presiding over the final collapse of the empire and condemned to spend his last days in exile in England.*

France's attempt at European domination – the first French empire – had been finally crushed at Waterloo. Louis XVIII was installed again as monarch by the allies, and presided over a wave of blood-letting as the royalists and their sympathizers took revenge on the former supporters of Napoleon and the one-time revolutionaries who had guillotined so many of the French aristocracy. But for all the disillusionment with the defeated Napoleon, there was little enthusiasm for the return of the Bourbons, and Louis' brother Charles, who succeeded him in 1824 as Charles X (r. 1824–30), was forced to flee some six years later.

All over Europe, the dynasties Napoleon had hoped to establish had collapsed with his own fall. In December 1848, his nephew Louis-Napoleon (1808–73) was elected as president of the republic, bringing with him memories of the glorious, triumphant days of the first empire. He unashamedly made political capital from his family connection with the former emperor and, after unilaterally dissolving the legislative assembly four years later, he declared the inauguration of the second empire. He himself, he declared, was the new emperor Napoleon III. (Napoleon Bonaparte's son, who was born three years before Waterloo and died at the age of 21, was considered Napoleon II, even though he never held any political office.)

Louis-Napoleon successfully fought to drive the Austrians out of Italy, paving the way for Italian unification, and worked to increase French influence in West

Africa, the Middle East and Indochina. For all that, the second empire was noted
more for its grandeur than its power. Louis could take Napoleon's name, but not
his reputation. When he was cajoled into declaring war on Bismarck's Prussia,
defeat at the Battle of Sedan in 1870 led to the fall both of the emperor and the
so-called empire. All that remained of the Napoleonic dream was a distant
memory. Though Napoleon I was famously short in stature – most estimates
suggest that he was no more than 1 metre 57 centimetres (5 ft 2 in) in height –
he was an infinitely bigger man than his successor. Louis-Napoleon had traded
enthusiastically on the memory and the legend of his uncle, but he could never
hope to match his achievements.

ABOVE *Twenty years after his
death on St Helena, Napoleon
was given a hero's burial in
Paris, where his remains lie in
a tomb of red quartzite in Les
Invalides, on the banks of the
Seine.*

Dem
Neuen Deutschland

Germany's 'third empire' – after the Holy Roman Empire (911–1806) and the second empire of the Hohenzollerns (1871–1918) – was supposed to endure for a thousand years, but lasted for just 12. Adolf Hitler never claimed the title of emperor, but the programme he and his Nazi Party espoused was unambiguously one of imperial conquest. It began with the plan to annex huge tracts of eastern Europe in search of *Lebensraum* ('living space') for supposedly racially superior Germans, and ended with Hitler's suicide as Berlin fell to the Red Army. The Third Reich brought about the death of 12 million civilians, including the systematic genocide of 6 million Jews, and presided over one of history's darkest chapters.

THE THIRD REICH
1933 – 1945

GERMANY'S FEDERAL ELECTION OF 1932 was fought with the country in the grip of economic gloom and social unrest. The National Socialist German Workers' Party, or 'Nazis' for short, from the first two syllables of the word *Nazional* – won 37 percent of the vote. In the ensuing stalemate, with no party able to form a government, Adolf Hitler (1889–1945) was chosen as chancellor the following year. It was a fatal misjudgement by the political establishment, which believed it could rein in his extremist policies.

After less than six weeks in power, however, he demanded new elections – the fifth in a year – which were preceded by a violent campaign of intimidation by Nazi stormtroopers. An arson attack on the parliament building, the Reichstag (allegedly by a deranged Dutch communist named Marinus van der Lubbe, but orchestrated by the Nazis) was used to whip up hysteria, and this time Hitler won 43.9 percent of the vote. He bullied parliament into passing the Enabling Act, which gave his personal decrees the force of law. Germany's democratic government had voted itself out of power.

A QUEST FOR RACIAL PURITY

Brutal purges followed, in which Jews, communists, socialists and trade unionists were dismissed from posts in the civil service. The Nazis' programme had been clear

LEFT *'To the New Germany' proclaims a campaign poster for the Nazi Party, showing a First World War infantrymen on the left and an SA stormtrooper on the right.*

ABOVE *The Axis dictators Hitler and Mussolini meet with the French prime minister Édouard Daladier and the British premier Neville Chamberlain during the Munich crisis of 1938, brought about by Hitler's territorial claims on Czechoslovakia.*

from the outset: in their manifesto of 1920, they had declared: '*None but those of German blood, whatever their creed, may be members of the Nation. No Jew, therefore, may be a member of the Nation.*' New laws now prohibited marriage between Jews and non-Jews and stripped Germany's 500,000 Jews of their citizenship. In November 1938, *Kristallnacht* ('the night of broken glass') marked the start of a wave of officially inspired attacks by brown-shirted Nazi stormtroopers on Jewish businesses, hospitals and homes throughout Germany. Synagogues were burned, and some 30,000 Jews placed under arrest.

Meanwhile, Hitler's colleagues Hermann Goering (1893–1946) and Heinrich Himmler (1900–45) were creating the secret police forces known respectively as the Gestapo (short for *Geheime Staatspolizei*, or 'secret state police') and the *Schutzstaffel* ('protective squadron'), or SS. One of the first tasks of the SS was to carry out mass arrests and killings of the original stormtroopers (the SA, or *Sturmabteilung*) whose campaigns of violence and intimidation had helped to sweep Hitler to power. Hitler needed to be rid of this thuggish element in his party in order to woo the industrialists and financiers who would be vital to his war effort.

HITLER SEIZES POWER

When President Paul Hindenburg (1847–1934) – the German leader who had been so confident of his ability to control the upstart Hitler – died in August 1934, Hitler unilaterally added the presidential powers and duties to those of the chancellor, and in February 1938 took personal command of all Germany's armed forces.

RIGHT *German troops cross the border during the* Anschluss *of Austria in March 1938. Most Austrians welcomed these forces with open arms and embarked on a vicious persecution of the country's Jews that surpassed even the terror enacted in Germany.*

All the elements of one-man, dictatorial rule were now in place. Hitler had the powers of an emperor even if – since the loss of Germany's overseas possessions after the country's defeat in 1918 – he had as yet no international empire to rule.

The policies that Hitler proceeded to introduce had been foreshadowed in Nazi speeches and pamphlets, and in his personal testament, *Mein Kampf* ('My Struggle') published in 1925. In an interview in *New York* magazine in 1923, he had warned that Germany's Jews, '*a ferment of decomposition*' would have to be purged from society.

In the same interview he set out his foreign policy with unmistakable clarity: '*We must expand eastward*', he said. '*There was a time when we could have shared world dominion with England. Now we can stretch our cramped limbs only toward the east. The Baltic is necessarily a German lake.*'

REARMAMENT AND ANNEXATION IN EUROPE

His first priority was to extricate Germany from the Treaty of Versailles which had ended the First World War and which limited the size and strength of the German armed forces; it also ruled that the Rhineland should be a demilitarized zone. Within months of coming to power, Hitler started a programme of rearmament, began the formation of a German air force and introduced military conscription. By 1936 he was spending over ten billion marks a year on weapons. On 7 March his troops invaded the Rhineland; Britain, France and the United States did nothing to stop him.

In 1938 Austria was declared part of 'Greater Germany', in an *Anschluss*, or annexation, with over 99 percent of Austrians approving this measure in a plebiscite. It was Hitler's first seizure of land in Europe, and it was rapidly followed by claims that the Czech government was discriminating against the German minority in the Sudetenland. Britain's prime minister Neville Chamberlain (1869–1940) headed an international diplomatic effort which included the Italians and French and resulted in the reluctant handover by Czechoslovakia of the Sudetenland and its three million population to Germany.

For a second time, Hitler had gained land without any military action, and in March the following year he seized the rest of Czechoslovakia, dividing it into two new German protectorates of Bohemia and Moravia, and leaving the rump as a nominally independent Slovakia. Next he announced the annexation of more territory in Lithuania which had been lost to Germany at Versailles. After this, Britain and

TIMELINE

1925 *Mein Kampf* published

1932 Nazis become the largest party in the *Reichstag*

1933 (January) Adolf Hitler appointed chancellor

1933 (February) *Reichstag* fire

1933 (March) First Nazi concentration camp at Dachau; Enabling Act

1934 Hindenburg dies; Hitler takes presidential powers

1938 (March) *Anschluss* declared with Austria

1939 (March) Hitler seizes Czechoslovakia

1939 (May) 'Pact of Steel' with Italy

1939 (August) Non-Aggression Pact with USSR

1939 (September) Germans march into Poland; Britain and France declare war

1940 (June) France defeated

1941 (June) Germans attack Soviet Union

1941 (December) Pearl Harbor attack by Japanese; Hitler declares war on US

1942 (November) Rommel defeated at El Alamein

1943 (January) Germans surrender at Stalingrad

1944 D-Day; Allies land in France

1945 (April) Hitler commits suicide in Berlin

1945 (May) Germany signs unconditional surrender; end of German Reich

France jointly pledged that they would go to war if the Germans invaded Poland, which Hitler needed to seize if he were to implement his *Lebensraum* policy.

WAR WITH BRITAIN AND FRANCE

In May 1939 Hitler formed an alliance, known as the Pact of Steel, with the Italian fascist dictator Benito Mussolini (1883–1945). In August, despite his opposition to communism, his purges of communists at home and his frequently repeated contempt for the Slavs of eastern Europe, Hitler also signed a non-aggression pact with Soviet leader Joseph Stalin (1870–1953). A secret protocol to the pact divided eastern Europe into 'areas of influence' for Germany and the Soviet Union. A week later, Hitler's tanks rolled into Poland, and on 3 September, 1939 Britain and France declared war on Germany.

For Hitler, war against the two western allies was always a distraction from the larger purpose of conquest in the east. Poland was overrun in less than a month. Then, early in 1940, he unleashed armoured *Blitzkrieg* ('lightning war') attacks in the west. The allies were powerless to stop his forces: Denmark and Norway fell, and German tanks smashed their way through Luxembourg, Belgium and the Netherlands, circumventing France's supposedly impregnable Maginot Line of defensive fortifications. Within six months France had surrendered, leaving Hitler in direct command of the north, while a puppet French regime ruled the south from Vichy.

BELOW *Germany's defeat of her old enemy to the west was swift and devastating, as French forces crumbled. Hitler relished his victory, forcing the French to sign the armistice in the same railway carriage that had been used to accept the German surrender in 1918. Here, German cavalry units pass through the Arc de Triomphe in June 1940.*

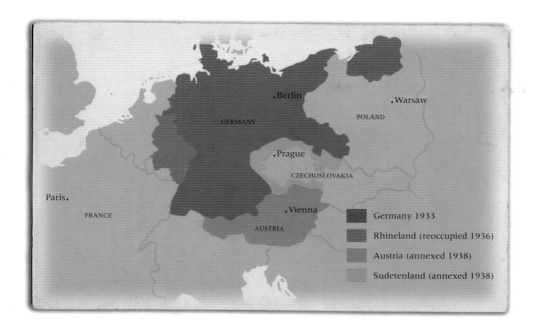

New campaigns also began around the Mediterranean, as German troops invaded Greece and North Africa in support of the Italians. The German leadership was convinced that the war in the west was won – Hitler's plan was to pound England by air attacks before launching a seaborne invasion the following spring. British victories in the air over southern England in the Battle of Britain forced him to delay and eventually abandon those plans, but with the whole of western Europe either under direct German rule or in the hands of its allies, he felt secure enough to pursue his original purpose in the east. In June 1941, in what he thought would be another swift campaign, he launched a surprise attack on the Soviet Union.

In less than a month, the three-pronged campaign seemed to be on the verge of success. One thrust had nearly reached Leningrad, the second was on the way to Moscow and the third had taken most of Ukraine in the south – the lands that Hitler had earmarked for German expansion. He had contemptuously predicted, *'We have only to kick in the door, and the whole rotten structure will come crashing down'*, and the success of his troops against the ill-prepared Russian defences seemed to have proved him right.

SETBACK IN RUSSIA AND WAR WITH THE US

But, just as it had done with the French invasion of Russia 130 years before, the bitter cold of the Russian winter, which came early, stopped the Germans in their tracks. The Soviet army, newly regrouped, launched a determined counterattack to protect Moscow. The campaign that Hitler had intended to be finished by Christmas was postponed until the spring of 1942. In the meantime, news arrived of a surprise attack by the Japanese – with whom Hitler had an alliance dating back to 1936 – on the American fleet at Pearl Harbor. It was already becoming clear that the US was likely to enter the war in Europe on the side of Britain, and in December 1941 Hitler declared war on the United States.

ABOVE *An American propaganda poster of 1943 depicting the Nazi threat as an assault on Christian values.*

THE HOLOCAUST

Hitler's persecution of the Jews started within weeks of his becoming chancellor. German Jews were first victimized by legal changes – the Nuremberg Laws, agreed at a Nazi convention in that city in 1935, set out a whole list of discriminatory measures. Marriage between Jews and non-Jews was forbidden, Jews could not be German citizens, they could not vote and they could not hold public office.

In the Polish capital of Warsaw, the Jewish population was forced into a cramped and insanitary ghetto. After a brave uprising in 1943, the Nazis cleared the ghetto and deported its inhabitants to their deaths.

what they termed the 'Jewish problem'. The first concentration camp at Dachau, near Munich, was built as early as 1933, and was originally designed for political prisoners. The industrial-scale mass murder of the Jews began with the invasion of the Soviet Union, when over four million more Jews came under Nazi control.

Public attacks on Jews, condoned and often instigated by the authorities, grew more common. The 1938 Kristallnacht, which followed the assassination of a German diplomat in Paris by a Polish-Jewish student, was another milestone on the road to genocide. Before long, thousands of Jews were being sent to Nazi concentration camps.

But it was the victories of 1941 in eastern Europe that cleared the way for the Nazis' master plan, the notorious 'Final Solution' to

German death squads followed behind the front-line troops, murdering any Jews they could find. This operation ceased in 1942 after some 1.5 million people had been killed – not because the Nazis were sated with the slaughter, but because the purpose-built death camps at Auschwitz-Birkenau, Treblinka, Belzec, Sobibor, Lublin and Chelmno – opened in 1941–2 – proved that gassing the victims was a more efficient way of carrying out the killings. By the end of the war, an estimated six million Jews and as many non-Jews had perished at the hands of the Nazis.

Despite the setback outside Moscow, the Russian invasion still seemed to be on the point of success. Even so, the declaration of war was a big gamble, with Britain still unconquered in the west, and German troops also committed in North Africa and the Mediterranean. But in terms of the amount of territory under German control, 1942 marked the high point of Hitler's power. The German army had conquered the whole of mainland Europe, from France to the outskirts of the Russian capital, and formerly independent states were ruled by Nazi puppet regimes. In North Africa, Field Marshal Erwin Rommel (1891–1944) seemed poised to smash British resistance, opening the door to Egypt and India.

ROLLING BACK THE TIDE

Late in 1942, the British pulled off a stunning vicory over Rommel at El Alamein. Early the following year the Germans suffered an even more significant defeat outside the southern Russian industrial city of Stalingrad (now Volgograd), where Soviet troops, initially forced to retreat, launched a fierce counterattack that overwhelmed Hitler's entire Sixth Army. With the surrender of the German and Italian forces in North Africa in May 1943 and the withdrawal of Italy from the war after Allied landings in Sicily, German forces were suddenly under pressure.

In 1944, as the Soviet army pressed forward from the east, British and American troops launched an invasion of mainland Europe on the beaches of northern France. Mass bombing raids on German cities had already taken the war to the heart of Germany – a single raid on Hamburg killed an estimated 40,000 people. Senior Wehrmacht officers, anxious to end the war before Germany was totally destroyed, tried to assassinate Hitler with a bomb at his headquarters. He survived, and the plotters were rounded up and executed. But now the Allied forces were advancing on three separate fronts towards Berlin.

DEFEAT AND SUICIDE

In January 1945, with his forces in full retreat, Hitler withdrew to his underground bunker in Berlin. There, on 30 April, 1945, he and several of his senior colleagues committed suicide. The Third Reich effectively died with him. In the chaos of defeat, Rear Admiral Karl Dönitz (1891–1980), commander in chief of the German navy, was named by Hitler as his successor.

The Allies insisted on nothing less than unconditional surrender. The Third Reich had already been crushed militarily, and now the state itself ceased to exist. Germany was in ruins, with its major cities reduced to piles of rubble by bombing raids. The country was divided into sectors, each one ruled by one of the victorious allies. The Nazis' empire, which they had once optimistically called the 'Thousand-Year Reich', was at an end.

BELOW *In 1945, Hitler's empire was squeezed by the Allied armies' thrust into Germany, until it became a narrow sliver of territory under constant bombardment. The final blow came when the Red Army captured Berlin, taking the capital in bitter hand-to-hand fighting. This famous image shows Soviet troops raising their flag over the Reichstag on 2 May.*

The communist leaders of the Soviet Union, which was established in the wake of the Russian October Revolution of 1917, never accepted that they had an empire. Instead, the USSR regarded itself as a single state comprising 15 'union republics'. Outside the Soviet Union, a group of eastern European states that came under Russian control at the end of the Second World War had nominal independence, but in truth were Soviet satellites. Dissent, either in the USSR itself or these client states, was not tolerated. One of the first Soviet republics to declare itself an independent state was Russia itself – probably the only example in history of a nation announcing its independence from its own empire.

THE SOVIET EMPIRE
1922 – 1991

A S A RESULT OF CONQUESTS from the 17th century onwards, by the start of the 20th century tsarist Russia was a vast empire, stretching over 11 time zones, and with ports on the Pacific, the Baltic, the North Atlantic and the Black Sea.

THE BOLSHEVIK REVOLUTION

The Bolsheviks, who emerged victorious from the October Revolution, were committed in theory both to improving the lot of the peasants, and to national self-determination for the non-Russian borderland areas of the empire. The Treaty of Brest-Litovsk (1918), which ended Russia's participation in the First World War immediately after the revolution, would have handed over vast tracts of territory in central Europe and the Black Sea to Germany and its allies. The handover meant that Russia lost a third of its population.

But the humiliating agreement was signed only because the Bolshevik leaders were desperate to get out of the war, not because they had any genuine desire to shed the tsarist empire which they had criticized so bitterly before they came to power. Once the treaty was annulled by the defeat of Germany in 1918, and once opposition to Bolshevik rule had finally been crushed in the Russian civil war of 1918–21, they acted quickly to force the former provinces of the empire back under their control.

LEFT *A poster from the October Revolution proclaims:* 'You – Still not a Member of a Cooperative: Sign Up Immmediately!'

By 1921, the Red Army had occupied almost all the newly independent republics, in the formation of what was effectively a new Russian empire – although the communists, wedded as they were to a policy of anti-imperialism, did not use the word 'empire'. Instead, in 1922, they announced the establishment of the new Union of Soviet Socialist Republics, which was made up of Russia, Byelorussia (now Belarus), Ukraine and the Caucasian republics of Georgia, Armenia and Azerbaijan. In theory, the USSR was established as a league of equal members, but in practice the Russian Communist Party was always in control, and the capital and seat of political power was accepted as being Moscow.

Finland and the Baltic states of Estonia, Latvia and Lithuania, which were protected by strong British and French support, remained outside the Russian umbrella. Likewise, an attempt by the Red Army to take control in Poland – which invaded Ukraine in 1920, in the hope of setting up an independent buffer state – ended with a crushing counteroffensive by the Poles. Under the Treaty of Riga in 1921, Soviet Russia abandoned its claim to large areas of Belarus and Ukraine, which were ceded to Poland.

CENTRALIZATION AND AGRICULTURAL REORGANIZATION

During the 1920s, the central authority of the Communist Party increased dramatically, with the ruling Politburo in Moscow increasingly taking decisions. This led inevitably to the draining of any residual powers from the non-Russian republics.

Soviet reorganization of agriculture, by which peasants had to hand over any grain that the government deemed to be more than they needed for their own consumption, led to a collapse of production. The cereal harvest in 1920 yielded only two-thirds of that in 1913, and a drought the following year coupled

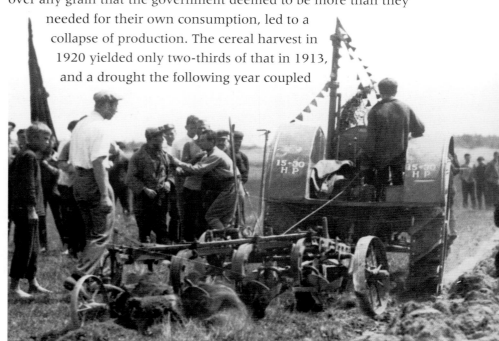

with this drastic shortage lead to widespread famine, in which over five million people are reported to have died.

Much the same thing happened in the 1930s, with the announcement of a series of five-year plans to increase agricultural production. This time the effect was intensified by a political campaign against the *kulaks*, or independent farmers, who were fined, dispossessed and forced off their land. Ten million or more are thought to have been deported to Siberia. The areas particularly affected by this reorganization programme were the 'bread basket' republics of central Europe, most notably Ukraine and the Caucasus.

Again, production slumped, and millions more died in the famines that followed. While 4–5 million people were dying in the Ukraine in the winter of 1932–3, the Soviet authorities – now under the leadership of Joseph Stalin (1879–1953) – actually exported more than 1.5 million tons of grain out of the region.

THE NON-AGGRESSION PACT

On 23 August, 1939, Stalin signed the Nazi-Soviet Non-Aggression Pact with Hitler's foreign minister, Joachim von Ribbentrop (1893–1946). Politically, the Nazis and communists were diametrically opposed, but as a piece of pragmatic manoeuvring, the pact had considerable attractions for the Russians. Firstly, it would keep them out of a potentially damaging war with Germany, at least in the short term. Moreover, secret protocols to the pact provided for the restoration to Moscow of the area of Ukraine and Byelorussia that had been lost to Poland in 1921. Estonia, Latvia and Lithuania would also be transferred to Russia.

Under heavy political pressure and the threat of direct military action, the three Baltic republics accepted the presence of Soviet troops on their soil, on the understanding that – at least in theory - there would be no interference in their internal affairs. Finland, where the Russians also wanted to post troops, was less willing to co-operate, and the Russians invaded. The Finns shocked Stalin with the strength of their resistance, and despite a 200:1 superiority in tanks, the Russians suffered a series of humiliating defeats. It was only after four months of fierce fighting that the weight of numbers forced the Finns to capitulate.

THE SECOND WORLD WAR

Just nine days after the signing of the Nazi–Soviet Pact, on 1 September, 1939, Hitler's troops blasted their way across the Polish frontier in the west; two days later Britain and France declared war on Germany. In the east of Poland, however, Stalin was sticking to the secret agreement he had made as part of the pact: the Red Army crossed the border on 17 September, crushing all resistance,

and by 1 October Russia and Germany had divided the country between them. An insight into the brutality of Soviet tactics in this conflict came some years later, with the discovery in woods near Katyn, in eastern Poland, of the remains of some 15,000 Polish officers and others, who had been summarily executed there on Stalin's orders.

Soviet expansion seemed unstoppable. The Baltic states were formally annexed in the summer of 1940, and Romania was pressured into handing over Bessarabia, which stretched north from the Black Sea, as well as northern Bukovina, in the east of the country.

ABOVE The bitterly fought siege of Stalingrad in the winter of 1942 was a key event not just in Russian history but also in the course of the Second World War. The surrender of Hitler's Sixth Army saw the tide finally turn against Nazi Germany.

Despite Nazi Germany's rapid *blitzkrieg* successes in western Europe, and encouraged by his deal with Hitler, Stalin was convinced that there would be no German attack in the east at least until 1942. In fact the invasion, and the tearing up of the non-aggression pact, came in June 1941, as German forces launched Operation Barbarossa againt the Soviet Union. The Soviet army was short of weapons and poorly trained, and many of its professional officers had been either imprisoned or executed in Stalin's political purges during the 1930s. It suffered a series of defeats, and retreated before the Nazis' heavy armour. The *blitzkrieg* was as successful in Russia as it had been in western Europe: by mid-October Kiev was in German hands, Leningrad was under siege and it seemed only a matter of time before Moscow was taken.

But a determined counterattack just outside the Soviet capital in the depths of winter stopped the German advance. A second thrust further south in the summer of 1942 took the Germans as far as Stalingrad (now Volgograd), but the Red Army cut off their strike force with a counterattack in November. More than 90,000 men of Hitler's Sixth Army were either killed or captured, and after a savage defensive battle during the summer of 1943 in Ukraine, around the city of Kursk, the Red Army began to advance. By the end of the year the Nazis had lost most of the territory they had gained since the invasion; in January 1944 Leningrad was relieved; and by April 1945 the Red Army was fighting its way through the streets of Berlin.

With Germany defeated, Stalin turned his attention to the east in August 1945, joining the Allied fight against Japan in time to share in the spoils of victory there as well. His forces overran Manchuria, and in the eventual peace settlement the Russians regained territory on the island of Sakhalin and the town of Port Arthur (now Lüshun), both of which had been part of the Russian empire in the 19th century.

In Europe, Red Army units were in control from the Soviet Union's own borders to Germany. One by one, the formerly independent countries of eastern Europe were taken over by communist governments, starting with Romania early in 1945, and ending with Czechoslovakia in February 1948. A Soviet-backed one-party regime was also installed in the Russian-occupied zone of eastern Germany, while American, British and French troops controlled the western sector of Berlin. In 1946, speaking in the US, the British prime minister Winston Churchill (1874–1965) declared: '*From Stettin in the Baltic to Trieste in the Adriatic an iron curtain has descended across the continent*'.

THE IRON CURTAIN AND THE COLD WAR

The countries of eastern Europe were now effectively satellite states of the Soviet empire. Although communist Yugoslavia under its leader, the former partisan fighter Marshal Tito (real name Josip Broz; 1892–1980), managed to maintain a belligerent independence from Moscow, elsewhere in the region Soviet economic and military power held complete sway. Even so, the citizens of the Eastern Bloc countries were not subject to the same degree of control from Moscow as those in the republics seized in the 1920s. During the war some three million people inside Russia were deported thousands of miles to Siberia and Central Asia. Ethnic Germans from the Volga region, Crimean Tatars, Chechens, Kalmyks and Turkic peoples of southern Georgia were uprooted from their homes in a concerted policy aimed at eliminating any nationalist aspirations. The deportations eventually involved more than 50 nationalities.

The communist seizure of power in Czechoslovakia in 1948, followed later that year by the imposition of a blockade of West Berlin to try to force the Western allies to abandon the city, and the first Soviet atomic bomb test in 1949, all led to the start of the period of international tension that became known as the Cold War. For the next 40 years, East and West would eye each other warily across the Iron Curtain.

Stalin's death in 1953 was followed by a period of relative liberalization

BELOW *In response to the Soviet blockade of West Berlin in 1948–9, which severed all road and rail links to the city, the western Allies organized a massive logistical operation to supply Berlin by air. After 11 months, the Soviets acknowledged defeat and lifted the blockade. By the end of the Berlin Airlift, American and British cargo planes such as that seen below had ferried a total of over two million tons of supplies to the beleaguered city.*

under Nikita Khrushchev (1894–1971) – but that did not imply any real freedom for the countries that had been forced within the Russian orbit after the war. The Warsaw Pact was established in 1955 to bind them together in a military alliance against the West's North Atlantic Treaty Organization (NATO), which had been set up six years earlier. When Hungarian communists and nationalists staged an uprising against Soviet rule in 1956, Russian tanks crushed the rebellion in a brutal reminder of the reality of Big Power politics. A similar response came in the 'Prague Spring' of 1968, when the Czechoslovak leader Alexander Dubcek (1921–92) sought to introduce what he called *'socialism with a human face'*.

International tension increased in the years following the Hungarian revolt, with the launch of the first Soviet intercontinental ballistic missile in 1957, and the building of the Berlin Wall in 1961. In 1962 the Soviets attempted to install missiles targeted on US cities on the island of Cuba, under communist control since 1959. This move, and the firm American response as the US navy blockaded the island, took the world to the brink of nuclear war. It emerged later that Russian commanders on Cuba had been given the authority to launch a missile attack if they believed an American invasion was imminent.

WORLDWIDE ADVANCE

In the Cuban missile crisis, Khrushchev eventually backed down, and the following year the USSR, the US and Britain signed a Nuclear Test Ban Treaty. It was the first real sign of a slight thaw in relations: both sides, perhaps, were shocked by how close they had come to nuclear annihilation.

Khrushchev was toppled in a party coup in 1964, and the new leader who finally emerged was Leonid Brezhnev (1906–82). The Russian economy was in the doldrums, relying on huge annual imports of grain. Although the country made huge strides in defence technology and space exploration, production and investment throughout the rest of Russian industry was experiencing a slump. Russia was caught up in a race for military supremacy that it could not afford.

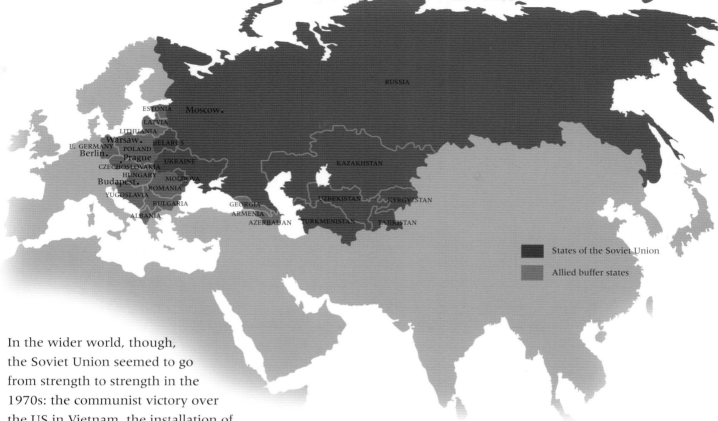

Moscow

RUSSIA

ESTONIA
LATVIA
LITHUANIA
E. GERMANY
Warsaw.
BELARUS
Berlin.
POLAND
Prague
UKRAINE
CZECHOSLOVAKIA
HUNGARY
MOLDOVA
Budapest.
ROMANIA
YUGOSLAVIA
BULGARIA
GEORGIA
ALBANIA
ARMENIA
AZERBAIJAN

KAZAKHSTAN

UZBEKISTAN
KYRGYZSTAN
TURKMENISTAN
TAJIKISTAN

■ States of the Soviet Union
■ Allied buffer states

In the wider world, though, the Soviet Union seemed to go from strength to strength in the 1970s: the communist victory over the US in Vietnam, the installation of communist-supporting governments in many new African states and a coup in Afghanistan that brought a friendly government to power there all seemed to underline the success of Soviet foreign policy. At the same time, ongoing talks eased the tension between East and West – SALT I and SALT II, signed in 1972 and 1979 respectively, limited the production of strategic weapons, while the Helsinki Accords of 1975 finally recognized the postwar frontiers in Europe. In return, the Soviets acknowledged that human rights in Eastern Europe were a matter of international concern. Nevertheless, the West's acceptance of the postwar carve-up of Europe was seen in Moscow as a considerable coup.

In Afghanistan, however, the fall of the pro-Soviet government led to fears in Moscow that a hostile regime might take power, and in December 1979 Soviet tanks rolled across the border to begin one of the most disastrous military operations in Russia's history. The invasion of Afghanistan led to the near collapse of international détente and tied down the Russians for the next ten years in a war they could not win.

The next year, US elections saw Ronald Reagan (1911–2004) come to power as president, determined to increase defence spending. The US had been worried by the apparent gains made by the Soviets around the world during the mid-1970s, so defence was already on the political agenda. Reagan had the additional aim of forcing the Soviet government to drive itself to bankruptcy by trying to keep up. It was a form of economic warfare: Nikita Khrushchev had once told the Western governments, '*We will bury you*', and Reagan was turning the threat back on Moscow.

ABOVE *The Commonwealth of Independent States, formed in December 1991, comprised Russia and ten former constituent republics of the USSR. By the time of its creation, the three Baltic states that had been under Russian control since 1940 and the former Soviet Bloc countries of Eastern Europe had freed themselves entirely from Russian domination.*

LEFT *A banner draped across a statue in Wenceslaus Square, Prague, announces support for the liberal reforms instituted by Czech communist leader Alexander Dubcek in 1968. Warsaw Pact forces were sent in to reimpose Soviet orthodoxy.*

REORGANIZATION AND REFORM

When the long-ailing Brezhnev died in 1982, he was succeeded as president by Yuri Andropov (1914–84), a committed communist, but a man who wanted to see step-by-step political and economic change. He encouraged the promotion of more reformers within the party's Central Committee – among them a party *apparatchik* from Stavropol in southern Russia named Mikhail Gorbachev (b.1931). Gorbachev was Andropov's chosen successor, although the sick and ageing Konstantin Chernenko (1911–85) was initially appointed on the death of the president as a stop-gap compromise candidate. When Chernenko died in 1985, after just a year in the job, Gorbachev took power.

ABOVE *Soviet leader Mikhail Gorbachev and US president Ronald Reagan met for the first time in November 1985 in Geneva, Switzerland. This summit resulted in a joint statement proposing that both sides should cut their strategic arms stocks by half. Later talks reached an agreement to eliminate land-based short- and intermediate-range nuclear missiles.*

From the start, he was committed to two key policies: *glasnost*, or openness, and *perestroika*, or political and economic restructuring. The country was in dire need of reform; the stagnation of the late Brezhnev era, exacerbated by out-of-control arms spending and economic inefficiency, had led to an economic crisis. By 1990 rationing was widespread, with long queues at shops even for basic commodities. Gorbachev pressed ahead with his political restructuring programme, allowing individual republics to elect their own supreme soviets. In the resulting elections, voters gave their verdict on the economic chaos – even where communist candidates were the only ones standing, they were often not elected, having failed to secure at least 50 percent of the votes cast.

Having tasted decentralized power, in March 1990 Lithuania took the logical next step of declaring itself to be a sovereign, independent state. The other Baltic republics had already made it clear they were heading in the same direction, as had Russia's satellite states. The momentous year of 1989 witnessed the collapse of the Soviet Union's proxy empire in eastern Europe, as 'people power' took hold behind the Iron Curtain. In quick succession, the citizens of Hungary, Poland, the German Democratic Republic, Bulgaria and Romania forced their governments to stand down and hold free elections. The greatest symbol of change was the opening of the Berlin Wall in November. In many cases, this seismic power shift passed off peacefully, while elsewhere it was marked by bloodshed.

In May 1990, the Russian supreme soviet declared Russia to be a sovereign state, with its own decisions taking precedence over Soviet laws. Gorbachev declared the move illegal, but was simply ignored. Russia, under its leader Boris Yeltsin (1931–2007), was in effect declaring itself independent from its own empire.

BREAK-UP OF THE SOVIET UNION

Internationally, meanwhile, détente was back on the agenda. The US was maintaining the pressure on defence spending, but Western leaders were keen to encourage Gorbachev to accept new arms reduction treaties. There was also

agreement on a Soviet withdrawal from Afghanistan, which was completed by February 1989. Nearly 14,000 soldiers had died in Brezhnev's disastrous adventure.

In a desperate rearguard action to preserve the communist state, hardline conservative politicians, supported by senior KGB officers and some elements of the military, staged a coup to remove Gorbachev from power, seizing him as he holidayed in the Crimea in August 1991. Gorbachev refused to resign, and Yeltsin, as president of the Russian Soviet Federated Socialist Republic, threw his weight behind him in a direct confrontation with the plotters. The coup failed, but the president's political credibility was fatally damaged. Different republics, worried that another plot might succeed, rushed to declare their independence from Moscow. First the three Baltic republics seceded from the union, then Ukraine, previously the second most powerful republic in the USSR.

The final nail in the Soviet Union's coffin was driven home in December 1991, when Russia, Ukraine and Belarus announced the formation of a new, loose confederation called the Commonwealth of Independent States (CIS). Seven other former Soviet republics joined them, although Estonia, Latvia, Lithuania, Georgia and Azerbaijan opted out. On Christmas Day, Gorbachev resigned the presidency, and on 26 December the Soviet Union was formally dissolved. There were no short-term economic or political solutions. Russia's economy remained in a parlous state, and remained embroiled in a bitter war in Chechnya – but the beginning of 1992 marked the end of a 75-year experiment with communism. It also saw the self-destruction of an empire dating back more than three centuries.

ABOVE *Muscovites unfurl a huge Russian flag in Red Square on 22 August, 1991, to celebrate the failure of the attempted coup by Soviet hardliners. The coup precipitated the incipient demise of the Soviet Union.*

By the end of the 20th century, with the Soviet Union in ruins, the United States had no challenger either economically or militarily as the most powerful nation in the world. Has the definition of empire changed with the advent of globalization and instant news coverage? And, if so, can the US be considered an empire?

A NEW WORLD EMPIRE?

THE US HAS ALWAYS PASSIONATELY DENIED ANY IMPERIAL AMBITIONS. Born, like the Soviet Union, out of revolution, it has its anti-imperialist credentials written into its own Declaration of Independence. Historically, there have been times when Washington's commitment to anti-imperialism seemed less than total – the end of the Spanish–American War in 1898, for instance, handed over control of the former Spanish colonies of Puerto Rico, the Philippines and Guam to the US. Moreover, much of the territory that now makes up the mainland United States was originally seized by military force from its original inhabitants.

Those who claim today that the US is at the head of a modern empire point not to history, but to the hundreds of military bases maintained in foreign countries all over the world. Most are there at the invitation of the host country's government, but that only prompts the question: is the military and economic dominance of the USA that leads to such invitations so very different from empire? What is more, some bases are a survival from earlier agreements with regimes that have long vanished. Guantanamo, on Cuba, for example, was occupied at the end of the Spanish–American War under a permanent lease that the Cuban government has long demanded should be cancelled.

According to those who subscribe to the theory of American imperialism, at the start of the 21st century the US, either by using its military muscle, diplomatic leverage or marketing clout, is extending its political and economic influence over more of the world than any empire in history.

Yet the US suffers some of the disadvantages of empire too: many people around the world blame the ills of their government or their region on American policy. The attacks of 11 September, 2001 only make sense as a strike against what is seen as a

LEFT *A plane being readied for deployment from a US aircraft carrier. From the Second World War onwards, these formidable weapons systems have been the instrument of US foreign policy around the globe.*

powerful and overbearing state. And such a view of the US is not limited to the Middle East. The Washington Consensus for free-market competition is widely perceived as being an ideology that serves the interest of an international and domineering empire at the expense of weaker countries and perhaps also of the less powerful classes in all countries.

On the other hand, although the US has more ways of projecting its power, whether by force or by indirect influence, than other imperial nations in history have enjoyed, it has less direct control over the day to day lives of people who live within its sphere of influence, and arguably less commercial power as well. Whereas the British administrators of the 19th century, for instance, could set up schools in India, hang thieves in Burma, or impose taxes in Uganda, the Americans of the 21st have no comparable imperial institutions or infrastructure. The British forced their colonies to trade almost exclusively with the mother country and usually to accept the role of raw materials supplier at that. Britain could go to war with China in the 19th century to force them to accept the opium trade, but the Americans have too much at stake in the multilateral economic system of international finance and the World Trade Organization to be able to impose their will so crudely. They have to reach trade agreements through negotiation, where their biggest leverage is not a gunboat but access to their vast consumer market. While that can be a very big stick in bilateral deals, it does not have any more impact than the European Union's in world trade rounds.

The argument over whether the US has an empire is partly one of definition – what exactly is an empire? But partly, it reflects the fact that in the age of globalization, instant communications, cheap and powerful weapons, and a much higher value set on human life in Western democracies than in empires of the past, empire in the old fashioned sense of control exerted by force by one country over several other peoples may simply no longer be possible. Globalization means that the economic costs of conflict are paid by the winner as well as the loser; television, the Internet and immediate communication mean that people at home can see the effects of warfare at first hand. And the availability of cheap and mass produced weaponry means that armies that were set up to fight major battles against other armies face grave challenges in dealing with low-level guerrilla attacks and insurgencies. For the Americans in Vietnam, Somalia and Iraq, or for the Russians and now the NATO allies in Afghanistan, the experience has been the same.

BELOW *An Islamic militiaman at an anti-American rally in Somalia, one of several 'failed states' in the post-Cold War world that have become breeding grounds for terrorism.*

Even in the 19th and the early 20th centuries, there were strong groundswells of opinion in Britain that thought that the moral and financial costs of policing the empire were too great. Such doubts are much more prevalent today. When nobody could see the carnage, 60,000 deaths on the Somme in a single day did not even dent the figures for new volunteers for the First World War; today, 4000 deaths in four years in Iraq, with constant and detailed news coverage, are causing serious domestic political problems in the US. When indiscriminately massacring opponents is rightly unacceptable, it forces the US as an occupier to try to win hearts and minds: an easy campaign for insurgents to frustrate by acts of terror and sabotage.

As to financial costs, the US is running up enormous international debts, at least partly because its taxpayers will not pay for its gigantic defence outlays. A country that is unwilling or unable to pay for its empire will not keep it long, as Britain found to its humiliation at Suez, the Soviet Union realized as its food queues grew longer, and as Spain had discovered centuries earlier.

But perhaps America may prove to be at the head of a subtle new sort of imperialism – one that is based on some of the same developments that make the old-fashioned military empires impossible. With globalization, the Internet and the worldwide presence of television, perhaps the new empire is a cultural, rather than a military phenomenon; people see the luxuries of a consumer society, and they want them. Globalized industry and commerce mean that they are available – and so one culture builds its dominance over others not on military strength, but on the power of its industry and economy.

Which, presumably, makes the 21st century likely to be, like the latter half of the 20th, an American century. Except …

In the Bible it is written:
> 'To everything there is a season,
> a time for every purpose under the sun.
> A time to be born and a time to die;
> a time to plant and a time to pluck up that which is planted.'

Or, for that matter, 'What goes around comes around'. It is the same message that is implicit in the story of every emperor who has ever ruled over a greater or lesser patch of the Earth – empires become over-extended, too far-flung, too complex for central rule, too expensive to hold together, too oppressive of their vassals. And those that are established to last for ever have one thing in common: they never do.

ABOVE *British politician Jack Straw (foreign secretary 2001–6), answers reporters' questions during an international conference on Iraq in Brussels in 2006. The controversial US and British invasion of Iraq in 2003 has only further destabilized the already volatile Middle East region.*

INDEX

FURTHER READING

Ascalone, E. *Mesopotamia: Assyrians, Sumerians, Babylonians* (University of California Press, Berkeley, 2007)

Bausani, A. *The Persians, from the Earliest Days to the 20th century* (Elek Books, London, 1971)

Beevor, A. *Berlin: The Downfall, 1945* (Viking, London, 2002)

Boxer, C.R. *The Portuguese Seaborne Empire 1415–1825* (Penguin Books, London, 1973)

Brown, A., and Kayser, M. (eds.) *The Soviet Union Since the Fall of Khruschev* (Macmillan, London, 1988)

Bryce, J. *The Holy Roman Empire* (Macmillan, London, 1968)

Bullock, A. *Hitler, a Study in Tyranny* (HarperCollins, London, 1991)

Chambers, J. *The Devil's Horsemen: The Mongol Invasion of Europe* (Weidenfeld and Nicolson, London, 1979)

Davies, N. *The Incas* (Colorado University Press, Boulder, CO, 1995)

Doherty, P. *Alexander the Great – The Death of a God* (Constable & Robinson, London, 2004)

Ferguson, N. *Colossus, the Rise and Fall of the American Empire* (Allen Lane, London, 2004)

Hemming, J. *Conquest of the Incas* (Abacus, London, 1972)

Hourani, A. *A History of the Arab Peoples* (Faber and Faber, London, 1991)

Hucker, C.O. *China's Imperial Past* (Duckworth, London, 1975)

Kinross, Lord *The Ottoman Centuries: The Rise and Fall of the Turkish Empire* (Harper Perennial, London, 1979)

Marshall, R. *Storm from the East* (BBC Books, London, 1993)

McCauley, M. *The Soviet Union Under Gorbachev* (Macmillan, London, 1987)

Meiggs, R. *The Athenian Empire* (Oxford University Press, New York, 1979)

Menzies, G. *1421 – The Year China Discovered the World* (Bantam Press, London, 2002)

Morris, J. *Pax Britannica, the Climax of an Empire* (Faber and Faber, London, 1968)

Motyl, A. *Imperial Ends – the Decay, Collapse, and Revival of Empires* (Columbia University Press, New York, 2001)

Munro-Hay, I. *Aksum: An African Civilisation of Late Antiquity* (Edinburgh University Press, Edinburgh, 1991)

Nilakanta Sastri, K.A. *The Colas* (University of Madras, Madras, 1955)

Ostrogorsky, G. *A History of the Byzantine State* (Basil Blackwell, Oxford, 1980)

Thompson, J.M. *Napoleon Bonaparte, His Rise and Fall* (Basil Blackwell, Oxford, 1963)

Tripathi, R.P. *Rise and Fall of the Mughal Empire* (Central Book Depot, Allahabad, 1966)

Wacher, J. *The Roman Empire* (J.M. Dent, London, 1987)

Warry, J. *Alexander 334–323 BC, Conquest of the Persian Empire* (Osprey Publishing, London, 1991)

PICTURE CREDITS

akg-images
40 © akg-images; 106–107 © akg-images; 122 © akg-images; 217 © akg-images

British Library
74 © 2008 The British Library

Corbis
8 © Gianni Dagli Orti/Corbis; 11 © Michael S. Yamashita/Corbis; 14 © Werner Forman/Corbis; 15 © Stapleton Collection/Corbis; 17 © Christie's Images/Corbis; 20 © Gianni Dagli Orti/Corbis; 23 © Gianni Dagli Orti/Corbis; 24 © Araldo de Luca/Corbis; 27 © The Art Archive/Corbis; 28 © Bettmann/Corbis; 29 © Gianni Dagli Orti/Corbis; 30–31 © Araldo de Luca/Corbis; 35 © Bettmann/Corbis; 37 © Stefano Bianchetti/Corbis; 38 © The Gallery Collection/Corbis; 41 © Roger Wood/Corbis; 42 © Bettmann/Corbis; 43 © North Carolina Museum of Art/Corbis; 46 © Smithsonian Institution/Corbis; 51b © Bettmann/Corbis; 51t © Bettmann/Corbis; 52 © Chris Hellier/Corbis; 54 © Vanni Archive/Corbis; 55 © Bettmann/Corbis; 57 © Bettmann/Corbis; 58t–59 © Bettmann/Corbis; 60 © Charles & Josette Lenars/Corbis; 64 © Araldo de Luca/Corbis; 66 © Stapleton Collection/Corbis; 68 © Charles & Josette Lenars/Corbis; 73 © Burstein Collection; 75 © Werner Forman/Corbis; 76 © Charles & Josette Lenars; 77 © Pierre Colombel/Corbis; 80 © Roger Wood/Corbis; 83 © Gallo Images/Corbis; 84 © Richard T. Nowitz/Corbis; 88 © Gianni Dagli Orti/Corbis; 89 © Werner Forman/Corbis; 90 © The Art Archive/Corbis; 91 © The Gallery Collection/Corbis; 93 © The Art Archive/Corbis; 96 © Gianni Dagli Orti/Corbis; 99 © The Art Archive/Corbis; 100 © The Art Archive/Corbis; 101 © The Art Archive/Corbis; 103 © Chris Hellier/Corbis; 105 © Elio Ciol/Corbis; 108 © Gianni Dagli Orti/Corbis; 111 © Burstein Collection/Corbis; 112 © Brooklyn Museum/Corbis; 115 © Werner Forman/Corbis; 116 © Burstein Collection/Corbis; 126 © Bettmann/Corbis; 127 © Arne Hodalic/Corbis; 129 © The Art Archive/Corbis; 130 © Stapleton Collection/Corbis; 133 © Burstein Collection/Corbis; 134 © The Gallery Collection/Corbis; 146 © The Gallery Collection/Corbis; 148 © The Gallery Collection/Corbis; 153 © The Art Archive/Corbis; 154 © Historical Picture Archive/Corbis; 156 © Bettmann/Corbis; 157 © Hulton-Deutsch Collection/Corbis; 158 © Atlantide Phototravel/Corbis; 164 © Historical Picture Archive/Corbis; 169 © Stapleton Collection/Corbis; 170 © Gianni Dagli Orti/Corbis; 171 © Bettmann/Corbis; 175 © Bettmann/Corbis; 176 © Gianni Dagli Orti/Corbis; 178 © The Gallery Collection/Corbis; 181b © Hans Georg Roth/Corbis; 187 © Bettmann/Corbis; 188 © Stapleton Collection/Corbis; 191 © Stapleton Collection; 193 © Francis G. Mayer/Corbis; 194 © Christie's Images/Corbis; 197 © Bettmann/Corbis; 197 © Brian A. Vikander/Corbis; 198 © Bettmann/Corbis; 199 © Bettmann/Corbis; 201 © Corbis; 202 © Hulton-Deutsch Collection; 203 © Fine Art Photographic Library/Corbis; 205 © Corbis; 207 © Bettmann/Corbis; 208 © Hulton-Deutsch Collection; 209 © Rykoff Collection/Corbis; 210 © Hulton-Deutsch Collection/Corbis; 211 © Bettmann/Corbis; 212–213 © Hulton-Deutsch Collection; 214 © The Gallery Collection/Corbis; 220 © The Art Archive/Corbis; 224 © The Gallery Collection/Corbis; 225 © The Gallery Collection/Corbis; 226 © Michael Nicholson/Corbis; 228 © Stapleton Collection/Corbis; 230b © Hulton-Deutsch Collection/Corbis; 232 © Hulton-Deutsch Collection/Corbis; 233 © Swim Ink 2, LLC/Corbis; 234 © Hulton-Deutsch Collection/Corbis; 235 © Yevgeny Khaldei/Corbis; 236 © Bettmann/Corbis 238 © Bettmann/Corbis; 239 © Bettmann/Corbis; 240 © Bettmann/Corbis; 241 © Bettmann/Corbis; 242 © Hulton-Deutsch Collection; 244 © Reuters/Corbis; 245 © Peter Turnley/Corbis; 246 © Les Stone/Sygma/Corbis; 248 © Albadri Abukar/epa/Corbis; 249 © Thierry Roge/Reuters/Corbis

photos.com
2–3; 4b; 5t; 5b; 18; 36; 48; 58b; 62t; 145; 149; 150–151; 172; 181t; 184; 185; 223; 230t

Shutterstock
4t © Tamir Niv; 12 © Michael Fuery; 32 © vieloryb; 45 © Massimiliano Lamagna; 56 © Andrei Nekrassov; 61b © Lagui; 62b–63 © Denis Babenko; 71 © Jack Cronkhite; 79 © gary718; 87 © Gustavo Fadel; 95 © Ilker Canikligil; 104 © manfredxy; 119 © Olga Kolos; 120 © Philip Lange; 162 © Mark Van Overmeire; 186 © Michael Stokes; 192 © pnicoledolin; 218 © Seet; 227 © TAOLMOR

TopFoto
61t © Roger-Viollet/TopFoto; 124 © 2004 AAAC/TopFoto; 137 © AAAC/TopFoto; 138 © TopFoto/Werner Forman; 139 © TopFoto/Werner Forman; 140 © TopFoto; 141 © 2004 AAAC/TopFoto; 142–143 © 2004 AAAC/TopFoto; 166 © Werner Forman Archive/TopFoto; 167 © TopFoto

Quercus Publishing has made every effort to trace copyright holders of the pictures used in this book. Anyone having claims to ownership not identified above is invited to contact Quercus Publishing.

AUTHOR'S ACKNOWLEDGEMENTS

For Harry and Jessica Taylor

1909–1987 and 1914–2008

How you would have loved working on this book with me.

I am grateful for the help and advice I have received from many friends, on subjects ranging from Arausio to the Zanj revolt, and most other letters in between. Chief among them are Julian Bene, Andy Boyd, Dave Bush, Martin Priestley and Tamsin Roberts, although there are many other individuals who have helped with particular queries. They have saved me from several embarrassments – whatever mistakes remain, of course, are my own.

I also owe a great deal, as always, to my agent, Mandy Little, to Richard Milbank at Quercus, and to Graham Bateman and the team at BCS Publishing.

The staff at the British Library, the Bodleian Library, and the London Library have never let me down, even when my requests for advice and assistance were particularly unreasonable.

My wife, Penny, has read the entire book in pieces, argued over most of it, and put up with my bad temper when things were not going well. And of course I remember, as I always do, Dr Tim Littlewood and his NHS team in the Haematology Department at Oxford's John Radcliffe Hospital. Without all of them, there really wouldn't have been a book at all.

First published in Great Britain in 2008 by

Quercus
21 Bloomsbury Square
London
WC1A 2NS

Copyright © Andrew Taylor 2008

A CIP catalogue record for this book is available from the British Library

Cloth case edition: ISBN-978 1 84724 513 7

Printed and bound in China

10 9 8 7 6 5 4 3 2 1

Designed and edited by BCS Publishing Limited, Oxford.